The Philosophy of Childing

The Philosophy of Childing

Unlocking Creativity, Curiosity, and Reason
through the Wisdom of Our Youngest

Christopher Phillips, PhD

Skyhorse Publishing

Skyhorse Publishing books may be purchased in bulk at special discounts for sales promotion, corporate gifts, fund-raising, or educational purposes. Special editions can also be created to specifications. For details, contact the Special Sales Department, Skyhorse Publishing, 307 West 36th Street, 11th Floor, New York, NY 10018 or info@skyhorsepublishing.com.

Skyhorse® and Skyhorse Publishing® are registered trademarks of Skyhorse Publishing, Inc.®, a Delaware corporation.

Visit our website at www.skyhorsepublishing.com.

10 9 8 7 6 5 4 3 2 1

Library of Congress Cataloging-in-Publication Data is available on file.

Cover design by Rain Saukas

Print ISBN: 978-1-5107-0326-1
Ebook ISBN: 978-1-5107-0328-5

Printed in the United States of America

To the loves of my life, Cecilia, Cali, and Cybele

Contents

Chapter I: A Childing We Will Go 1

Chapter II: Ages and Stages..11

Chapter III: Ripeness Is All 72

Chapter IV: Play's the Thing 130

Chapter V: Through the Looking Glass................................. 180

Chapter VI: Sweet Child of Mine 218

Acknowledgments 233

Chapter 1

A Childing We Will Go

Children and Adults First!

"WHICH CAME FIRST, THE CHICKEN OR THE EGG?"
I've just posed this philosophical oldie but goodie to a group of third graders in Iowa. Elementary schools are a frequent stop in my sojourns around the world holding Socratic give-and-takes. The meetings inspire those taking part to share an array of thought-provoking perspectives on questions we explore together. As I note in *Socrates Café*, my first book about my philosophical adventures, "I need children to philosophize with. No one questions, no one wonders, no one examines, like children. It's not simply that children love questions, but that they *live* questions." My view is kindred to that of the influential German existentialist philosopher Karl Jaspers (1883–1969), who held that "spontaneous philosophy"—the inescapable urge to ask profound questions and seek out answers, of a type that lead to a whole new host of questions, and answers—is in children's DNA. For kids, this "Socratizing" is an existential thrill ride. The more unexpected twists and turns, the more surprising and novel the insights, the merrier they are.

I myself got the Socratic bug at age twelve, after my Greek grandmother, my *yaya*, Kalliope Casavarakis Philipou, gave me a handsome leather-bound English translation of Plato's Socratic dialogues. She tweaked my cheek, as Greek grandmothers do, told me I had the blood of Socrates, and predicted that one day I would repeat his feat in modern contexts, engaging people anywhere and everywhere in philosophical inquiry. I read the book from cover to cover, again and again. Socrates rocked. His notion that each of us could and should become our own best questioners and thinkers spoke to me.

Martin Heidegger (1889–1976), the German philosopher who made a lasting name for himself with his existential explorations, considered Socrates the "purest thinker of the West," because the Athenian believed that the questions posed were more important than the answers arrived at. My affinity with Socrates lies more in the fact that, to him, even the most convincing answers were never meant to be final, but merely a way station for using one's imagination and experiences to develop a whole new host of questions. The long and short of it is that my *yaya* ruined my life. From that point forward, the idea of having normal career aspirations would not do. I wanted to be a Socratic seeker. Which is who I've become.

I started my first Socrates Café way back in 1996 in a cozy coffeehouse in Montclair, New Jersey. I shared the sensibility of the fifth century BC philosopher that continual close encounters with others of a philosophical kind, engaging in impassioned yet thoughtful exchanges of ideas and ideals, is a portal to sculpting what the Greeks of old called *arete*—all-around excellence of a sort that is an individual and collective pursuit rolled into one. Socrates Café went on to become something of a phenomenon, an oasis of reasonableness in a desert of rising intolerance and fundamentalism taking place around the world. Hundreds of groups now convene far and wide in public places and spaces, including cyberspace, but also in brick-and-mortar locales like schools, churches, community centers, nursing homes, prisons, shelters for homeless families, libraries, even daycare centers.

Socrates Café still has momentum after all this time. As motley people break philosophical bread together on a regular basis, close connections are often forged among the strangest bedfellows. If you were a fly on the wall at one of these gatherings, you'd see that Socrates Café-goers in action are an inquisitive, open, curious, and playful bunch—childlike, in a word.

I'm fond of saying that Socrates Café is for "children of all ages," because these gatherings bring out our innate inquisitiveness and sense of wonder. Speaking of children, over the years I have held thousands of dialogues around the globe with our youngest, both inside and outside the hallowed halls of formal learning. Their beautiful minds think in a brilliant array of colors, and their often-jarring and mind-bending insights help me see old conundrums in new lights.

At this latest philosophical soiree, no sooner do I put forward the chicken-and-egg question than eight-year-old Eva says right back to me, "Look, I know we're in Iowa, and this is farm country and all, but I don't know the first thing about chickens and eggs. I *do* know something about how human babies are born. My mom is an obstetrician. If I can refer to *Homo sapiens* instead of chickens, then I can tell you something about who comes first."

Without waiting for my permission, Eva continues in a schoolmarmish tone, "An adult male and female member of the species have to mate in order to fertilize the female's egg—and by adults, I mean *biological* ones who can produce eggs and sperms that can make babies." She looks at Ms. Bunn, her third-grade teacher, and asks, "Is it sperm or sperms?" She gets no immediate reply from her disconcerted teacher, so goes on, "In real life, it boils down to this: the male has to impregnate the female with one of his sperm. If the impregnation is by artificial insemination, it still requires a mature male sperm. Once that sperm fuses with one of the female's eggs—whether in the uterine tube or the test tube—the process of fertilization begins. Eventually, if everything goes as planned, the fused cells form a zygote, or fertilized egg, which keeps dividing in more and more specialized ways. Then, about nine months later, a fully developed baby is born."

She turns her attention back to me. "I have no idea where these first baby-makers—much less chick-makers—came from. But they *had* to have come first, because they are the possessors of the eggs and sperm, or sperms—unless there is something like . . ." Eva struggles with the word "parthenogenesis," and settles on "asexual reproduction." She then goes on

to say, "As is the case with flatworms and sharks, where the begetter and begettee are one and the same."

Seth sort of nods. He's not sure he has altogether understood Eva, to whom he's taken a shine, but nonetheless he's determined to support her. "Adult chickens and adult humans must have come first, because babies or chicks wouldn't last long without them. Once the baby human or chick enters the world, then at least one adult has to be ready to take on the role of parent and raise it. Human babies, every bit as much as baby chicks, are helpless and defenseless creatures. Someone has to nourish them, watch over them, fend for them, or they're not long for this world. In the case of humans, sometimes the adult or adults who care for a baby aren't the same ones who made the baby. Sometimes it isn't even an adult, but an older kid. But usually, it's one or more of the original parents."

Katrina now says, "Seth is right. Human parents have a job to do: it's called *parenting*—raising children from babyhood, so they can grow into happy and healthy adults. You don't ever hear anyone talking about *childing*, do you?"

"There *should* be a word like childing," says Lauren. "Children give birth to parents. There wouldn't *be* parents without children. Not only that, children *raise* parents. My mom and dad all the time tell me how they learn important lessons in life from me. They say I help them grow as human beings."

"Children don't just raise their own parents; they raise all of us of adult age who are privileged to be part of their lives," says Ms. Bunn.

Then she says to me, "Earlier in the year, I'd shared the joyful news with my students that I was expecting a child. When I had a miscarriage, I tried to think of how to tell them. I kept putting it off. Then, one by one, each came to me in a private moment. They knew just what to say, and what not to say. Several told me that their moms had had miscarriages, but went on to have babies. I found strength and comfort in their gestures. They lifted me up from sorrow. I learned a great deal from how they reached out to me about how to reach out to others in their time of need."

We sit in comfortable silence for a spell, until Eva says, "My parents aren't the only ones who raise me. Ms. Bunn raises me too. So do other adults. There should be a word to describe that—adulting!" She thinks some more. "My friends raise me too. They stand up for me, protect me, call me on the carpet when I'm not being kind. They're like an extended part of my family."

To which Lauren says, "When it comes to raising one another, we're all in this together, children and adults. We need one another to make sure we don't shrivel like raisins."

This inspires Seth to say, "Does that mean we all come first?"

A Childing We Will Go

Are these kids onto something? Many adults speak in glowing terms about how their lives are incalculably enhanced by the youngest among us. But do we really consider our brethren at the other end of the age spectrum our peers in matters of raising one another? Do our actions often belie our words?

When I enter the word "adulting," my spell-check software changes it to "adulating." The nerve. As if all adults merit adulation. When I refuse to let spell-check have its way, it remonstrates me with fiery red squiggly underlining. The message: this word does not exist. Just to be sure, I do an extensive search in a variety of dictionaries. Sure enough, adulting is not in our lexicon.

Then I type "childing." Spell-check again tells me I'm barking up the wrong etymological tree. This time, I'm inclined to accept the verdict. Still, I double-check. Lo and behold, an enormous *Merriam-Webster* dictionary, a childhood Christmas gift, reveals that this word does indeed exist. It turns out that "childing" has been around for centuries, even if it did fall out of favor long ago.

Childing first arrived on the scene around 1250 AD. According to *Merriam-Webster*, the word denotes "being pregnant" or "bearing a child."

Robert Southey made use of the word in his stirring poem "The Battle of Blenheim," published just before the turn of the nineteenth century. In it two children "with wonder-waiting eyes" ask a man named Old Kaspar what the 1704 war—in which allied troops under the Duke of Marlborough defeated the French and Bavarians under the French Marshal Camille d'Hostun, duc de Tallard—was all about. He tells them:

> With fire and sword the country round
> Was wasted far and wide,
> And many a childing mother then,
> And new-born baby died;
> But things like that, you know, must be
> At every famous victory.

About a century before Southey, William Shakespeare made matchless use of the term in *A Midsummer Night's Dream*. Oberon and Titania, the king and queen of the fairies, are engaged in a torrential tiff over whether a little boy from India whom Titania has taken under her wing and mothered since infancy belongs to her or to Oberon, who refers to the boy as his "charm," as if a mere trifle. The acrimonious barbs the immortals hurl at one another reach such a crescendo that Mother Nature herself is thrown out of kilter. When Titania takes a moment to catch her breath, she surveys the aftermath.

> The childing autumn, angry winter, change
> Their wonted liveries; and the mazed world
> By their increase, now knows not which is which.
> And this same progeny of evils comes
> From our debate, from our dissension;
> We are their parents and original.

Just when autumn is aborning, winter muscles its discontented way into the picture. Not only have Titania and Oberon managed to upend the order of the seasons, but they've stirred autumn and winter into such a frenzy that it's impossible to pry the two apart. Titania acknowledges that she and Oberon have "childed" this mayhem. The cautionary tale: be mindful of your actions, lest you "child" in unintended if not disastrous

ways. If Titania subscribes to the Gaia hypothesis, which holds that all the world's creations, inorganic and organic alike, are intimately interlocked, then she must have been dismayed that their immortal ability to throw the seasons into disarray confounded all the world's creations.

I do some more digging. I unearth an old edition of *Collins American Dictionary* and find another definition of childing: "bearing a cluster of newer blossoms around an older blossom." Such a rendering, if applied to the human condition, would indicate that there is no shedding of the old as we add the new, but a continual super-adding of the new to the old.

How can we best see to it that we blossom like flowers rather than shrivel like raisins? Is a philosophy of childing in order, as Lauren of the Iowa elementary school put it?

Never before has our culture been as child-centric as it is today, and yet, never before has childhood been as strained and pinched. Its serendipity and spontaneity is fast disappearing in our heavily vocationalized, over-scheduled culture. Kids are expected to be adults-in-training and to be thinking about college by the time they're in third grade. To the extent that we've bought into this hyper-utilitarian notion of childhood, we not only do tremendous damage to kids, but to ourselves, severely constricting our possibilities for being all that we can be.

Sir Isaac Newton (1643–1727), one of the most important scientists of all time, singled out for praise René Descartes (1596–1650), dubbed the father of modern philosophy, for deepening and expanding his horizons for knowing both the inner and outer cosmos. "If I have seen a little further," Newton claims in a February 6, 1675, letter to a friend, "it is by standing on the shoulders of giants."

What if in order to see further in matters of human prospering, we must stand on the shoulders of our youngest? What if kids are giants when it comes to being paragons who chart groundbreaking paths of seeing and being and doing?

A "philosophy of childing" is called for, a systematic philosophical take grounded in powerful evidence from the human sciences about how we should treat children and what we can learn from the way young people process the world. Because in matters of human flourishing, we at times must take our cue from those with the least number of physical years under their belts. This is based on the perhaps-unsettling assertion that, without the able assistance and guidance of kids, we are apt to shrink mentally, emotionally, and cognitively with the passage of time. If we're not vigilant, our sense of who we are can become fuzzier over time, diminishing our prospects for further development. Indeed, if we persist in denaturing our original nature, we'll mistake rottenness for ripeness.

But all is far from lost; kids can show us the way out of this pitfall. By tapping into their unique talents and capacities, we can continue on an upward path of growth and development our whole lives. And we can return the favor in spades by ensuring that our youngest also have full and ample opportunity to flourish from a healthy core.

We can greatly expand our horizons regarding our development by taking a radically different approach to the boundaries between childhood and adulthood, paying far more attention to the former. By doing so, we can sustain our development along the meteoric lines with which it began, rather than let it lapse, as it too frequently does, into apathy, bitterness, and dullness as we become adults.

As I set about challenging and debunking much of the received "wisdom" about children, I draw on the gripping observations and arguments of a band of mostly modern philosophers who make a convincing case for the indispensable role that kids play in helping us become all we can be at every age and stage of our lives. These philosophers have the pluck to take on three of the most lionized philosophical and humanistic luminaries of all time—Plato (427/488–347/348 BC), Aristotle (384–322 BC), and Michel de Montaigne (1533–1592)—whose perspectives on themes central to human flowering—on human ages and stages, growth and shrinkage, play and work, identity and spiritedness—continue to play an outsized role. Leading developmental specialists across the disciplines (not to mention self-help gurus) have long been hoodwinked by their persuasive but unsupported prejudices about the youngest (and also, at times, the oldest) among us and what they have to offer if we are to thrive singly and together.

My principal aim, though, isn't to "deconstruct" and just dismantle flimsy philosophical perspectives on children formulated by idolized ancients; rather, it's to construct something more compelling and substantial in their place. To that end, I don't just radically reassess long-dominant notions of what optimal "human being-ing" can be; instead, I attempt to do so in ways that present new possibilities to be considered. In doing so, I draw on the thinking of an alternative coterie of philosophers, many revered in their own right, whose philosophical thinking on the unique capacities of kids has received lamentably short shrift. Their iconoclastic if not heretical perspectives presage many of the groundbreaking findings today by researchers in cognitive science, psychology, and neuroscience, among other human sciences disciplines, who are confirming empirically some of their more disconcerting and exhilarating insights. Far from settling matters, this opens up new lines of inquiry for how we optimally can grow one another.

Why "grow" rather than "raise"? The verb "to raise" fits the bill in many ways: to lift up, to elevate, to set upright. The verb "to grow" incorporates various meanings of "to raise," but it also offers additional avenues for evolution in the human sphere. The definition of "to grow" that is most profitable for my purposes is this one offered by *Merriam-Webster*: "to develop from a parent source." A parent source that "childs."

To better understand our potential for childing, I convene hither and yon with people of many ages and at many stations of life with an unquenchable love of asking "Why? Why? Why?" It's my experience that it's in a certain kind of group setting, with a method of inquiry that requires the sustained and thoughtful consideration of a variety of objections and alternatives to any given point of view, that we can most effectively hash out our highest ideas, our values, our visions for ourselves and one another, in this case about how we best unfold. And as I assert in *Six Questions of Socrates*, in crafting the dialogues for my books, I take my cue from Plato, and "use some license in fashioning the dialogues adapted here from the dialogues in which I took part, in order to reflect *more* faithfully the tone and tenor and substance of what took place. To this end, the actual dialogues best serve as a template from which to cull and structure and compose."

As always, my objective as a speculative philosopher in the Socratic mold is not to come up with the last word, much less have the pretense to be all-encompassing. Rather, it's to present promising new vantage points for consideration.

In the acclaimed journals of author Anaïs Nin (1903–1977), which she began writing at age eleven, she observes that "some people remind me of sharp dazzling diamonds. Valuable but lifeless and loveless. Others, of the simplest field flowers, with hearts full of dew and with all the tints of celestial beauty reflected in their modest petals." She makes clear her preference for the latter, who have "a warmth and softness" that is lacking in those with "mere brilliancy and coldness" who are both the willful parents and originators of a host of ills. By all outward appearances, they may have grown up and out in brilliant fashion, but as we know, appearances are deceiving.

How can we child one another so that we are not crushed into diamonds, but able to flourish? As I set off in search of promising answers, I do so as a husband and a father of a young family who hopes to build on his modest efforts to help make this uncertain world a bit more livable and loveable, so that those "with hearts full of dew and with all the tints of celestial beauty reflected in their modest petals" can shine.

Chapter 2

Ages and Stages

Stagecraft

WHAT IS MAN? A STAGE-CRAFTER, FOR ONE, IN THAT IT'S A NATURAL impulse to define and assess the various stages of life. Witness the relentless attempts over the millennia to carve out sets of ages and stages that tell the definitive story of our growth and development. Two of the most influential modern stage-crafters focused only on childhood, due to their premise that the first years of life are all-determining in the formation of our adulthood personality.

The theory of Sigmund Freud (1856–1939) of our psychosexual development describes a process during which our personality and sexual drives, instincts and appetites evolve in a series of five fixed stages from birth to adolescence. The eight cognitive stages of Swiss developmental psychologist Jean Piaget (1896–1980) detail our intellectual progress from infancy to the latter years of youth. The developmental psychologist and psychoanalyst Erik Erikson (1902–1994) and the Swiss psychoanalyst Carl Jung (1875–1961), on the other hand, carved out human stages that run the course of our lives; they maintained that we continue to grow and change in distinctive ways well into our adult years. Erikson distinguished eight stages of psychosocial development, each with its unique crises that one must confront and overcome in order to have a healthy sense of self. Jung marked out four broad stages in our personality's progression through distinct levels of consciousness, which starts out hazy but becomes increasingly heightened, until one reaches old age. Though not as well-known, even more types of stages have since been "discovered." For instance, Yale psychologist Daniel Levinson (1920–1994) identified four adult stages—pre-adulthood, early adulthood, middle adulthood, and late adulthood—in each of which one's life outlook and commitments alter markedly.

These stage-crafters' attempts to divvy up stages and come up with distinguishing characteristics for each are meant to be scientific and as such, provide a theoretical explanation and foundation for determining how best to go about flourishing in an optimal way. According to each theorist, only successful completion of each stage will leave us with an elevated sense of well-being and a healthy self-image. On the other hand, failure to do so usually takes a lasting toll and results in aberrant development.

Once upon a time, philosophers got in on the stage-crafting act in a big way, lending to the undertaking their peculiar slants on the world of human experience. Greco-Roman philosopher, mathematician, and astronomer Ptolemy (90–168 AD) asserted that the universe's seven heavenly spheres held sway over seven matching stages of human life. He was convinced that each planet influenced our life stages by its speed of movement around the zodiac, with the fastest—the moon, which speeds around the earth—associated with birth, and the slowest, Saturn, tied to the last years of life. The enlightenment philosopher Jean-Jacques Rousseau (1712–1778) identified six ages of human maturation—the age of infancy (birth to age two), the age of sensation or nature (three to twelve), the age of ideas (at the onset of puberty), the age of sentiment (puberty to age twenty), the age of marriage and social responsibility (from age twenty-one on), and finally, the age of happiness. Rousseau believed that the older we get, the more richly and deeply we experience life—until about age sixty, when our powers begin to wane. The Spanish liberal philosopher José Ortega y Gasset (1883–1955) believed the four biological stages mirror our advancement in "the knowing of life." As he put it, "What are called the ages of man—childhood, youth, maturity, and old age—more than differences in the condition of our bodies signify different stages

in the experience of life," with each offering its singular set of insights.[1]
The Danish philosopher, theologian, and social critic Søren Kierkegaard
(1813–1855) contended that humans potentially ascend three stages: the
aesthetic (the life of pleasure), the ethical (in which one grows up and
accepts responsibility for one's conduct), and at the apex, the religious
stage (in which one becomes, as he put it in his famous work *Fear and
Trembling*, a "knight of faith" and embraces God). To Kierkegaard, we
pass through these stages—which represent modes of being—"on life's
way" toward realizing our true self. But many of us may never advance
beyond the first or the second stage and attain the ultimate stage, the religious. Kierkegaard's stage are aspirational; we can only ascend them with
will, purpose, and direction. Even if these assays at stage-crafting reveal
as much or more about the individuals who devised them as they do the
rest of us, they've driven the way we relate to one another, govern one
another, raise and educate our young. The typical aim is to "universalize"
the human equation in some way. This facilitates, for better or worse, the
creation in modern times of standardized models for assessing our development and for implementing one-size-fits-all gauges of our cognitive,
emotional, mental, and motor development.

Whatever stage theory or theories you subscribe to can be a kind of self-
fulfilling prophecy. If the stage theory you embrace holds out the promise
that you can continue to evolve, adapt, create until your dying day—
perhaps in unanticipated or far different ways than when you were
younger—this can have a decisive influence on how you live. But if it
leads you to conclude that your growth path is largely foreordained, this
can prove a convenient crutch to justify doing little with your life, or at
least, not as much as you otherwise might.

When it comes to human flowering, do any of the stage theories invented so far come close to circumscribing our growth and development? Are
they overly constricted, distorted, or do some—or some combination—
get it just about right?

---

1 Translated citation of Ortega y Gasset from *A Pragmatist Philosophy of Life in Ortega y Gasset*, John
T. Graham, Columbia, MO: University of Missouri Press, 1994, p. 53.

Exit Stage Left

I'm with a group of sixth graders and seniors—a baker's dozen of each—at a community center near Montclair, New Jersey, where I established my first Socrates Café group in 1996 (the group continues to meet weekly after all these years). At one of the first Socrates Cafés I convened all those years ago, I met Ahmed, now seventy-one, the center's activities director who invited me to preside over this latest session. Once a month, the school kids rendezvous with seniors here. I relish opportunities to inquire with our youngest and oldest together. Those close to the beginning and the end of the human life cycle have a kindred curiosity, openness, and honesty, and they share enthusiasm for following a line of inquiry wherever it happens to lead. (Another reason they have such an affinity might be that they have a common antagonist—adults of parenting age.)

In the days leading up to this gathering, I'd immersed myself in the works of luminaries who'd constructed influential stage theories. By the time I arrive, my mind is swimming in stage theory. I survey my captive audience, seated around tables in groups of four—two adults and two children at each—sipping coffee, tea, or juice. I find myself wondering if any of the stage theories I've read about remotely do them justice? Before I know it, I find myself asking them, "What stage of life are you in?"

No sooner has the question popped out of my mouth than eleven-year-old Whitney says, "I'm in a forgetful stage. When my mom or dad or teacher asks me to do something—power down my iPod, submit a homework assignment to our online Blackboard site, take out the compost—next thing I know, I've forgotten all about it. I'm not trying to be difficult, as they choose to think. It's just that I have so much else on my mind. This is the first time I've fallen in love, and it's all I can do to think about anyone or anything else but my true love." If I'm not mistaken, her beau gives himself away with sudden face-reddening and seat-squirming.

"You're not in a forgetful stage," Isadora, eighty-three, tells her. "When I was your age, I went through the same thing. My parents called me 'flighty.' My mind was in a million places at once. The wonders of the world, the dawning of love and romance, my own rising awareness of myself as a living, thinking, creating human . . . my goodness, it's enough to make anyone forget run-of-the-mill tasks. You'll learn how to better compartmentalize your thoughts and feelings over time."

"You're not going through a stage at all. You're going through a phase that's a normal part of your stage of life, early youth," Isadora next says to Whitney. "A stage marks a clear transition, while a phase is part of a series of passages within a stage. For instance, there are phases within the three stages in childbirth."

The children (who like most their age are fascinated by the topic of birth) ask Isadora, who was a midwife for more than forty years, to tell them more.

"The first stage marks when labor begins," she says. "It has early, active, and transition phases that take place before the changeover to the second stage, when the mother begins to push the baby out. In the third stage, the baby enters the world, and the placenta follows. The fourth stage is recovery, when, if there are no medical issues to attend to, mommy and baby spend some quality time bonding."

"Isn't there a fifth stage?" says Maia. "After the baby is born and becomes an official part of your family? That was a distinct transition for me. I'd been an only child for seven years when my triplet sisters were born."

"Well, that's right," Isadora says. "I hadn't thought about it that way, but that should be considered a stage too." She thinks some more. "The same could be said for other distinct changes in our lives—becoming a parent or grandparent, losing a parent or grandparent, getting married, divorced. All of those could be considered stages."

"Are those stages or milestones?" I ask.

"Maybe milestones," she says after some thought. "Or maybe stepping stones—watershed moments that lead to new possibilities for your development."

"I can't decide whether I'm in the 'what do I want to be when I grow up' stage or phase," I then say. "I've never grown out of it, so does that mean it's a phase that extends throughout my life? Among other avocations, I still hope there's time to be a lawyer, a toymaker, an actor, an astronomer, a novelist."

"I ask myself all the time what I want to be when I grow up," says Harry, ten. "Maybe for some it's a stage, and for others, like you, it's kind of a permanent phase. For my dad, it was a stage. He decided when he was my age that he wanted to be a fireman, and that's what he became. He's never dreamed of being anything else."

"For me, it's a recurrent phase," says Isadora. "It comes out like clock-work with great intensity every several years, and then goes back into hibernation. I still dream of being a veterinarian, an actress, a songwriter." She sighs. "Those will just remain dreams." Then she turns to Whitney and says, "While you're going through a forgetful phase in your childhood stage that you'll get over, I am getting more and more plain forgetful. It will only get worse. It's part of aging, the process in which your biological parts, including your thinking parts, wear out over time. It's a stage I won't exit from until I die."

"Can it be a stage then?" asks Whitney. "Isn't a stage something you pass through?"

"A stage is something you enter, sometimes by choice, sometimes not, just as it's not always something you exit, even when you could if you wanted to," says Ahmed. "You can enter, or exit, some stages kicking and screaming. I entered the old-age stage of life that way, I didn't want any part of this biological stage, even if it can't be avoided if you live long enough.

"With more and more infirmities to deal with, it does limit me from doing many of the things I most enjoy. On the other hand, just because I'm in this stage doesn't mean I have to become a grumpy old man and resign myself to the belief that now that I'm on the dark side of the biological mountain, I can't have an enjoyable life. I read more now, think more. I've taken up painting, even dabbled in poetry. If I was as active now as I was even a few years back, I wouldn't be doing these things, which I've come to enjoy tremendously. I plan to leave this world just as I entered it—kicking and screaming. I love each day, and I rebel against the idea that this stage of my life can't be as meaningful in its way as my earlier life stages."

This brings eleven-year-old Chad to say, "My dad says I'm in a 'rebellious stage.' By that he means I'm questioning and challenging authority—his authority. I used to never question him. Even if he said something outrageous like, 'I would never trust a Muslim,' I let it slide. These days, I take him on. I'm at a stage in life where I want reasons. My dad would like to think that what I'm going through is just a phase. He says he's more careful about what he says around me now, for fear I'll jump down his throat. I've done no such thing. He should appreciate that I want to know why he's coming from where he's coming from. That helps me figure out better my own views on things."

Virginie, seventy-nine, has given Chad her undivided attention as she crochets a shawl with intricate patterns. "My husband thinks I'm in a rebellious stage, too. 'Go along to get along' was my motto. Our relationship was in a well-established forty-three-year rut. I never thought of it in terms of good or bad. It was what it was. That began to change after one of my granddaughters invited me to a 'stitch and bitch' knitting session at her house. At first, I blushed to high heaven at some of the things they shared openly. I didn't hold my own in the conversations—what did I have to say of any interest?—but I was a good listener. They kept inviting me back, and soon I began to open up. Soon I became an excellent 'bitcher' in my own right.

"My husband is slow to the take but even he began to detect the change in me. I've become what he calls 'sassy,' what you here would call bitchy. I want in my relationship what those young women have, to be equal partners in an intimate relationship. My husband remains convinced that what I'm experiencing is 'just a phase' I'll pass through. Not pass through as in go forward, but as in, go backward, regress to being who I used to be. If anything, I'll just get bitchier. I want what I want. He's in the Stone Age stage. I'll keep trying to bring him into what is commonly referred to as the twenty-first century. If he doesn't come along for the ride, I'll leave him and move into a group home with some other bitchy and rebellious old ladies."

Everyone claps.

Soon afterward, Meng, seventy-nine, says, "My wife and I went our separate ways several years ago, after a half-century together. Ever since I entered the old-age stage, I've been in a state of crisis. I sailed through midlife, no crisis at all. But I had a late-life crisis starting around the time I turned sixty-five. I pined for my youthful years. I got bogged down in what I didn't do rather than what I've accomplished, and can still accomplish. My therapist has helped me understand that I've gone through distinct stages within this stage—denial, anger, and a stage she calls 'replay,' where I attempt to return to my lost youth. My wife loved me, showed great understanding for what I was going through, and for my frailties, but even she had her limits. I don't blame her for leaving me. She forgave me after my first affair, but not the one that followed. Only after we divorced did I seek help and begin to deal with my crisis.

"At last I can safely say I'm entering the stage of acceptance—but not resignation." His wizened face breaks into a smile. "I'm still finding my way, but I'm enjoying this stage of life now. In some ways, without pretending to be any younger chronologically than I am. Being in one's seventies is 'the new old age.' Hell, with life expectancy so much greater these days because of all the advances in medicine and in preventive care, I still have time to write the great American novel I've always dreamed about. I'm trying to make my second act in life memorable. *Carpe diem* is my motto these days. I hope to have quite a curtain call."

This theme of a "second act" in life is at the center stage of *O My America!: Six Women and Their Second Acts*. Biographer Sara Wheeler chronicles six nineteenth-century women who in their fifties—which typically proved in that era to be the "last gray chapters of female lives"— reinvented themselves entirely. For instance, Frances Trollope set off in her fifties for Europe, and even though she "had grown up with the entrenched idea that life was more or less over for a woman at fifty," she went on to write a bestselling book about American manners and a number of acclaimed social protest novels. She disproved F. Scott Fitzgerald's assertion in an unfinished novel that there are no second acts in American lives, and inspired her son Anthony to become an author himself (and a praised and prolific one at that).

"My mother had me when she was forty-seven," says Harry. "When I turned ten, she had an older-age crisis. She had plastic surgery. It made her happy, and that made me and the rest of the family happy. She's now with a guy just a few years older than my older brother. I guess she's in a 'forever young' stage. I hope for her sake that it turns into a passing phase. All I want is for her to be happy. I can tell she still isn't, not really. The guy she's with will leave her eventually. I feel sad for her that she had a family who loved her just like she was, but it wasn't enough to make her happy."

"Hopefully she'll find her way through this stage," says Virginie. "One of my sisters went through something very similar when she was your mother's age. Her way of addressing it was not to address age head-on, but to get involved in something so important that she forgot about her age. If there's a protest for a cause she believes in, she marches in it. I have no doubt that if she gets too feeble to march, she'll have someone push her in a wheelchair. She was just accepted into law school, so she can be of even more service to the causes she supports. Maybe she'll keel over during her bar exam, but at least she'll end her days full of life and fight."

After a short time passes, Christine, eleven, makes eye contact with Meng as she says, "My youngest brother was diagnosed with autism. It was hard for all of us to accept. My parents especially had a difficult time. They went through stages close to what you shared with us—denial, anger, confusion, depression. We became educated on autism spectrum disorders. We learned how the developmental stages for kids with autism are different than for other kids, yet how, except in the most severe cases, they can live a rich and full life, with the help of specialists and a family's love and support. My brother is amazing with art. Our rooms are plastered with his work. If only I were a hundredth as talented.

"All of us in my family are in the stage of acceptance now. It still isn't easy, but is any stage, whether denial or acceptance, ever totally easy? Moving from one stage to another means there's change, and that can mean there's some sort of passage we have to experience. Going from being an infant to a toddler to a child wasn't easy. I'm sure being an adolescent isn't going to be easy, if my older siblings are anything to go by."

This prompts Chad to say, "What would it be like to be at an easy stage of life, with all the pieces in place, no stresses, trouble free, no big changes to dread or look forward to?"

"It would make life less interesting," says Phil. "Or I suppose it depends. One of my childhood friends left Jersey right after turning eighteen and has lived by Surfrider Beach in Malibu for almost six decades. He still surfs, still plays the drums with young and old companions at night. I visit him on occasion. He dreamed of living an endless summer-type existence, and that's what he's done."

"My romance with my husband was of the endless summer variety—if that term can be applied to describe a life together of near-endless bliss and a love deep and true and changeless," says Isadora. "It was never a rut, never boring. It was the soil for endless growth." Directing her attention at Christine and then at Meng, "Those stages you both described fit almost to a tee the stages of grieving. My husband—my best friend, my soul mate—died fifteen years ago. We never had children. It was just me and Frank. We loved our life together. We didn't want to share each other with children. We traveled, took all kinds of classes, from pastry making to salsa dancing. We learned languages, lived here and then there, the world our oyster. I wouldn't change a thing about how we lived. I only wish our life together had lasted longer."

"Well-meaning people gave me books that dealt with the stages of grief," she goes on, "so I could recognize and confront each of them as they came along. I was assured that I'd learn not only to live with grief but to 'get past' it. I have gotten on with my life, but I'll never get past my grief. Why would I? It's a permanent state, not a stage. Frank was the love of my life. Really, the term grief doesn't begin to do justice to the enormity of the loss."

Until now, Anna had listened intently to others' offerings, but had not spoken herself. Looking at Isadora, she says, "I wish I'd had that kind of relationship. Mine was more like Virginie's, in a well-grooved rut. My husband, Herbert, and I raised a family—nine children!—and were married fifty-seven years when he passed. I did go through the stages of grief as they were described in Elizabeth Kübler-Ross's book, *On Death and Dying*—denial, anger, bargaining, depression—sometimes several at the same time. At last I entered the final stage, acceptance. But even then, it wasn't smooth. There was some back-and-forthing, some refusal on my part to give in—sometimes swimming against the current, other times resisting the current.

"After over a year had passed, I began to reflect more honestly about our life together. I realized that I never had been in love with Herbert. Yes, we were quite fond of one another, committed, devoted to our family. There was love of a sort, but it didn't grow. I felt guilty acknowledging this to myself at first, but truth will out."

Despite her serious tone, she smiles. "I had a boyfriend, Henry, during my middle school years. As you young people here know, you can love deeply when very young. Henry's family had to move to California. His father was military and that was his new base. I was heartbroken. My parents thought I'd get over it, that I couldn't possibly know what it was like to be in love. His family moved two more times in the years to come, and we did fall out of touch eventually.

"About nine months ago, Henry tracked me down. I don't have a Facebook account, but he does and he located me through one of our mutual friends who keeps a Facebook page. When he asked her if she knew how to reach me, she gave him my contact info. When he called and I heard his voice again, how my heart pounded.

"His wife had died several years back. They raised a beautiful family, had a nice life. Their relationship was better than mine was with my husband. But Henry said he'd never stopped thinking about me over the years. He started phoning me regularly. Then we opened Skype accounts, so we could have video chats. I was worried that when he saw me, he wouldn't be so keen on staying in touch. But that wasn't so. He's still handsome, his smile still kind and warm. He's still the same Henry I'd known, and loved, all those years ago."

"He's flying here to see me this weekend. His fourth visit in two-and-a-half months. Henry proposed to me his last visit. Can you guess my answer? My children don't approve—except my youngest, bless his heart. To the rest, this is just a phase. They think I'm behaving like a silly schoolgirl. What they don't understand is that my love for Henry is of the permanent variety. It had deep roots and now is growing again. The best love has stages, stages of ascent."

Whitney claps her hands in delight. "Yes! The love I feel inside for one particular person is eternal, just like yours. My mother and siblings think our love is just a phase, just like my love of princesses. But my love and I—I won't say his name here; I don't want to embarrass him—we know better. He told me just yesterday that I'll always be his princess."

A World of Stages

Almost all stage theories are based on the conviction that human growth and development is progressive in bent—or at least, an uphill climb before there is any downhill slide—and that if and as we successfully pass through each stage, we augment our capacity to grasp ever more complex realms of experience. In instances, this capacity may peak at middle age or soon after, but in almost all instances, these stage-crafters hold that we start out life at the bottom of the developmental heap, and that the only direction to go from there is up.

An exception is Shakespeare, whose plays the famed German philosopher and social critic Friedrich Nietzsche (1844–1900) says in *Human, All Too Human* were "so full of ideas they make all others seem empty." At the time he penned his famous "all the world's a stage" soliloquy for *As You Like It*, the notion that man's journey from cradle to grave had distinct ages was old hat. As historian Philippe Ariès (1914–1984) notes in *Centuries of Childhood*, one popular fourteenth-century version depicted them this way: the age of toys, the age of love, the age of war and chivalry (considered the peak stage), the age of love for learning, the age of the hoary scholar, and finally, the age of infirmity and death. In the hands of Shakespeare's irascible Jacques, these ages of man are given a jaded twist: Man makes his debut as an infant "mewling and puking in his nurse's arm." He then becomes a "whining school boy." From there, he transitions to the age of the lover, his claim to fame his ability to sigh "like a furnace, with a woeful ballad." He goes on to become a soldier, all puffed up and full of himself, "seeking the bubble reputation." The fifth age is likened to a well-fed, well-heeled justice "full of wise saws and modern instances." By the time he reaches the sixth age, he is reduced to a "slipper'd pantaloon," his voice a "childish treble." His "strange and eventful history" winds up in stage seven, marked by "second childishness and mere oblivion," "sans teeth, sans taste, sans everything." To Jacques, it's as low as we can go—but it's not as if we started out on a high note to begin with.

Jacques does not trace the trajectory of stages for women, but it's safe to assume they would be just as miserable. Jacques's philosophy of stages challenges any notion that each successive stage of man represents some sort of advance in the lived experience. What he offers us is a "human shrinkage" theory of man: we start out puny, then have a spell in which we engage in a bit of puffery to deceive ourselves into thinking we're growing, when in truth we remain puny, and if possible, get ever punier. There is no progression, no ascent, no peaking.

For those who insist that there is a highest stage, it usually makes its appearance when we're in the so-called prime of our lives. But what if it turns out that in many respects we are at our highest when we are at our lowest on the human totem pole, when we are mewling, puking infants and whining schoolboys and schoolgirls?

Karl Jaspers, for one, maintains, as he puts it in *Way to Wisdom*, that adults "overlook the fact that children often possess gifts which they lose as they grow up." In contrast to adults, "the child still reacts spontaneously to the spontaneity of life; the child feels and sees and inquires into things which soon disappear from his vision." The legendary social philosopher and educational reformer John Dewey (1859–1952) maintains in *How We Think* that we make our entrance into the world with a surfeit of beneficent habits crying out to be further cultivated. Yet often they are neglected to the point that they become supplanted by "habits of hasty, heedless, impatient glancing over the surface . . . of haphazard, grasshopper-like guessing . . . of credulity alternating with flippant incredulity, belief or unbelief being based, in either case, upon whim, emotion, or accidental circumstances." Dewey's use-it-or-lose-it philosophy is that "the only way to achieve traits of carefulness, thoroughness, and continuity . . . is by exercising these traits from the beginning"—traits which we possess from the outset but must polish if they are to remain in good condition. He rues that many seem willfully to exorcise these traits in themselves and do further damage by allowing them to atrophy in children under their care.

Following Dewey, one of my esteemed mentors, the lamentably unheralded Matthew Lipman (1922–2010), founder of the Institute for the Advancement of Philosophy for Children, at Montclair State University, decried the fact that human stages are crafted in a way that place adulthood at the pinnacle and childhood at bottom, as if childhood is "to be viewed as only a means to an end or as an incomplete condition moving toward completeness." The operating assumption, according to Lipman—who left his professorship at Columbia University to devote himself to nurturing children's natural abilities to philosophize—is that "adults know and children don't know":

> Children must, therefore, acquire the knowledge with which grownups are so richly endowed. Thus, . . . if children are not moving in the direction of what we adults know and believe and value, there must be something wrong with their "development."

Lipman's iconoclastic outlook was not arrived at intuitively, but rather was based on comprehensive experience. He realized after philosophizing extensively with children that in many respects they were more adept at reasoning than his Ivy League students and older adults. Lipman ridicules prevailing notions that stage-by-stage advancement is *ipso facto* progressive. He notes that boosters of hierarchically-based developmental stage theories "are always careful to select those criteria which will reinforce the case they are trying to make, while ignoring other criteria through whose use that case might be weakened."

> Those who uphold the development thesis make sure not to select such criteria as artistic expression or philosophical insight, for to do so might make their case seem less compelling. Why do children create such impressive paintings while in early childhood? Why do they ask so many metaphysical questions while still young, then seem to suffer a decline in their powers as they move into adolescence? How can children learn the terms and syntax and logic of a whole language—indeed, often, of several languages—while they are still toddlers, a feat beyond the scope of most grownups?

For Lipman, the challenge that we need to recognize and meet is "to *sustain* the child's development along the meteoric lines with which it begins, rather than let it lapse, as it now so frequently does, into apathy and bitterness" as we become adults. We need to nurture their inborn artistry for achieving a well-rounded life. To do this, those charged principally with growing our children must first acknowledge and appreciate the high note at which they start out their lives. The view of Lipman, whose philosophical specialty was aesthetics—his little-known *What Happens in Art* is a tour de force—is reminiscent of Pablo Picasso's oft-quoted assertion that "every child is an artist. The problem is how to remain an artist once he grows up."

Ralph Waldo Emerson (1803–1882) pinpointed well over a century ago the chief obstacle to sustaining children's special way of and approach to unfolding. The quandary, he observes in one of his journals, is that "children are all foreigners"—or at least, "we treat them as such. We cannot understand their speech or their mode of life, and so our education is remote and accidental and not closely applied to the fact." The physician, researcher, and etymologist Lewis Thomas (1913–1993) agrees. The poetic philosopher of science and medicine, revered for his striking meditations on the unexpected or heretofore unexplored implications of research in the human and biological sciences, bemoans in *The Fragile Species* that "we seem to have forgotten, or never to have learned, what young children really are, and how special their minds are." He wrote:

> Most of us tend to think of early childhood as a primitive stage of life, a sort of deficiency in the mind that will, in time, be outgrown. What we keep overlooking is the sheer tremendous power, unique in the brain of the young child, never to be matched again in later life, for *learning*.

By learning, Thomas does not just or primarily mean the formal type, and he is by no means only alluding to the well-known ability of children to master different languages, if given the opportunity. Rather, he is "persuaded, by things written by some of the specialists who have spent their lives studying young children, and also by observations of my own, that young children that are fabulously skilled at all sorts of feats." He surmises that this is due to the fact that "they have receptors wired in for receiving the whole world."

Thomas's speculative insights, shared more than twenty years ago, turn out to be spot-on. Alison Gopnik, professor of psychology and affiliate professor of philosophy at the University of California at Berkeley, is among those cognitive specialists whose cutting-edge research is debunking long-reigning assumptions "that babies and young children are limited to the here and now—their immediate sensations and perceptions and experience," and "that babies and young children were basically defective adults—irrational, egocentric, and unable to think logically." Gopnik, author of the acclaimed *The Philosophical Baby* and coauthor of *Scientist in the Crib*, maintains that, to the contrary, "new studies . . . demonstrate that babies and very young children know, observe, explore, imagine, and learn more than we would ever have thought possible." A panoply of data across the science and social science disciplines make it abundantly evident that "babies' brains are actually more highly connected than adult brains; more neural pathways are available to babies than adults." Far from being "primitive grownups gradually attaining our perfection and complexity," Gopnik insists in an essay published in the *New York Times* that the youngest among us are "in some ways . . . smarter than adults."

Gopnik has a particular ax to grind with Jean Piaget, the founder of developmental psychology and cognitive development, whose view "that children were egocentric and amoral and that they had a very limited ability to understand or perceive abstract ideas such as causality" has long held sway. Her problem with Piaget and his legions of followers ever since is that they observe and assess children using methods with built-in biases—including asking questions that are bewildering and intimidating and even unintelligible to a child. Thus they confirm their preexisting views about kids' limitations.

Much of today's empirical research does debunk Piaget and his acolytes. In an article, "How Babies Think," in *Scientific American*, Gopnik points to studies that prove that "even the youngest children know, experience, and learn far more than scientists ever thought possible." Abundant research now shows that children are adept at figuring out probabilities and predicting future events, that they can engage in logical thinking, that their play activities are exercises in deep exploration, that they can understand cause and effect, and that they are adept at entertaining the perspectives of others.[2] If this is so, then it is hard to dispute the claim that childhood is our primary launching pad for research and development, a time of life when learning is more intense than at any other, when children gain the critical knowledge and skills that can help ensure that the human species as a whole remains adaptable. Yet children too often remained stymied at doing what they do best, and will continue to be, until we remove our blinders, face up to the fact that they have uncommon capacities, and as a result, quit viewing them as a big bundle of deficits.

Deficit Schmeficit

Piaget needn't be blamed. The principle culprit for the still-prevailing "deficit view" of children originates with the Greek polymath Aristotle.

---

2 For instance, a study by Fei Xu and Vashti Garcia at the University of British Columbia, reported in the journal *Nature*, shows that babies have an intuitive grasp of statistics that enables them to predict the likelihood of the occurrence of future events. Gopnik has learned in her own research that preschoolers not only employ probabilities to learn how things work, but that they take this a step further and use this innate ability to imagine new possibilities. A study carried out by Laura Schulz and Elizabeth Baraff Bonawitz at Massachusetts Institute of Technology demonstrates that when young children engage in exploratory play—figuring out how things work—they are for all intents and purposes examining cause and effect.

The student of Plato and teacher of Alexander the Great, hands down one of the most influential figures in Western intellectual history, relegates children to the bottom of the human heap. Children, he contends in two of his enduring classics, *Nicomachean Ethics* and *Politics*, are an amalgam of appetites run amuck, incapable of reasoning in even a rudimentary way. He considers kids so dissolute that he's sure they'd raze civilization without the continual vigilance of adults, whom he charges with wresting them from their inborn wanton habits and inculcating virtue, wisdom, happiness. The best that Aristotle can say about the youngest among us is that they are *capable* of becoming decent human specimens, with the proper nurturing and guidance of adults, their superiors in every respect. His negative notions of children have influenced aspiring stage theorists ever since.

Yet the evidence is convincing today that we begin our lives with a moral and intellectual bang. To be sure, if we adults want to make sure kids grow optimally, we have to be there for them and make sure they cross the street safely, don't trip over their shoelaces, don't touch a hot stove, get enough sleep. This frees them up to do what they do best—explore, experiment, learn, understand, imagine, create. However, just as children are fragile in certain ways and must be protected if they are to develop optimally, so are adults. Indeed, adults enter into social contracts (including treaties) and lots of other kinds of binding agreements to ensure they are protected from one another's worst impulses. Humanistic advances are sporadic at best, while the constant is that adults make a mess of things, with children the ones who suffer the most as a result. Children do need to be protected, yes, but mostly from the tragic blunderings of adults.

Deficit Surplus

It has been discovered that one big reason children excel in certain ways is because they have a blend of cerebral over- and underdevelopment. While they have an undeveloped prefrontal lobe, they possess an inordinately active occipital cortex (in the back of the brain) and parietal cortex.

This enables their beautifully overcharged minds to do everything from see the world in more holistic ways, to adjust and adapt more readily to unforeseen events and new information. It's the wellspring for their unique approaches to reasoning, imagining, and empathizing. It makes them uninhibited, open to experimentation. These qualities in kids endow them with what one might call "attention surplus order," qualities which might be of immense help to their older counterparts in charting new strategies for everything from personal growth to problem-solving of many sorts.

What do these exceptional capacities of everyday kids make of us adults? Nincompoops in comparison? Or just different, with different strengths, and weaknesses? One of Alison Gopnik's important points in *The Philosophical Baby* is that "children and adults are different forms of *homo sapiens*. They have very different, though equally complex and powerful, minds, brains, and forms of consciousness, designed to serve different evolutionary functions." Children shine in their "distinctive capacities for change, especially imagination and learning." Adults, on the other hand, are stand-outs in "long-term planning, swift and automatic execution, rapid skillful reaction." This creates an "evolutionary division of labor." Children and adults need each other's talents and skills equally if each is to develop to the full.

What if we start looking at adulthood not so much as the end of certain incapacities and deficits, but as the beginning of a new set that differs from those of childhood? What distinctive qualities, virtues, and skills do adults lack that children have in abundance, and vice versa? In which developmental areas do children surpass adults, and in which do adults have an edge? Do adults "naturally" lose their advantage with certain capacities over time, regress even? If so, can this be forestalled, even allayed? Would we want to preempt them if we could, or can some adult deficits be seen as pluses? Among other things, are they opportunities to reach out to and cooperate with those who are younger?

When Alison Gopnik contrasts children and adults, she treats adults as a single category. Yet there are often remarkable similarities between children and older adults, who tend to go about questioning and learning and experiencing in more fluid modes than those in middle age. Those doing cognitive comparisons between older and younger people are starting to distinguish between fluid intelligence, demonstrated by acute short-term memory and analytical ability, and crystallized intelligence, which is all about accumulated stores of knowledge and skills. Such studies indicate that we have the most fluid intelligence when young, making memory itself more fluid, and that the older we get, the more crystallized it becomes. So, for instance, it might take a senior a longer time to retrieve a word from his memory, but far from an automatic indication that his memory is on the decline, this slower and more deliberative process of word retrieval can be due mainly to the fact that a well-educated person in advancing years will have so many more words stored in his brain to sift through.[3]

While such findings begin to quash long-held notions about the elderly and their diminishing cognitive capacity,[4] I believe that one day we'll learn that the oldest and youngest have some kindred types of fluidity. No matter how many times I screw up raising my daughter on any given day, she wakes up the next morning and, even though all is not forgotten, it is forgiven and not dwelt on. When we turn off the lights at night, she also says "good night" to any unpleasantnesses foisted on her by yours truly. Starting the next morning, I have a new chance to get it right. I know these days will soon end, that her emotional intelligence will become more

---

3 See, for instance, *Topics in Cognitive Science*, "The Myth of Cognitive Decline: Non-Linear Dynamics of Lifelong Learning" by Michael Ramscar,* Peter Hendrix, Cyrus Shaoul, Petar Milin, and Harald Baayen. Article first published online: Jan. 13, 2014. The lead researcher, Michael Ramscar, told Benedict Carey, medical and science reporter for *The New York Times*, that before conducting this study, he'd "totally bought into the idea of age-related cognitive decline in healthy adults." But the study results "slowly forced me to entertain this idea that I didn't need to invoke [cognitive] decline at all" in describing what becomes of the cognitive ability of most seniors. This sets the stage not only for unraveling a century's worth of cognitive research into the elderly, as Carey notes, but it also for undermining the long-held prejudice about seniors that has been around since Aristotle first exaggerated their deficits. Carey believes these new findings will "add to a growing skepticism about how steep age-related decline really is."

4 Studies on Alzheimer's and other forms of dementia are starting to question whether the onset is at a much younger age, though it is not yet possible to detect outwardly the symptoms. If so, this would chip away at the notion that these are triggered mainly by old age. As *New York Times* medical and science writer Benedict Carey notes, "doubts about the average extent of the [cognitive] decline [in the elderly] are rooted not in individual differences but in study methodology. Many studies comparing older and younger people, for instance, did not take into account the effects of pre-symptomatic Alzheimer's disease."

crystallized like mine, and this will impact her affective dimensions. But for now, she has the fluid emotional intelligence exemplified by seniors, who also more easily brush off hurts and slights. Children and seniors don't forget, but they typically don't allow hurts to fester.

In Picasso's later years, when he was known as the "Old Master," he experienced a phenomenal surge of creativity, which is saying something, given how many extraordinary works he'd already produced. In a way, he went full circle, revisiting the subjects of his earliest years as a painter, but this time around making so much more of them. When he died at age ninety-one, he'd reached yet a new zenith as a painter. What if we could manage, like Picasso, to cultivate our fluid intelligence our whole lives, so that it doesn't so much give way to crystallized intelligence, but instead combines with it? Is sustaining an artistic dimension key to "childing" throughout all stages of our lives? Can this lead to new kinds of creative, intellectual, and emotional fluidity—an ever more full yet open heart and mind?

Grumpy Old Men

Those of various cultures and eras differ over when old age begins, just as they do on whether it's a mostly good or bad stage, or a mixed bag. To Aristotle, however, middle age is our peak physical, mental, and creative moment in life. After that, we've passed our prime. Aristotle offers up a dismal view of old age. In his *Rhetoric*, he contends that there is no such thing as aging gracefully. For those who reach old age:

> Life on the whole is a bad business. The result is that they are sure about nothing and *underdo* everything. . . . They are cynical, that is, they tend to put the worst construction on everything. . . . They are small-minded because they have been humbled by life. . . . They are cowardly and always are anticipating danger. . . . They are too fond of themselves. . . . They are not shy but shameless rather. . . . They lack confidence in the future. . . . They live by memory rather than by hope.

For anyone who takes Aristotle's words to heart, is it any wonder they'll try to fend off old age at all costs? Even Immanuel Kant (1724–1804), the emblematic philosopher of the European Enlightenment and a true believer in the possibility of human perfectibility if ever there was one, was taken in by Aristotle. As the deconstructionist philosopher Jacques Derrida (1930–2004) notes in *The Beast and the Sovereign*, Kant's view (which Derrida agrees with) was that "vice is a thing of old age, and to get old is to turn vicious."

Thankfully, there are other compelling perspectives, such as that of Epicurus (341–270 BC), who devoted his philosophical life to worrying over how we can become happiest (which to him means living devoid of physical and mental pain). He asserts that our elder years can be happy and fulfilling ones, but for this to be so, we have to learn early on in life to maintain good habits of exercise, nutrition, and stress management. If successful, Epicurus believes, we stand a good chance of repelling infirmities that keep us from remaining independent when old, so we can continue to do those things that most give us pleasure.

The Roman intellectual jack-of-all-trades Cicero (106-43 BC)—a remarkable philosopher, statesman, orator, lawyer, and political theorist— acknowledges in his essay *de Senectute* (*On Old Age*) that most thinkers of his day took the Aristotelian tack that old age (which to them started at about age sixty) is a problematic and fraught-filled stage. He then rebuts point by point their "four reasons why old age appears to be unhappy: first, that it withdraws us from active pursuits, second, that it makes the body weaker, third, that it deprives us of almost all physical pleasures, and, fourth, that it is not far removed from death."

Addressing gripe one, Cicero holds that you're never too old to make yourself useful. For instance, an older person can put his vast expertise to service to his community in an advisory capacity. Cicero further believes that memory loss can be staved off by continual exercise of the mind. To support his view, he points out that the Athenian statesman and lawmaker Solon (630–560 BC) never experienced dotage, but instead was as productive as ever in his senior years—so much so that he was even "boasting in his verses that he grows old learning something every day." What about complaint number three, that old age makes the body weaker? To Cicero, that's all the better, since that frees up a person to focus on cultivating mind and character. How about the loss of physical pleasure? Again, that's also to our advantage, because it enables us to concentrate our energies on cultivating reason and virtue.

Cicero was influenced by Plato, the incomparable philosopher, poet, and dramatist of the life of reason, who believed we should welcome and embrace old age, see it as a stage that affords us the last best chance to gain insight into what really matters in life. To Plato, whether you view old age as a bane or boon depends on your outlook on being young. While he recognized that physical and mental aging can lead to a hardening of the mind and heart, he convincingly pointed out that such hardening can just as well take place when one is young, depending on one's disposition.

In his still-influential *Republic*, which Plato wrote when he was sixty-eight years old, the octogenarian Cephalus argues that old age is what you make of it. He has no pity for "men of our age [who] flock together [and] bemoan, 'I cannot eat, I cannot drink, the pleasures of youth and love have fled. . . .' They will lament to anyone who will listen of all the evils of which their old age is the cause." In the same vein as Cicero, Cephalus makes the case that the intellectual pleasures of conversing, wondering, and inquiring increase in proportion to one's waning carnal desires. His message to his fellow old men is that they should quit grousing about their decline in physical prowess and celebrate the fact that old age has liberated them from the libidinous (Gloria Steinem, who turned eighty-two in March 2016, said that "the brain cells that used to be obsessed are now free for all kinds of great things.") If Plato's "you're not getting older, you're getting better" philosophy of old age was subscribed to today, drugs to curb sexual dysfunction might no longer enjoy such robust sales. But what if physical pleasure stimulates intellectual pursuits? Surely it depends on the person, just as it depends (as it does at most any age) on whether one has kinds of afflictions that make it challenging if not impossible to enjoy or immerse oneself in those things that matter most to a person.

When my father, Alexander Phillips, retired in 1990 at age seventy, this most emotionally even-keeled of people experienced a depression. At first, all was well. He got to experience a first childhood, since he'd missed out on the one of his early years. When my father was seven, his own father, at age fifty-seven, dropped dead right in front of him of a heart attack. In a sense, my father's childhood was over. He took on several jobs to help provide for his mother, brother, and sister. It was arranged with his teachers that he cram a full day's worth of work into half a day. While there was next to no idle time for play and exploration, he did teach himself to play piano by ear and brought in a decent amount of money to his mother by playing at local gathering spots. My father excelled in whatever he took on; he had a single-minded discipline, drive, and determination that thankfully rubbed off on me. After a stint in the army, he went on to become a designer of aircraft carriers and then an electrical engineer. He later earned a business degree, becoming the first person at the university to earn his diploma by taking all of his classes in the night school program. Long after I went to bed, he was still studying at the dining room table, his books covering almost the entire surface.

After retiring, my father finally had a stab at childhood. He read piles of books, took long walks on the beach, danced the night away. But he missed his work terribly, as he told me often. Idle time made little sense to him unless it was bounded by a job. He picked himself up by getting back to work; he became a consultant, lending his forty years' worth of know-how in naval ship-building to firms doing business with the United States' Department of the Navy, where he had made his career, rising to the highest civilian post. In his spare time—which he enjoyed once again, now that he had structure—he took up playing the piano again and became a regular in early a.m. hours at the local Wendy's, where seniors gathered each morning to engage in spirited inquiries on political and philosophical matters. When I visited, I was invited to moderate the fray. It was a marvel to watch his nimble mind in action as he put his views through the Socratic wringer, all the while parrying and pondering those of others. He would have made Cicero and Plato proud.

My father weathered tremendous physical ups and downs in his final years. Yet such was his love for life that he had a second open-heart surgery, at age seventy-five. After a lengthy recuperation, it was as if he was ten years younger; modern medicine worked its magic, for a while. When he did decline again, the gloomiest thing he'd say was, "It's no fun getting old. But I take each day at a time and treasure it as best I can." He never felt sorry for himself, never allowed himself to wallow in regret over things he still wanted to do but couldn't, such as fulfill a decades-long dream to go to Greece to visit the tiny volcanic island of Nisyros from which his parents had emigrated. We had become particularly close the last two years of his life. His car even became a portable library for my books. As much as he told me how proud he was of the legacy I'm leaving, I was prouder of my dad's own legacy of achievement, of surmounting difficult odds to leave a positive mark on the world. And I was grateful for the gift he and my mother had given me—an ideal childhood and youth—that made it possible for me to imagine and carve out a kind of creative adulthood that they could not dream of. My father asked me to promise him that I'd go to Greece in his stead and hold lots of dialogues there. He knew that if I went, he would in a sense be going along for the ride—not just in spirit, but because he's such a part of me in every way.

Stages of Age

The Christian theologian St. Augustine of Hippo (354–430), whose writing had a decisive influence on the course taken by Western philosophy in coming centuries, was far from original with his division of the life cycle into six stages (with old age beginning at sixty). What is novel is his notion, as elaborated in his sermon *Ad competentes*, of how these stages impact us:

> By means of these divisions, or stages of age, you will not change from one stage to another, but staying the same, you will always know newness. For the second age will not follow so that an end may be put to the first; nor will the use of the third mean the ruin of the second; nor will the fourth be born so that

the third may die; nor will the fifth envy the staying power of the fourth; nor will the sixth suppress the fifth. Although these ages do not come into being at one and the same time, they continue in harmony with one another in the soul, . . . and they will conduct you to the everlasting peace and tranquility of the seventh stage.

One need not adhere to his or any other religious faith to find significant the view that the stages we experience never disappear for good, but remain with us. What about Augustine's claim that the stages we experience contribute to the development of a harmonious and tranquil yet evolving self—that each new stage naturally accrues to the old in a way that makes who we are richer rather than poorer? Each stage might give rise in us to a newer display of curiosity, rationality, imaginativeness, playfulness, and compassion than the one that came before, the transformation so indiscernibly smooth that we'd never really be aware of what we've undergone.

Augustine's philosophy of stages is based on an idealistic notion of a kind of enduring self that is fertile grounds for continual blooming throughout one's life. He conceives of stages as contiguous, seamlessly connected platforms that as a matter of course generate newness out of sameness, much as composers craft new songs or symphonies out of the same sets of notes and bars.

Even if any given stage is far from tranquil, even (or especially) if it has considerable disequilibrium, it can prove grist for one's development and that of others. It might lead one to produce an outpouring of works and deeds that continue to move people long after one's own life has ended. While much depends on happenstance, on circumstances beyond one's control, the most admirable people refuse to be defined by the worst things that happen to them, and sometimes manage to make beauty out of them of a kind that transcends self, time, and place.

While Augustine is a believer in transitionless stages, the venerated Swiss physician and author Paul Tournier (1898–1986) believes it's the "experience of being in between," the transitions between one stage and another, rather than the stages themselves, that matter most in our development. To him, the most important life journey lies between the time we leave home and arrive at our destination; between the time we leave adolescence and arrive at adulthood. . . . It is like the time when a trapeze artist lets go the bars and hangs in midair, ready to catch another support: it is a time of danger, of expectation, of uncertainty, of excitement, or extraordinary aliveness.

What if you're not ready to let go, even if there's another support for you to catch hold of? What if you experience "detachment anxiety" and you cling for dear life to the support you're on? Some trapeze artists, even with years of practice under their belts, fail to let go of the bar at the critical moment; they realize or intuit that something is not quite right. They swing all the way back to the original platform, take a deep breath, and start again (once in the bluest of moons, they decide not to tempt fate any longer, and quit). Tournier recognizes the danger and uncertainty involved in transitions, as well as the accompanying jolt of excitement and aliveness. Timing is everything. Yet even when things are in ideal sync, something might go wrong. On the other hand even when one's timing is off, near-instantaneous adjustments sometimes can be made and all turns out fine. One experiences a thrill and shudder that one has evaded a tragic mishap. It might give one a new or renewed appreciation of life, might even radically change one's approach to living.

The contemporary poet Alfred A. Poulin Jr. (1938–1996), who deserves a much wider audience, in "Saltimbanques" ("Acrobats"), likens those who are "magnetized into each other's time and space by love's stranger law of gravity" to a "troupe of seasoned acrobats" who risk it all to experience a kind of free flight in which their only support is "the midair of imagination." Even if they accomplish this "but for a moment," what a moment it is, to love another with all one's heart and mind and might. There are those phenomenal few who have a romance with humanity itself and somehow apply this kind of intimate and affirming love. Whether on a grandiose or personal scale, our petals might get bruised or broken in the process. Worse, we might lose our grip on the one or ones we dare to risk or sacrifice it all in the name of love, and plummet in midair. The poem claims that it is worth it, that it is the all-out attempt that matters most and that defines us—"for what we do, we do for nothing other than all we are, all we've chosen to become."

The Human Garden

In *Being There* by Jerzy Kosiński (1933–1991), the gardener known as Chauncy—or "Chance"—has next to no contact with anyone outside of the home where he lived and worked as a gardener for as long as he can remember. When the master of the house dies and he's made to leave, by uncanny coincidence he comes to be taken care of by Benjamin Rand, one of the nation's most influential captains of industry, who takes Chance's simple reflections on gardening for deep wisdom. Chance winds up rubbing shoulders with society's muckety-mucks. He even has an audience with the President, who seeks his opinion about stimulating growth. Chance replies: "In a garden, growth has its seasons. There are spring and summer, but there are also fall and winter. And then spring and summer again." He goes on to say, "As long as the roots are not severed, all is well and all will be well." This brings the President, who marvels at the "good solid sense" of his insightful new friend, to say, "We welcome the inevitable seasons of nature, yet we are upset by the seasons of our economy. How foolish of us!"

What if we applied Chance's philosophy to the human garden? The indigenous Mayan groups with whom I held frequent dialogues when my wife and I lived in Chiapas, Mexico, believe that each of the four biological stages of childhood, youth, adulthood, and old age spark important types of growth and change, which they mark with special rites of passage. By their belief system, the stages in the human life cycle are best represented in the form of a circle, without hierarchy, like nature's seasonal cycles. When a member of their group dies, usually in the winter of life, it is a time not only for circle ceremonies of remembrance, but also for ones of rebirth and renewal. It's not just that they consider their community as a whole to be greater than the sum of its parts, but that, once someone is part of their world, he is part of it forever, his roots never severed.

Where the Childhood Things Are

About twenty interested inquirers—a mix of children, youth, parents, sin-
gles, seniors—are gathered with me at a public library in southern Maine.
When I was fresh out of college and a camp counselor in the area more
than thirty years ago, I visited this library whenever I had time off. Its rib-
vaulted ceiling, stained-glass windows that have been part of the structure
since it was built in the early nineteenth century, and eclectic book collection made for an inviting sanctuary. Most of all, I enjoyed the company
and conversation of Gaby Schaefer, the head librarian at the time. Gaby
and I had a shared love of all things Jane Austen, Charles Dickens, Edith
Wharton, and even Charles Portis.

By the time my summer job ended, my homesickness for my native
Virginia stomping grounds had abated, and I was no longer anxious to
return anytime soon. Maine seemed an ideal place to begin what I hoped
would be a writing career. I got off to a promising if inauspicious start
when I landed a job as a cub reporter for a family-owned weekly newspaper. Gaby, now eighty-five, tipped me off about the opening. When I did
finally return to Virginia, for another newspaper position, she and I stayed
in touch. I went on to become a freelance journalist for national magazines. My search for a good story—my forte was sharing the tales of our
unsung heroes—took me all across America. I sent Gaby a postcard from
whatever point on the map I happened to land on. She mounted each and
every one of them in a scrapbook, which she promised one day to give me
so I'd have a memento of my peregrinations.

When I left journalism to devote myself to Socrates Café, Gaby—now
librarian emeritus, but as involved as ever—issued to me a standing invitation to convene dialogues at the library in this once-insular town that now
enjoys considerable ethnic diversity and suffers from the development of
sprawl. I had not seen Gaby in more than a year. As always, her vivacious
hazel eyes swim behind large-frame glasses, and her hair is arranged in a
long bun resting over one shoulder. She hadn't told me in our correspon-
dences that she'd been confined to a wheelchair after a spill on the stairs at

her home six months earlier. She brushes off my shows of concern. "Let's not talk about things we can't fix." She asks about my daughter, Cali, whom she has met twice and who was to accompany me here. I tell her that Cali has a high fever, and so, much to her disappointment, she had to stay home for this long-planned weekend trip of ours to Maine. Before her school years got underway, Cali was an even more frequent companion during my Socratic travels. I've worried out loud to Gaby whether our worldwide gallivanting—which began when Cali was two months old—without a permanent home base for the first six years of her life, has hindered her development and made me remiss as a parent. One time at age five she said to me, with eyes aglow, as we moved into yet another furnished apartment, "Daddy, we have so many homes!" Yet I've fretted that she'll look back at her childhood one day and regret it didn't include a consistent stable of friends and a room to call her very own.

As the participants on hand know from the library announcement, I'm keen to investigate a question that has to do with some facet of the ages or stages of life. It is Gaby herself who poses a question. With a knowing look directed at me, she asks, "What is the ideal childhood?"

"I have my own strong ideas of what makes for an ideal childhood, and how that can lead to an ideal adulthood," she says, "but I'm wondering what those here think it is."

"I bet they're wondering what your own thoughts are," I say.

She smiles. "Not going to let me off the hook so easy." She is prepared for my query. "I subscribe to the view of childhood offered by Jo's mother in Louisa May Alcott's *Little Women*. She believes that 'children should be children as long as they can.' I take that to mean that children should be as carefree and have as uncomplicated a life as possible. Yes, they should have responsibilities, and no matter how protective a parent is, they no doubt will be exposed to worries and sorrows. But parents should make sure their kids have time to just be kids, to live outside of everyday hours, and explore and wonder to their heart's content. No tiger moms cracking the whip. No 'helicopter parents' hovering over their every move."

"That sounds nice in theory, but the world today is more dog-eat-dog than ever," says Onika, forty-three, a hospital administrator, "what with the soaring cost of living, and good-paying jobs fewer and further between. It's all hard-working parents can do to keep a decent roof over their kids' heads. It's going to get worse in the years to come, as globalization makes competition for decent jobs even more cutthroat. We parents have to do what we have to do to make sure our kids get ahead in the world. We're obligated to exploit every opportunity in this time of their lives to develop their abilities to the fullest.

"That means that today's version of an ideal childhood must be chock-full of the right kinds of activities. My son and daughter are enrolled in after-school classes in computer programming, foreign language studies, science enrichment, and they still have time to take part in sports too. Maybe they are overscheduled by yesterday's standards, but this is the new deal, the new ideal."

Her view that when childhood begins and adulthood ends can have changing boundaries dovetails with that of Hannah Arendt, (1906–1975), one of the most consequential philosophers of the twentieth century, who asserted in an essay, "The Crisis in Education," that "where the line between childhood and adulthood falls in each instance cannot be determined by a general rule; it changes often, in respect to age, from country to country, from one civilization to another, and also from individual to individual."

Onika goes on, "I am tiger mom-ish. And I *do* hover, to make sure they're not slouching. It's up to parents to steer them, discipline them, mold them, so they can have an ideal adulthood." She wraps her arms around her kids, seated on either side of her. "They're well-adjusted and happy enough. Really, they don't have any other type of childhood to compare theirs to. The childhood they have is the childhood their friends have. They understand they have to start preparing for adulthood now."

"What about my best friend Mason's sister, Mishi?" her twelve-year-old son, Kishan, asks. "She's got acute leukemia. She might not live to see adulthood." He directs his attention to the rest of us. "Mishi's parents and siblings make a lot of sacrifices so she can enjoy life right here and now. Since Mishi's diagnosis, her parents have stopped pushing their other kids so much. They understand that now is all you've got."

His mother is silent for some time. Eventually she says, "I haven't thought about this in too long a while, but I lost a friend when I was about Kishan's age. One day Mychal just quit coming to school. My mom told me she was sick. Months passed and I didn't see her. Then my mom took me to her house to say good-bye. I thought she meant Mychal was moving someplace else. She was real sick. I hardly recognized her. She died the next week."

Onika squeezes Kishan's hand. "It's true, you know, you never know if a child is going to make it to adulthood. You need to live in some ways like today is all you have."

Their exchange brings to mind a vignette the Russian novelist and moral philosopher Leo Tolstoy (1828–1910) shared in his memoir, *Boyhood*. He became so struck as a child by the philosophical view that "death awaited me at any hour, at any moment, [that] I made up my mind . . . that man can be happy only by making use of the present, and not thinking of the future." Tolstoy relates his youthful take on how this philosophy was best applied: "For three days. . .[I] neglected my lessons and did nothing but . . . enjoy myself by reading a romance and eating gingerbread with Kronoff mead, for which I spent the last money I had."

Onika goes on to say, "But you still have to prepare them for that, even as you try to make sure they have time to treasure each day in itself. It's a balancing act. I have to put a lot more effort into that balancing act."

I'm soon prompted to ask the group, "If the ideal childhood is one in which kids can be kids for as long as they can, is that the same as saying that adulthood is something to fend off until it's no longer possible?"

"Not if you have the right kind of adulthood," says Josie, ninety-one, a whirling dervish who is involved in just about every community activity there is. "Though you wouldn't know it by Wordsworth's 'Ode: Intimations of Immortality from Recollections of Early Childhood.' He called childhood"—she stands up, puts her hands behind her back like a child set to recite a passage at school—"'a time when meadow, grove, and stream/The earth, and every common sight/To me did seem/apparell'd in celestial light.' In contrast, he believes adulthood is filled with nostalgia and regret: 'The clouds that gather round the setting sun/do take a sober colouring from an eye, that hath kept watch o'er man's mortality.'"

"Wordsworth's answer to your question," she says to me, "would be, 'Yes, keep adulthood at bay for as long as possible.'" She shakes her head. "I'd like to grab him by the collar and say, 'It doesn't have to be that way.' The ideal childhood should transition into an ideal adulthood, and from there, into an ideal elderhood, where curiosity and wonder and a sense that all is wrapped in celestial light are more a part of your life than ever."

"In my childhood home in rural North Carolina, my parents let our large backyard grow wild," Onika tells us. "It was a universe for me, a place where I could explore and get in touch with nature and myself. Yet I've forgotten that language of nature." She falls silent, but then says in a barely audible voice: "'Once I understood each word the caterpillar said/once I smiled in secret at the gossip of the starlings/. . . once I spoke the language of the flowers. . . ./How did it go?/How did it go?' That's from Shel Silverstein. Part of his message is that you can be wisest to the wonders of the world when you're youngest."

This also is the perspective of the pre-Socratic philosopher Democritus (460–370 BC), not to mention Plato, neither of whom considered wisdom an automatic byproduct of age or experience.

"I don't want my kids to forget how such things go," Onika says next. "If you lose the ability—or never learn it in the first place—to be conversant with the things of nature, a lot of childhood's luster is lost. Children might also lose out on opportunities in adulthood. If they become close to nature when young, they might decide to pursue a career in the sciences." She thinks some more. "Let me take off my practical hat and say it might also inspire them to be a poet, or novelist, or explorer of some sort, like an astronaut. That wouldn't be bad."

Then Vitaly, who came to Maine from his native Ukraine a quarter of a century ago and has a popular family-operated bakery-café, says to us, "My father never had time to learn any other language but that of harsh reality. He put me to work selling newspapers on a street corner when I was five. But my mother made sure I still had time to play.

"My adult life has been all about hard work too, but I leave work early on Saturday, and never work on Sunday. Whenever possible, I take my kids on an outdoors adventure of some kind while my mother—at her insistence—minds the bakery. My mother believes that a childhood can't be ideal unless you have lots of opportunities to explore the world around you." He holds up a careworn book for all to see. It is *A Sense of Wonder*, by the biologist Rachel Carson, who sparked the global environmental movement. "My mother, who I'm sure would have become a scientist if given the chance, gave us this book. It is a bible for me. Carson tells about the first time she took her nephew, an infant at the time, to the ocean shore of Maine, and how he 'laughed for pure joy' at the song of the wind and the deafening surf and the pitch darkness. Her nephew delighted in the life around him." He thumbs the pages until he lands on the passage he's looking for: "'The sight of these small living creatures, solitary and fragile against the brute force of the sea, had moving philosophic overtones. . . . It was good to see his infant acceptance of a world of elemental things . . . with baby excitement.'"

"I make sure my kids get a regular dose of nature," he then says. "My nine-year-old wants to be a botanist. He is already learning on his own—and teaching me and his grandmother—the fascinating scientific language of nature. It's not a forbidding language to him, but a kind of poetry."

If so, his son may prove wrong the view of Henry David Thoreau (1817–1862) that "the child plucks its first flower with an insight into its beauty and significance which the subsequent botanist never retains." His son may be one who will always study flowers and plants as if seeing them for the first time.

"That book is a favorite of mine," says Gaby. "Like Rachel Carson says, if a child is to retain her inborn sense of wonder all his life, she needs the regular companionship of at least one adult who can share with her 'the joy, excitement and mystery of the world we live in.'"

"I wish my great grandkids appreciated the great outdoors more," says Josie. "If they had their way when they visit me, they'd spend all their time playing the interactive games on their tablets. So much of what they see on TV or online is hard to control, even when their parents supervise. They have access to limitless information and images. No question, children today are more worldly-wise. They're so much more sophisticated in what they say and in how they carry themselves than I was at their age. They seem like little adults. I can't pass judgment on whether it's ideal for children today, but it wouldn't have been for me when I was their age. There will be plenty of time in later years to lose their innocence about the darker side of the ways of the world."

"Just because you process a great deal of information and images as a child doesn't mean you're a little adult, and I'm not sure it always means you lose your innocence," says Tracie, forty-three, who runs a thriving horticulture business. "It amazes me how my kids can absorb and process so much information, while it leaves me mystified and overwhelmed. But you should experience things as a child in an active and hands-on way, for childhood to be ideal, rather than the passive way too many experience it. I did lose my innocence about the world's darker side early in life, but I also had opportunities to deepen my sense of wonder that few children have."

"My parents worried that I had a disadvantaged childhood," she says next. "It definitely was unconventional. They were judged harshly by a lot of friends and family who felt they should have settled in one place after I was born—as if, once you have a child, living a nomadic life would have been pure selfishness on their part.

"I had the world at my fingertips. By the time I was twelve, I'd circled the globe twice with my intrepid parents, both photojournalists. I was exposed to some beautiful things, and some not so beautiful. I met indigenous children throughout Latin America who were put to work in the fields or selling handmade wares as soon as they'd mastered walking. I was in parts of Africa where people die of preventable illness. I also encountered a tribe in the Amazon that has no concept of time, their lives spent like some would conceive an ideal childhood to be like. I saw Machu Picchu, the Eiffel Tower. I visited Nepal and Tibet. They were wonder-filled years. Sometimes I still feel like I'm catching my breath from it all. I definitely am still processing it. Traveling did mesh with my personality at the time, thankfully for my parents, and for me. And yet now, as an adult, all I want to do is stay in one place."

Looking at Tracie, Gaby says, "You make me wish I'd had your childhood—or that of Chris's daughter, who already has seen so much of the world, and from all I can tell, almost lives to travel as much as her father. It would have fit my nature. My childhood was a lot like Jane Austen's. I never strayed far from my hometown and did my traveling through the books I read. Like her, I had access to a huge assortment of books in my father's library, though in my case, I had to sneak inside to read them when I knew he wouldn't catch me.

"I read some things that I wasn't ready for—D.H. Lawrence, Henry James, Anaïs Nin. I didn't understand a lot of what I was reading. I drank in passages with rapturous language and heavenly if erotic descriptions." She pauses, puts her hands to her cheeks. "Oh my, I am feeling like a hypocrite. A complaint I've had about today's children is that I've felt, like Josie, that they're exposed to too much 'media' before they're ready, and that that is the furthest from ideal. Yet you could make a similar complaint about my own childhood, and I'm no worse for the wear."

She then says, "I carried over my love of the written word into my adult life. I never became a great writer, but as a librarian I'm surrounded by the written word. Every day I'm with people of all ages who share my love for it. For me, it's made for an ideal life. Unlike Mr. Wordsworth, no clouds have ever gathered around my sun and taken a sober coloring from my eyes."

The short silence lifts when Josie again speaks up. "I had a child when I was not yet sixteen. It was with the person who'd been my sweetheart since kindergarten. Our baby was conceived just before Ronnie went to fight in the Korean War. My parents made my transition from youth to the responsibilities of adulthood and parenthood as ideal as anyone in my circumstances could hope for, in that era or any other. They made it clear I was still their child, and they would love me and take care of me as always, but that they'd also have to prepare me to take full responsibility for my daughter. With their support, I graduated from high school on time, then went on to nursing school and then became a registered nurse. After Ronnie came back from his long tour of duty, we married. We had four more children. I eventually left my nursing career. We raised our brood on a farm, tried to give them all the time in the world just to be kids, though it was mixed with farm chores. Each left Maine—except my oldest, who took over the farm, which is now in the hands of his oldest daughter—and went on to do something distinctive and creative with his life. We have in the family a boat-builder, a cinematographer, an internist, and an art curator. I like to think that their childhood had something to do with that."

Josie is silent, lost in thought. When she looks at us again, she says, "The week after Ronnie and I first became an item in kindergarten, he gave me a rose. It was the first day of spring. He picked it from his mother's rosebush. She gave him what for. Until he died three years ago, he continued the tradition. I have eighty-three dried roses in an album. I touch the brittle petals of the first rose he gave me, and I touch my idyllic childhood."

Childhood Interrupted

The French philosopher Gaston Bachelard (1884–1962), who made important contributions to poetics as well as the philosophy of science, holds in *The Poetics of Reverie* that we adults never lose the essence of our childhood, which "remains within us a principle of deep life, of life always in harmony with the possibility of new beginnings." What about those who did not have much if any childhood—who essentially had to become little adults at a young age? For instance, the deep and harmonious life that Bachelard extols was not part of the upbringing of Jean-Jacques

Rousseau. After his mother died at nine, his father, a watchmaker, remarried and left Rousseau to fend for himself with an abusive uncle. His childhood irretrievably lost, Rousseau fled Paris for Geneva, where he slaved away at a variety of odd jobs. Likely both despite and because of his harsh younger years, Rousseau went on to become one of our most celebrated philosophers, his keen insights on moral and political thought influencing not only the French Revolution, but the evolution of modern political, social, and educational theorizing. In *Emile*, his famed treatise on education published in 1762, he made the impassioned argument that the all too fleeting stage of childhood should be cherished. Rousseau exhorted parents to allow children to "love childhood, indulge its sports, its pleasures, its delightful instincts."

> Who has not sometimes regretted that age when laughter was ever on the lips, and when the heart was ever at peace? Why rob these innocents of the joys which pass so quickly, of that precious gift which they cannot abuse? Why fill with bitterness the fleeting days of early childhood, days which will no more return for them than for you?

Perhaps he was thinking of his own father's neglect when he went on to write these moving words:

> Fathers, can you tell when death will call your children to him? Do not lay up sorrow for yourselves by robbing them of the short span which nature has allotted to them. As soon as they are aware of the joy in life, let them rejoice in it, so that whenever God calls them they may not die without having tasted the joy of life.

Rousseau anticipated forceful objections to his stance: "I hear from afar the shouts of that false wisdom which is ever dragging us onwards, counting the present as nothing, and pursuing without pause a future which flies as we pursue." Yet when he was a young parent, Rousseau himself did not practice what he came to advocate in *Emile* as a fifty-year-old. After his stint in Geneva, in his twenties, Rousseau returned penniless to Paris, where he had five children with his lover, a seamstress. Rousseau relates in his *Confessions* that, unable to care for his brood, he persuaded his mistress to leave them at a foundling hospital. At the time, child abandonment was commonplace in Paris among poor parents. A decade later, Rousseau tried, to no avail, to find his children. They likely had not survived; at the time, the infant mortality rate hovered at 50 percent.

Even if Rousseau's perspective that parents should do all they can to make sure their children have a rich childhood had been conceivable, much less doable, it would have met with resistance in his era and earlier ones. Philippe Ariès asserts in *Centuries of Childhood* that from the medieval era until the latter part of the nineteenth century, childhood was widely looked on in the Western world as "an unimportant phase of which there was no need to keep any record." To be sure, stages of childhood had long ago been carved out by now-anonymous thinkers in the Middle Ages—stages like *infantia*, which lasted from birth till age seven, *pueritia*, which lasted until about age twelve, then *adolescentia*, and then a stage known as *juventus*, which served as a bridge between adolescence and full-fledged adulthood. Even so, while childhood might have been a recognized stage of life, it was not a valued one.

Perhaps, then, one should not be surprised, even if one can't help but be disappointed, that Michel de Montaigne (1533–1592), the influential French Renaissance philosopher and founder of modern skepticism, openly confessed to having few pangs over the loss of a child: "I have lost two or three children in their infancy, not without regret, but without great sorrow." His stoic recollection is so hazy that he can't so much as recall how many of his children died. This hardly conforms with Montaigne's reputation as one of our most regarded humanists. Failing to grieve over the loss of one's children would be unthinkable, indeed unpardonable, to most modern parents, much less the modern humanist. Yet like Aristotle, Montaigne doesn't think much of kids. He went so far as to characterize the doings of children as "puerile nonsense." As far as he was concerned, their sole reason for being was "for our amusement, like monkeys." Given his lowly view of kids, it's little wonder he hardly laments the loss of his own.

What is the ideal adulthood? For most adults, it's one in which they enjoy a considerable measure of autonomy and choice. Throughout the ages, though, this has been an unreachable ideal for many. Yale historian and philologist John Boswell (1947–1994) notes that it's taken for granted that in modern Western societies "everyone of sound mind achieves independent adult status on attaining a prescribed age," because their "social and political capacities are ripe;" and so they're "inducted into the world of the adult, with all the privileges and responsibilities that entails, and that everyone undergoes this rite of passage." Yet this ideal is a myth that can't be reconciled with the reality of most lives. The fact is that "during most of Western history only a minority of grown-ups ever achieved [social and political] independence: the rest of the population remained throughout their lives in a juridical status more comparable to 'childhood,' in the sense that they remained under someone else's control—a father, a lord, a master, a husband." Then, as now, most adults hope for their shot at an idyllic adulthood, even as they continue to be treated like children, in a demeaning sense. They live in circumstances in which they have little control over their destinies, no matter how hard they work, and next to no time to wonder, explore, sate their curiosity—and yet many, no matter how oppressive their straits, somehow make sure their own kids have a childhood that they'll one day look back on as ideal.

Act Up

"What does it mean, to act your age?" asks Alonzo, fifteen.

I'm at a co-ed summer camp for inner-city children and youth. The camp is situated along a pristine lake in upstate New York. One of the directors, a participant in a Socrates Café held at a diner in Brooklyn, hit upon the idea of holding nightly philosophical exchanges at the camp. When he asked if I'd venture there to preside over a dialogue, I jumped at the chance. Nothing better than philosophizing under the stars. Besides that, kids at this season in life are uncommonly perceptive, and I had no doubt that they'd help me gain further philosophical insight into age- and stage-related matters. So it is that on a midsummer evening, in a clearing surrounded by yellow birch trees, I'm sitting around a campfire with a group of thirteen- and fourteen-year-olds, the heavens above a veritable planetarium.

"My teacher last school year was all the time telling me, 'It's time you learned to act your age,'" Alonzo says, imitating his teacher's voice, after I told them about the theme I'm investigating. "But I *am* acting my age. Kids my age act up from time to time. What Ms. Michaels really means is, 'Act like I want you to act.'"

"What she *means*," says Vivienne, who'd been his classmate, "is, 'Act according to how I think kids your age should be acting *in my class.*' Ms. Michaels told us from day one how she expected us to behave. She's a serious teacher and she demands serious, mature students."

"You're mistaking being serious for being mature," says Hector. "You can be silly and mature. When I go to a baseball game with my dad, he whoops it up like a kid. That man works hard, and going to a game is his way of forgetting everyday concerns and letting that kid inside him come out."

"Sure, it's fine to act that way at a baseball game," Vivienne says. "But you better believe that if he whooped it up at a symphony performance, then he'd be kicked out, as well he should. Acting age appropriately is situation-specific. That's why Alonzo is all the time in trouble at school. He acts in a classroom situation as if he's at a baseball game."

Aristotle holds in *Nicomachean Ethics* that one should act with "firm and unchangeable character" regardless of the situation. But he's not as rigid as he might seem at first glance, since his view is that you might moderate or "temper" your character, without being untrue to it, if or as the situation warrants.

Vivienne goes on, "Whether you're a child living in the ice age, the Stone Age, the space age, or the information age, there's only one appropriate way to act when you're a student learning from a teacher, and that's serious and respectful and attentive—in a word, mature. If you would make an effort to act mature, you'd soon start feeling mature.

You'd feel better about yourself and everyone else in class would feel better about you."

Unbeknownst to Vivienne, she is advancing the view of the American philosopher and psychologist William James (1842–1910), one of the leading thinkers of the late nineteenth century. "Action and feeling go together," James claims, "and by regulating the action, which is under more direct control of the will, we can indirectly regulate the feeling, which is not." So if you want to feel happier or more mature or more adventuresome, just start acting happier, more mature, or adventuresome, and the rest will take care of itself—that's who you'll become for real.

Alonzo begs to differ with Vivienne's outlook. "Says you. There's no guidebook that spells out what it means to act your age at age fourteen as a whole or in any specific situation."

"There *should* be," says Yahaira. "Some sort of series of books, including, *Act Your Age, or Else: The Adolescent Years*. That way, when you don't act your age, you can refer to the book and understand why an adult like a teacher has lowered the boom on you for acting up in an age-inappropriate way."

"Who would author the book?" I'm curious to know.

"People who are authorities on the subject," she says. "Like, someone with a PhD in adolescent studies."

"What you need is a whole group of author-experts to put their brainpower to work on the book," says Alonzo. "Besides that PhD, some of the others joining forces on it should be teens. Who's more expert about teens and teen behavior than teens themselves? We'd be the best 'teenologists.' With this book, we could dictate our own terms on appropriate adolescent etiquette. Because adults like Ms. Michaels forget what it's like to be a teen, and all the pressure coming at you from every different direction—friends, parents, teachers—to act a certain way. Better yet, it should be written only by teens. I bet Ms. Michaels wouldn't want teens to coauthor a book on etiquette for adults. After all, I'm no 'adultologist.' So why should adults take part in writing a book about teen-appropriate behavior?"

"What if we were writing a book about age-correct behavior for a prodigy?" asks Moises, warming to the subject. "There needs to be a special book tailored just for them. They don't act like anybody else their age. They're prodigies, so they act their age *for a prodigy*."

"Most prodigies are super-humanly serious and disciplined professionally," he goes on. "Tiger Woods was a golf prodigy. When he became an adult, he graduated from being a prodigy to becoming the best professional golfer in the history of the game. But he didn't act his age in his private life, not for a married man with children. Until he got outed, he acted like a kid in a pornographic candy store. I have to hand it to him, though; he's turned things around. Since that crisis, he's started acting mature and become the right kind of role model."

"For an adult, acting your age should be the same as acting like a grown-up," says Yahaira. "Maybe I'm no 'grownup-ologist,' but I do know that whether you're silly or serious by nature as an adult, you're supposed to be responsible, since being a grown-up is all about taking your commitments seriously." She thinks some more. "I suppose that can apply to kids too, but with adults, who are supposed to be our role models, it applies even more."

"My dad still dreams of being a successful inventor," says Alonzo. "He manages to do enough odd jobs to help get the bills paid, barely, but he spends all the time he can tinkering in a big closet that he's turned into a little workshop. He hasn't made much money, so far. I guess that's why my mom up and leaves him—leaves all of us—from time to time. She gets exasperated. She calls him 'an overgrown child.' She keeps coming back, so far. She knows we can't get by without her."

"A famous seventeenth century poet and playwright by the name of John Dryden called men 'children of a larger growth,'" I tell them. "Dryden meant by this that adult appetites are 'as apt to change as theirs, and full as craving too, and full as vain'—that we can be, in other words, as immature as kids, present company excepted. But can't holding onto and nurturing some youthful attitudes and behaviors in our later adulthood years be a good thing?"

Speaking for the first time, Roy, the camp director, says, "Not if you're so irresponsible that you don't take care of your responsibilities and obligations as a spouse and parent." Then, looking Jonathan's way, he says, "This brings to mind a passage in the Bible: 'When I grew up, I put away childish things.' It sounds like your mother wants your father to put away his childish things and act more his age."

Vivienne becomes the unexpected ally of Alonzo's father. "His dad may be unrealistic, but he doesn't sound so irresponsible. He's helping pay the bills even as he tries to make his childhood dreams come true during his adulthood years."

"If you're a responsible person, no matter your age or circumstances, you act in a respectful, appropriate and responsible way," says Taunya. "Those adults who don't do so aren't grown-ups. Like, John Edwards: he's an adult, but he's not a grown-up. Same with Arnold Schwarzenegger. They're of adult age, but their behavior is the furthest thing from grown-up behavior. When they had babies with other women, they cheated not just on their wives, but on the other members of their family, on their country, on all those who worked with them, who voted for them."

"Their behavior *is* disgusting," says Alonzo. "But they *were* acting their age *for people of their kind.* I come across stories all the time about politicians and celebrities and sports stars womanizing and cheating like there's no tomorrow. If that's how so many of them act, if that sort of behavior is normal *for* politicians and sports stars and celebrities, then that's normal *for them* when it comes to acting their age. If some of us normal people approve of their actions, or even look up to them, then shame on us. It means our society as a whole has a lot of growing up still to do."

"I can't abide by everything you're saying," says Vivienne. "At the very least, acting your age as an adult should be to act more responsibly than your average kid. It doesn't mean you have to be perfect, but that you should try to be responsible, own up to your mistakes, and be aware of the *consequences* of your actions. When you're reckless, when you don't care how your actions affect your loved ones and all the others who've devoted themselves to your life advancement, it means you only care about pleasing yourself, no matter the toll it takes on others. People like that are un-adult; they're anti-grown-ups."

She pauses before going on to say, "Acting your age in my own life situation means to pitch in whenever and wherever in ways that keep my family's head above water. This is the first time in my life I've been out of the city, much less on a vacation. When I'm at home, I have to take care of my kid brothers and sisters, because my mom is single and has to work. Once she gets home around 6:00 p.m., it's my turn to go to work, as a dishwasher at a restaurant, to help bring in more money for the household.

"The camp is paying for daycare for my brothers and sisters so I can be here, and I was given time off from my job. Since arriving here at camp, I've been thinking that acting my age *should* be having more time for fun and leisure. I don't mind being super responsible at home, but I didn't realize how tired I was and how hard it can be for someone my age to have so much responsibility, until I came here and had time just to chill."

"I'm starting to wonder more and more what acting your age is really all about," says Yahaira after a short lull. "Last summer, I went to Disney World with my YWCA group, and I saw old people there dressed like Disney princesses. Some of those in my group made fun of them because they didn't think it was appropriate for older people to dress like that. But they were so happy, and they weren't hurting anyone. What's wrong with dressing like a Disney princess, no matter your age?"

"Can't some things that you do be ageless, have nothing to do with age?" asks Moises. "Those old ladies were going against most people's beliefs about what people their age should wear. I admire them. I hope I act that way when I'm their age."

This brings Vivienne to say, "My own grandmother says she's growing up backward, toward youth. She says she's becoming impulsive, irresponsible. She worked hard all her life. It's about time she got to 'un-act' her age."

"So why don't you admire me for being me, myself, and I in class?" Alonzo asks her.

"Because all you're doing is going against classroom etiquette. You're not acting in an ageless way. You're acting *up* in an immature way."

Alonzo isn't ready to cede the point. "Well, Peter Pan was ageless *and* mischievous. If it's good enough for him, it's good enough for me. He and the Lost Boys never grew up, and they lived happily ever after in Neverland. That's the life for me."

"Michael Jackson, may he rest in peace, created a home that he named Neverland, after the place where Peter Pan lived," says Taunya. "It was meant to get across that he's a person who never wanted to grow up. I wouldn't want to be like that. He wasn't the man-child he's often described as. He was just stuck. Acting your age doesn't apply when you're stuck like that. He was ageless, but not in a good way, because he had no way forward."

"Last school year I read *Catcher in the Rye*," Moises then says. "It's about an adolescent, Holden Caulfield. He doesn't want to have anything to do with becoming an adult, because he feels the adult world is one of phonies. To Holden, acting his age—acting as others expect him to act— would mean selling your soul, and he doesn't want any part of it. But he's paying a price: he's all alone and troubled and sad. As far as he's concerned, it's him and his kid sister, Phoebe, against the world. I wonder what'll happen when his sister keeps growing up and changing, while he stays unchanging."

He is silent for a good bit, thinking hard. "You know," he then says, "I'd thought the book was about an adolescent who refuses to grow up. Now I'm thinking that it's a book about an adolescent who *can't* grow up. That's the way it was with Michael Jackson, too. I would never want to be ageless in that way."

"That makes me think of Mr. Schuester, or Mr. Schue as he's known, on the TV show *Glee*," Vivienne says. "He's the director of the high school's glee club. He's described as a 'strange weeping man-child who has lotion in his hair but no adult friends.'

"Now, that Mr. Schue is unlike any adult I've ever laid eyes on in the real world. But he gets the best out of those kids. He even recruited a jock football player—the quarterback!—to be in the singing group. That quarterback is one brave dude, facing up to the taunts of his jock peers to be in the glee club, which isn't a jock thing to do. He's not so much acting his age as he is being his true self, his best self, no matter what others say or think. In my book, that's acting agelessly."[5]

Acting One's Age

How do we go about best determining what is and isn't age-appropriate? Do kids mostly leave it up to those who rear them to clue them in? Is that a big, if not the biggest, part of what parenting is all about? Surely part of the reason why books on parenting sell by the bushelful is because parents need guidance on such things. But what if parents themselves act in age-inappropriate ways?

The verb "to parent" is defined in *The Free Dictionary* as "the rearing of a child or children, especially the care, love, and guidance given by a parent." There are other verbs that have made their way into the child-growing lexicon—mothering and fathering, and most recently, sistering and brothering, who also clue young family members in need on the ins and outs of age-appropriate behavior. All connote the positive roles played by family members in the raising equation. Probably one day there will be additional affirmative participles—youthing, relativing, adulting, which (if I have anything to do with it) will fall under the umbrella of "childing."

What about the babies in the family? Do they play a key role in raising us? If so, then the existing definition of the verb "to baby" doesn't do justice to how a baby helps us grow. Instead, it connotes an unflattering way some parents treat their children. It signifies parents and other adult caregivers who are hell-bent on keeping kids in a state of immaturity that soon becomes age-inappropriate. According to *Merriam-Webster*, such parents

---

5 Shortly after this dialogue, the actor Cory Monteith, who played the show's star quarterback, died from (according to autopsy) a "mixed drug toxicity." He was thirty-one.

"tend to indulge with often excessive or inappropriate care and solicitude." But the baby, in her gibberishy way, doth protest: "That is not babying; I had nothing to do with this folderol." Rather, that is bad mothering, or fathering, parenting, or adulting, mollycoddling of the worst kind.

Babying merits a different definition. It deserves the same kind of uplifting spin as its counterparts. If the baby is the one doing the baby-ing, then she is lending her special abilities to nurture others—parents, siblings, relatives, neighbors, strangers who pass her by and whose eyes light up, momentarily swept up in the hope and promise of a new life that personifies fascination, wonder, exploration. Babying should be specified as the process by which babies lift up those of us who have had the honor of being part of their universe.

The well-known political theorist Benjamin Barber would not agree with me. In his book *Consumed*, the political theorist asks us to picture a universe made up of and run by "infantilized" people. If you go along with his characterization, ours would be one in which adults were governed by appetite, for whom self-aggrandizement and self-gratification is all. Barber claims that America today is a nation operated by adults behaving just like this—"kidults" he calls them—poster children for crass and gluttonous consumption driven by out-of-control commercial markets. He argues that adults around the country are failing to comport themselves little if any better than infants, and are triggering our country's downfall. Our only hope for survival is for them—or put another way, us—to quit this asinine nonsense.

The standard dictionary definition of "to infantilize" is to reduce to a childhood state or condition. Aristotle surely would have agreed with Barber that adults acting in an age-inappropriate way fit this definition. But is adults' behavior in fact infantile? Or is it an abysmal form of "adul-tishness," and of the pot-calling-the-kettle-black to boot? Just because an adult fails to act like a responsible grown-up is no cause to impugn kids. Irresponsible adults are just that. Leave kids out of it; enough scapegoat-ing already. Why liken adults behaving badly to the conduct of a child or an infant? Why equate their excessive wantonness and waywardness to the run-of-the-mill behavior of youngsters? Whenever adults spend beyond their means, are mindlessly voracious consumers, throw virtue to the wind, whenever they have a temper tantrum, why not call a spade a spade and leave kids out of it?

If my own daughter, Cali, and some of her friends are any indication, children can at times be unequaled in exercising discipline and willpower. My daughter regularly thwarts my attempts to buy something for her when we're out and about. She much prefers to make things—books, cards, kites, stuffed animals, fairy wings—than buy them, since that would mean that others are doing the imagining and creating for her. When I gave her a Valentine's card, she gently remonstrated me. "Daddy, why didn't you make one?" It leaves me scratching my head in amazement how few manufactured products she desires compared to most adults I know (including me). She is far from "infantilized." Is my daughter an anti-consumerist, do-it-yourself saint? Nope. She likes her new skates, her Barbie sneakers and dolls, her Polo summer dress. She likes even more buying, and selling, at consignment stores, because she likes "to give things a second and third life."

Let's overhaul the definition of infantilization with its current meaning misinformed by Aristotle's perverse notions of our youngest. From here on out, infantilized should be a laudatory term. It should mean to be inquisitive and connected to others, to care and share in ways that are natural to infants. Such a definition would go a long way toward undoing the damage done by its current usage, reflecting adults' newfound understanding that infants are typically not at all the self-absorbed creatures that they have been discredited with being for too long.

In *The Making of the Modern Mind*, the American pragmatist philosopher John Herman Randall Jr. (1899–1980) rhapsodizes about those whose "infancy is prolonged" and as a result are "able to continue learning when others have reached the limits of their powers and natural resources." In this vein, what if infantilization signifies the process of prolonging one's infancy in ways that facilitate one's continual unfolding throughout life? What if it implies the ability to stay inquisitive to the core, one's heart full of feeling for one's fellow humans?

While we're at it, let's give a different spin to the term "acting child-ishly." C. S. Lewis (1898–1963) opines that "critics who treat 'adult' as a term of approval, instead of as a mere descriptive term, cannot be adult themselves." He goes on to say:

> To be concerned about being grown up, to admire the grown up because it is grown up, to blush at the suspicion of being childish; these things are the marks of childhood and adolescence. And in childhood and adolescence they are, in moderation, healthy symptoms. Young things ought to want to grow. But to carry on into middle life or even into early manhood this concern about being adult is a mark of really arrested development. When I was ten, I read fairy tales in secret and would have been ashamed if I had been found doing so. Now that I am fifty I read them openly. When I became a man I put away childish things, including the fear of childishness and the desire to be very grown up.

If Lewis had his way, we'd embrace childishness and shun "adultish-ness." When adults consume beyond all sane limits, when they max out their credit cards, fritter away leisure hours planted in their media centers, shirk any constructive limits on consumption, care not a whit about civic involvement (or consider civic involvement tantamount to closing traf-fic lanes on a busy bridge between New Jersey and New York as payback against those who do not support their political whims), they are not feckless kids or infants, and we're doing a disservice to the Nth degree by typifying their behavior as childish or infantile. Moreover, when children and youth live in the grip of adults who place few if any limits on them-selves, is it little wonder that their progeny, contrary to their nature, often end up capitulating and behaving likewise?

Childish Things

The full biblical passage cited in part by the camp director goes: "When I was a child, I spoke and thought and reasoned as a child. But when I grew up, I put away childish things."

How do children speak and think and reason? Is it different from the way adults go about it?

John Locke (1632–1704) maintained that children have inborn reasoning capacities, albeit in unpolished form. "We are born free, as we are born rational," he posits in his *Second Treatise of Civil Government*. But he qualifies this: "Not that we have actually the exercise of either. Age that brings one, brings with it the other too." In his view, our reasoning capacities can only improve with "the improvement of growth and age," and only then when adults "supply the defects of this imperfect state." To this end, Locke enjoins parents to "reason with children." What he means is that practice makes perfect, so if we want children to become adept at their innate reasoning capacity, we need to reason with them on a regular basis.

What if the adult "suppliers" are in an imperfect state in their own reasoning capacities? What if they never learned to practice them properly in the first place? At least, what if, when reasoning with children, adults operate from the premise that their young counterparts can help them become more skillful practitioners themselves?

John Dewey challenged the prevalent opinion in his day that "childhood is almost entirely unreflective—a period of mere sensory, motor, and memory development," and that it is only as we grow older that there arises "the manifestation of thought and reason." Dewey's decades of observation and evaluation of children and youth prompted him to conclude in his landmark *How We Think* that we are no babes in the woods when it comes to high-order thinking, not even when we are, well, babes in the woods:

> Thinking begins as soon as the baby who has lost the ball that he is playing with begins to foresee the possibility of something not yet existing—its recovery; and begins to forecast steps toward the realization of this possibility, and by experimentation, to guide his acts by his ideas and thereby also test the ideas.

To Dewey, though, "only by making the most of the thought factor, already active in the experiences of childhood is there any promise or warrant for the emergence of superior reflective power" as we grow older.

How do we go about making the most of it? If children practice their reasoning skills and adults do their part to encourage this practice by engaging with them—each bringing their unique stores of experience and the wisdom that can result from that to the "reasoning table"—then Dewey is optimistic that by the time a person reaches adolescence, she will experience "an enlargement of the horizon of childhood, a susceptibility to larger concerns and issues, a more generous and a more general standpoint toward nature and social life." This in turn "affords an opportunity for thinking of a more comprehensive and abstract type than has previously obtained." This does not gainsay but rather supports his assertion that "thinking itself remains just what it has been all the time, . . . a matter of following up and testing the conclusions suggested by the facts and events of life." At least, thinking of the highest order, which is not a childish thing, not an adultish thing, but an excellent human thing.

Are kids masters of such sound and well-reasoned thinking? They are forever on the lookout for solid explanations to back up their reasoning. The developmental psychologist Henry Wellman, a professor at the University of Michigan, has found in his involved studies that it is part of the everyday existence of children as young as two and three to ask why things happen, and then come up with their own answers, using whatever supportive evidence they can muster. But is that the same as *good* supportive evidence, even when they are a bit older? When it snowed on a spring day, my then-four-year-old daughter had this explanation at the ready: "The clouds got confused. They meant for it to rain but they stirred in the wrong mix of water and temperature, so it snowed." How cute, right? But given what Cali knew so far about nature's workings, it's a pretty darned good explanation. Or am I being too charitable?

Consider the case of the Roman poet and philosopher Lucretius (99 BC–55 BC). He would have found much to praise and little to cavil over in my child's reasoning prowess. In his two-millennia-old poem "On the Nature of Things," Lucretius set forth a paradigm-shattering principle, namely, that the unforeseen, unpredictable movement of matter—the "swerve"—was no violation of nature, but its essence. He influenced everyone from Leonardo da Vinci to Galileo, Francis Bacon to Machiavelli, all of whom in their own right prompted cultural, scientific, technological, and political paradigm shifts.

Yet this most brilliant and sophisticated of thinkers was perfectly capable of reasoning—like a typical child. As Stephen Greenblatt, author of the Pulitzer Prize–winning book *The Swerve*, points out, Lucretius "thought that worms were spontaneously generated from wet soil, that earthquakes were the result of winds caught in underground caverns, that the sun circled the earth." His rationales were based on the best evidence he had at hand. Yet we don't give kids an equal break when they engage in their own earnest attempts to describe how and why things are the way they are, doing their level best to offer the most valid explanations they have in their experiential arsenal to underpin their views. We consider their attempts cute, fanciful, but not "scientific." Yet Lucretius would applaud them for what he would consider brilliant attempts at making cause-effect connections. When they do have more hard evidence at their disposal in years to come, if they have not been intimidated into thinking that their explanations are juvenile when they do not match up with the "right" answers that adults already know, they may wind up, in their older years, seeing things that no one else has yet seen—just as Lucretius did.

The English poet, literary critic, and philosopher Samuel Taylor Coleridge (1772–1834) lauds "intuitive reason," which he characterizes as "that intuition of things which arises when we possess ourselves as one with the whole." To Coleridge, it is only through this form of reason that we feel intimately connected to the immensity, and proceed with reasoning from that sensibility—not a childish capacity to "put away," but to hold onto for dear life. We adults, he laments, "think of ourselves as separated beings, and place nature in antithesis to the mind, as object to subject, thing to thought, death to life," and so our reasoning, such as it is, moves forward from that standpoint. Most importantly, in extolling intuitive reason, which is practiced par excellence by children, Coleridge effectively debunks William James's view—subscribed to, alas, to this day, even by many of our most exceptional adult philosophers—that children see the world as a "blooming, buzzing confusion," as James put it in his 1890 volume *Principles of Psychology*. Our youngest in fact see the world more clearly than they likely ever will again.

In the same vein, Alison Gopnik insists in *The Philosophical Baby* that children "are vividly aware of everything without being focused on any one thing in particular." They do not see things in a blur; they see clearly, wholly. I won't be surprised if one day cognitive scientists come to find that children have the capacity to focus on any one thing and everything at one and the same time. Children not only look at the world holistically, but with a sense of oneness. To them, there are no neat divides between their inner and outer cosmos, no more than there are between parts and wholes. The mind-bending questions they pose reflect this—and the more we take the time and trouble to inform them of what we're inquiring into, the more probing their questions. If only all our laboratories were peopled with children milling about, poring over the work of scientists, who felt obliged to explain to them in intelligible terms what they're up to, I have no doubt that the questions the children would then pose to them would further their experiments and explorations by leaps and bounds. Just as I'm sure that if children were given the same license to study adults that adults have to study children, and if they were ever made genuine co-inquirers in the quest for understanding self and other, the advances made would be far greater and more helpful to all concerned.

Coming and Going of Age

What about adolescents? Are current notions of their capabilities as off base and even put-downish as those many harbor of babies, toddlers, and kids, or have we come a long way since the days of the pioneering psychologist and educator G. Stanley Hall (1846–1924)? In his landmark work, *Adolescence*, Hall claimed that adolescence was a time of unparalleled "storm and stress." Adolescents, he alleged, were a rebellious lot nearly as physically strong as adults, yet at the mercy of raging hormones, making them capable of doing much damage to our social fabric if left unchecked. Parents and educators of his day, already convinced that adolescents were a vexing problem in need of solving, welcomed his "empirical" findings. Hall's take on youth, though, was colored by his embrace of the Darwinian notion that the development of each human individual mirrored the evolution of the human species as a whole. By this view, adolescents are at a middling and ill-formed stage, little better than children and their bundle of uncontrolled appetites, yet far more dangerous, because of their physical strength and mental smarts.

Coming to society's rescue, Hall developed a set of "pedagogical imperatives" to deal with adolescent degeneracy. Under his plan, teen girls were to be educated in finishing schools that prepared them, at a great distance from male teens, for marriage and motherhood. For teen boys, the order of the day was "manhood training," which amounted to a combination of sports, exercise, and educational curricula that drilled into them the importance of loyalty and patriotism. Hall called for universal abstention from sex for adolescent males and females, since he considered them too emotionally and intellectually immature. His remedies were widely put into use in his day and influenced everything from the development of educational curricula to Boy Scouts practices to rehabilitative strategies for so-called juvenile delinquents.

Taking direct aim at Hall's account of adolescents, Margaret Mead (1901–1978), in *Coming of Age in Samoa*, argued that it is not at all the case that adolescents necessarily experience a storm and stress phase. The observations she shared of Samoan cultures revealed a society in which adults give adolescents the space to work out the changes they're experiencing, without judgment or pressure. As a result, adolescence is a tranquil stage for them, with nary a whisper of destructive or aggressive behavior, much less bullying. Mead concluded that in those societies in which adolescents experience great conflict, this is due not to their nature but to the nature of their society. A recent cross-cultural study of 175 tribal and traditional societies further confirms Mead's findings, namely, that a period of psychological crisis, or rebelliousness, is not at all typical, much less universal (or inevitable) among adolescents.[6]

Yet to this day, in American society, adolescents are still considered the most problematic among us. Nancy Lesko of Columbia University's Teachers College, a specialist in adolescent development studies, takes the stance that adults must cease and desist considering adolescents as a group that has an inherent set of natural or inevitable characteristics, and falsely characterizing them as irrational beings controlled by raging hormones who are outside of history and society. To the contrary, she maintains, such widespread views of adolescents have no basis in fact. She challenges us to quit seeing adolescence as a problem and instead to look on this special stage as an opportunity, one in which we actively draw on their unique talents and make them full partners in the civic enterprise, since she considers them perfectly capable of making well-reasoned and responsible choices. The important questions posed by Lesko in *Act Your Age!: A Cultural Construction of Adolescence* are:

> Can we work to enhance youths' life conditions without the confident characterization that youths are at a different psychological stage from adults? Can we work to improve youths' life conditions without the hierarchy of adult over youth? Can we consider youth as more than *becoming*?

To which one should add: Can we consider adults as more than *being*, as if they have "arrived"? If adults looked at themselves in this way, might they treat those younger than them with more humility, even treat them in a more egalitarian way? Moreover, wouldn't this seismic shift in how we adults view ourselves enable us at long last to learn a great deal from adolescents, and in ways that would help us—and them—flourish?

Lesko holds that "in these times of fast capital and welfare state downsizing, we need a new vision of adolescence." In her estimation, "with

---

6 Schlegel A, Barry H. *Adolescence: An Anthropological Inquiry.* New York: Free Press; 1991.

these current challenges come new opportunities for re-visioning them; if we are to advocate for youth today, the images and reasoning about their slow coming of age are not viable." Yet it's precisely because we live in times of fast capital and welfare state downsizing that any sort of new re-visioning of adolescence, much less implementation of a new vision, isn't likely to happen. Certainly it won't be driven by the adults who have a vested interest in keeping things as they are.

It's not as if adolescents are somehow predisposed to be disconnected from society, any more than they are naturally directionless or cynical, much less aggressive to the extreme. Yet the "system" itself can breed such traits in them, making it almost a self-fulfilling prophecy, since any group that is ignored and deliberately made powerless to be included in decisions that affect them directly might lash out at such tyranny in self-destructive ways. This in turn can mislead adults into believing that such qualities come naturally to adolescents, or can serve to justify some adults' deep-rooted and distorted prejudices about them.

When Dewey asserts that everyone has the right to fit into society, he is not equating "fitting in" with conforming. Rather, he means that we should be able to mold society in ways that make it possible for all of us to be part of it. Those adolescents, for instance, who challenge the commonsense wisdom or mainstream values of their day are, by his yardstick, "conforming" to the ideals of a democratic society, in that they are doing what they do best to make it so they are included in its circle. If one is in agreement with Dewey's conception of what self-realization is all about, adolescents who challenge the system in ways that might strikingly alter the status quo aren't just rocking the boat for the sake of it, but are fitting in, adolescent-style.

Ralph Waldo Emerson declares in his essay "Self-Reliance" that "whoso would be a man, must be a nonconformist," which he characterizes as one who questions conventional society's ways and challenges the commonsense "wisdom" of the day. Such skeptics are thorns in society's side in the best sense; they refuse to accept that society is virtuous or good just because those who steer it insist that it is. Emerson might just as well have asserted, "whoso would be an adolescent, is a nonconformist." They have

built-in hypocrisy detectors, and a piquing social conscience and intellectual integrity.

Emerson himself had a dreary view of American society, which he likened to a joint-stock company comprised of unquestioning sycophants to
whom "self reliance is its aversion." In fact, in established societies throughout history, he finds the joint-stock analogy apropos. Emerson takes heart,
though, in the fact that there always have been a few standout citizens
in any given time and place who have what he called the "character of
Socrates," and as such keep everyone else in their society on their p's and
q's by telling it like it is, and also like it should be. The lesson that such
people impart, to Emerson, is that "to be great is to be misunderstood."
Granted, many who are misunderstood are far from great. Even so, who is
more misunderstood than adolescents?

While it may come naturally to adolescents to be rebels with a cause,
John Stuart Mill (1806–1873) considered rebelliousness in and of itself
a good thing. Mill maintained in *On Liberty* that "the mere example of
non-conformity, the mere refusal to bend the knee to custom, is itself
a service."

> Precisely because the tyranny of opinion is such as to make eccentricity a
> reproach, it is desirable, in order to break through that tyranny, that people
> should be eccentric. Eccentricity of character has always abounded when and
> where strength of character has abounded; and the amount of eccentricity in a
> society has generally been proportional to the amount of genius, mental vigor,
> and moral courage it contained. That so view now dare to be eccentric, marks
> the chief danger of the time.

We need colorful people, people who think in colors. The young have
few preconceptions, and even fewer prejudices, about what they are seeing;
they are not wedded to belief systems that would prescribe certain rigid
lenses for how they should see, much less how they must see. As a rule, they
don't want what is patently in flux to stay still, to be fixed and anchored,
and they have no desire to ward off the world of colors and filter what they

see through monochrome lenses. They are at home with those qualities that give color to the world's palette—ambivalence, doubt, uncertainty, incompleteness, skepticism—also a sign of an "Emersonian" intellectual maturity that can lessen or even wither on the vine altogether as time goes by.

Ageless

What would it mean to be genuinely ageless? Would this give us the capacity to ward off permanently the encroaching years? Would we remain just as we are at this moment from here on out, physically, mentally, emotionally frozen in time? If so, would that be a sort of eternal hell?

In the preface to his Pulitzer Prize–winning *Doubt*, playwright John Patrick Shanley writes of his days attending Catholic school in the Bronx in the 1960s: "Looking back, it seems to me, in those schools at that time, we were an ageless unity. We were all adults and we were all children." According to Shanley, children and adult alike in that era

> flocked together for warmth and safety. As a result, we were terribly vulnerable to anyone who chose to hunt us. When trust is the order of the day, predators are free to plunder. . . . As the ever widening Church scandals reveal, the hunters had a field day. And the shepherds, so invested in the surface, sacrificed actual good for perceived virtue.

If the adults were in fact the shepherds, then much as they might have pretended to be indistinguishable from their flock, their task was to protect the children. Rather than an elegy to agelessness, Shanley's is a cautionary tale about what happens when adults who put themselves in positions of crucial responsibility don't shoulder it as they should.

Some scientific researchers are devoted to discovering the molecular switch that can postpone or even stop in its tracks the aging process. If they one day succeed, would we change the way we go about living our days? Would we "make the most" of our time, or the least, given that we conceivably have limitless days to come in which to make the most of it? Would we fritter away even more hours if our lifespans were extended?

In the movie *It's a Wonderful Life*, one character memorably says, as George Bailey misses out on an opportunity to give Mary Hatch a passionate kiss when it looks like no one is looking, "Aw, youth is wasted on the young." What if youth was wasted on the old, and we had endless opportunities to experience it? Would we squander it even more expertly?

Are there ways in which we can grow more youthful over time? For instance, innocence is usually attributed to youth. Even if adulthood does represent the loss of certain kinds of innocence, new kinds enter the picture as we grow older. How many adults have thought themselves worldly-wise, only to find that they're still innocent—in some ways, to the good, in others, not so at all—about the ways of the world?

Does every age have its own potential fountain of youth with its own blends of idealism, innocence, dreams, and hopes? What if, instead of agelessness, we strive for "agefulness," to squeeze every drop out of whatever age we are in life, to take advantage of the signal sets of strengths and limitations, challenges and experiences, and "event horizons" that it offers us?

To Epicurus, the purpose of life is to grow more youthful, which by his conception is the ability to become ever more adept at divining wisdom about how to attain what the Greeks of his era called *ataraxia*, the happy and tranquil liberation from fear, dread, and anxiety—not tranquil in a *Brave New World* way, but one born of hard-won experience and effort. "Let no one be slow to seek wisdom when he is young nor weary in the search of it when he has grown old," Epicurus opined in one letter. "For no age is too early or too late for the health of the soul." He's ready to take on those curmudgeons who might claim it is either too early or too late for such a pursuit: "To say that the season . . . has not yet come, or that it is past and gone, is like saying that the season for happiness is not yet or that it is now no more." Epicurus's "don't worry, be happy" philosophy of life and living amounts to a kind of wisdom-seeking aimed at giving one an ideal measure of youth, no matter one's age: "Both old and young alike ought to seek wisdom, the former in order that, as age comes over him, he may be young in good things because of the grace of what has been, and the latter in order that, while he is young, he may at the same time be old, because he has no fear of the things which are to come."

There's an old saw that one is "with child," meaning that one is so excited, curious, and inquisitive about something that one is about to burst. To be ageful would be to remain "with child'"throughout our lives, at every age and stage.

Chapter 3

Ripeness Is All

All the Ripe Stuff

A CCORDING TO *MERRIAM-WEBSTER*, TO BE RIPE IS TO BE "MATURED, not mature." Something or someone ripe is "fully grown and developed." As in, you can't get any riper than this. As in, it only goes downhill from here. Some might delude themselves into thinking they've reached peak maturity, when nothing could be further from the truth. Alternatively, some might well have reached a kind of peak maturity that's the furthest thing from an admirable or enviable sort—one might peak in meanness or outright cruelty, for instance. The sooner such a person unpeaks, the better. On the other hand, lost dimensions of certain "good" kinds of ripeness might inspire you to develop ripeness in other areas. You might lose your physical agility to some extent, yet compensate in other ways. A baseball pitcher might no longer be able to zip a fastball past a hitter, so he becomes wilier, uses his vast knowledge of the game, and of his opponents, to continue besting his opponents. Physical peakness is supplanted by a combination of rising psychological astuteness and technical prowess.

What about peak parenting?

Studies show that children born to young adults have longer life spans. Does that mean that those of us who've passed our childbearing or child-rearing prime but still have (or try to have) children are somehow remiss? An adult may be ripe biologically to have a child, but not ripe mentally or emotionally, or not ripe enough financially. Some might declare, upon deciding to be a parent, "I'm as ready as I'll ever be." But that might just mean they aren't going to get themselves any readier than they already are—even if they're not very ready at all, and are in fact in a state of woeful unpreparedness. When making monumental life decisions, such as to become a parent or to have another child, or to radically change course in life in some way, it might be prudent or even wise to take an honest tally of where you are, or think you are, in various dimensions of ripeness. Still, no matter how carefully you've considered momentous decisions, they often require a leap of faith over a moat of uncertainty and even anxiety. Is what matters most one's combined ripeness and readiness to attempt the leap, succeed or fail?

Ready or Not

The nine couples attending the first week of my wife Ceci's natural childbirth course look on as she points to a chart that provides a preview of a baby-in-the-making's journey from conception to birth. When she reaches the part of the chart that details what will happen between months four and five of conception, our daughter, Cali, sitting cross-legged on the floor, a plastic diapered baby in her arms, sets it down gently, swaddles it, and stands up. "The fetus is really starting to grow at a fast pace," she tells the group. "So the uterus has to get bigger, and in a special way. It has to make room for the changing size and shape of the baby, now about a third of the weight it'll be when born." She takes the pointer from Ceci and traces an invisible circle around the uterus on the diagram: "As you can see, the top part of the uterus, here between the fallopian tubes, is stretching up toward the mommy's chest."

The students are impressed. Their amber-haired, agate-eyed teacher, nearly five-and-a-half years old at the time, knows her business. As well she should. Cali is a natural childbirth junkie. She has been sitting in on her mommy's classes since infancy and is well versed on the ins and outs of the subject. Such is Cali's fascination with the world of birth that odds are just as good that she'll be found at home absorbed in watching one of Ceci's collection of birth videos as one of the more "child appropriate" DVDs in her own collection.

Ceci and I had been together ten years to the day when Cali entered the world with the assistance of a midwife at 6:40 a.m. on Friday, August 18, 2006 at the birthing center at Roosevelt Hospital in Midtown Manhattan. Her entry was dramatic. Ceci had twelve hours of active labor and then a difficult transition. Her strength was already at an ebb when Cali got stuck in the birth canal. That put pressure on the umbilical cord and slowed down her heart rate. The midwife called the Labor and Delivery ward on the floor above us. A gurney was rolled into the room so my exhausted wife could be transferred. A C-section seemed inevitable. Nurses had her prepped so that IVs could be inserted. An oxygen mask was put over her nose and mouth. Somehow, just then, Ceci mustered the strength to make one more big push. Next thing, our baby was crowning. Ceci pushed once more. Cali swooshed into my welcoming arms. Our drama queen came out a tad bluish, and perfect, and with her right arm extended—that's why she'd been stuck—waving at the world.

We named her Caliope after the ancient Greek muse of wisdom and poetry. I had just turned forty-seven when she was born. Much as I thought I'd readied myself for life with a bundle of joy, it turns out I was pretty clueless about how to deal with the quantum change. I had been juggling the writing of a new book as well as a doctoral dissertation. All of a sudden, I could not, did not want to, do my work. I made feints at writing at the start of each day. But all I wanted to do was stare at my baby girl, watch her every drool and gurgle, revel in her company as she slept or screamed or pooped or fed at Mommy's breast. I missed deadlines for the first time in my life. Both my editor and my dissertation supervisor read me the riot act.

More than six years have passed. I finished the book, *Constitution Café*, and my dissertation (on the topic of whether Socratic inquiry contributes to a participatory democracy), becoming "Dr. Phillips" at age fifty. Along the way, I came up with a new writing routine. My most productive work time had always been in the tranquil morning hours. Cali, though, is at full volume from the moment she wakes up—and no matter how early I start my day, she somehow senses it, and insists on greeting the day with Daddy as he savors his first cup of coffee. Now I do the bulk of my writing after she's asleep.

Once every week or so, Cali and I have a standing date. We go to a restaurant of our mutual choosing. Over the course of our meal, we convene a mini-Socrates Café. The questions Cali poses are as varied as they are provocative: Why are you my daddy? Is it better to want something or need something? Why are there words? Would life be better without time?

I share the bemusement of Karl Jaspers that when a child comes up with "really serious questions," many adults assume that "the children must have heard all this from their parents or someone else." He is amazed that it doesn't occur to them that children are quite capable of coming up with jaw-dropping queries without any outside assistance. After all, it's part of their makeup.

Cali's questions and answers stay with me and continue to command further consideration. One question of hers that took me a while to wrap my mind around was: "Why do I get so upset when things that aren't real are suffering?" While in kindergarten, Cali had been given a series of booklets to learn the alphabet. Each book featured one of the "letter people." One of them she couldn't bear to look at—Mr. Z, who had a zipper for a mouth. She decided to make her own booklet. In her version, Mr. Z had a normal mouth. When she showed me her own Mr. Z creation, she explained, "People are always saying, 'zip up your lips.' But you should never put a real zipper on someone's lips." Cali felt that Mr. Z's creator had made his character suffer needlessly. She knows he's not real, yet to her, suffering is suffering, whether a real person or a fictional character. She feels their pain, and if it's in her power to alleviate it, then by golly she will. Whenever she sees a look on my face that appears to be of self-reproach over something I've said or done earlier in the day that has to do with her, she takes my hand and says simply, "Daddy, nobody's perfect." She is a practitioner of the description of empathy offered by Scottish moral philosopher Adam Smith (1723–1790): "We enter as it were into [another's] body, and become in some measure the same person with him." What I become ever more appreciative of is Cali's role in helping me become a better parent, a better person. She is in many ways my teacher, my guide.

Cali wraps up her presentation to the childbirth students with this avowal: "When my mommy gets pregnant again, I'll help take care of her placenta."

Ceci and I, eyebrows raised, share a look across the room. Though the rest in attendance are not quite sure what to make of her pronouncement, we're not so taken by surprise. Over the Christmas season, when Santa asked her what she wanted for a present, she told him point-blank, "I want a baby, a real baby." This was new territory for Santa. He looked to us for guidance. But Cali filled in the picture. Looking our way from her perch on his lap, she said, "Mommy and Daddy, I want a baby brother or sister. I'm ready."

Such is our daughter's influence that Ceci and I soon began discussing the possibility. The prospect of an expanded family came more and more to appeal to us. Still, we had valid concerns, not least of which was my age, and our ever precarious finances. For the time being, we stayed in the "thinking about it" stage.

After class ends, as Ceci chats with a couple of her students and Cali and I pack up the teaching materials, I say to my daughter, "What did you mean, you'll take care of the placenta?"

"I'll make sure Mommy gets lots of rest, does lots of healthy exercise, like gentle yoga and low-intensity Zumba. I'll see to it that she meditates, so she'll be stress-free. I'll make sure she eats only good things, doesn't drink anything with caffeine. That way, her placenta will be in tip-top shape. Because the placenta nourishes the uterus where the baby will be growing. So if I take care of Mommy's placenta, then the uterus can do its job."

"Let's say we go along with your plan and you become a big sister," I say. "Mommy and I will have to spend a whole lot of time with your little sibling."

"I'll spend a lot of time with her too, Daddy. I'll help raise the baby."

"That's great, sweetheart, it really is. But I want to make sure you understand that if and when we have another child, we'll have another family member to whom we'll have to devote a lot of time and love and attention."

"Of course you will, Daddy. Daddy, are you listening to me? I'll raise the baby too. I'm ready—to help care for her, love her, give her lots of big-sister attention. I'm ready to help you and Mommy figure out her needs, so you know how to care for her in a way that makes her giggle more than cry.

"It isn't easy being the newest member of a family, Daddy," she goes on. "You're always telling people—the students in birth class, your friends, even people we don't know that well—how difficult it was to get used to having me around. You say this right in front of me. It doesn't hurt my feelings so much anymore, but you don't realize that I had to get used to you and Mommy, too. Especially you. You wanted Mommy's attention at the same time I did. You still pout sometimes when she and I are doing something together and you're not included. I know all about how you and Mommy were together for ten years to the day when I was born. I've heard a thousand times how life as you knew it has changed. Now, I've tried my best to give you some quality time with Mommy, once I figured out what was what. I knew you still needed love and care, too. But you could have taken a little more time to figure out my needs."

Before I can get a word in edgewise, Cali goes on, "Like, you had no idea how to bathe me. I couldn't put into words that you kept bathing me in water that was too cold. So when I was having a fit, screaming and waving my arms and legs every which way, it meant that I wanted you to wrap me as tight as can be."

How can she remember such things? Can she really?

She's not done with me. "Daddy, *baby* raising is about being in tune with baby needs. I'm closer in years to a baby, so I *know* better where they're coming from. I know you've seen how I can calm down a screaming baby, even when their own parents can't. You've seen me do it at airports, at the park near home, even once at the movie theater. When I cross paths with a baby, they can see right away, 'Here's someone who understands.'"

Like a lawyer summing up her case, she then says, "Daddy, I'll help raise that baby boy or girl or twins. I'll have my baby radar on and will help you and Mommy make sure her baby years are really happy ones."

My turn to talk at last: "Can I offer you a blanket apology for all my many mistakes?"

"No apologies needed. You're a wonderful daddy. I just want to make sure you know how much I have to offer a baby."

"You've convinced me. *You* are ready." To myself, "Am I?"

"You'll do fine, Daddy," says my little mind reader. "You're readier than you know. So is Mommy. You should see how you two look at other people's babies with dreamy looks on your faces."

"Sweetheart, maybe I am ready in many ways, but I'm not so ripe for daddyhood anymore."

Cali's look is thoughtful. She takes her time with her reply, making sure each word is just the right one: "That nice lady, Mrs. Heaven, she knew what she was talking about." Cali is referring to the woman who owns a soul-food diner we frequent. "The last time we were there, she asked you, 'When are you gonna give your daughter a little brother or sister?' You said you weren't sure you would, because of your age. What did she say? 'You're at the perfect age. You'll give her so much of yourself, just like you do your daughter here.'"

Then Cali says, "Daddy, I need you and Mommy to make a baby if I'm to fulfill my identity goal."

"Your what?"

"My identity goal, of being a big sister. Being a big sister is who I'm meant to be. Wasn't one of your identity goals to be a daddy?"

"It was." Well, it was, but only after my wife set to convincing me it was, much as Cali is now trying to sway me that becoming the father of two children should be my new identity goal. Fact is, I'd been content as a childless hubby. Then one day in early 2005, over dinner at a restaurant near in our home in Chiapas, Mexico, Ceci took me off guard when she said, "I want to have a child." One look at her was sufficient to know there was no room for debate. I stumbled for a way to convey that I wasn't sure that parenthood was the right path for me, for us. Don't get me wrong, I was no extreme cynic about parenthood like the great twentieth-century Romanian philosopher-pessimist E.M. Cioran, who in *The Trouble with Being Born* declared himself "to have committed every crime but that of being a father." But it wasn't on the top of my "to be" list.

Still, parenthood intrigued me. Friends with kids made it an unsolicited point to share that they've gained so many fresh insights, from the theoretical to the practical, the ethical to the metaphysical, since becoming parents. True, many philosophers across the ages with the most penetrating understanding of things human were sometimes lousy parents, or were never parents, or had miserable upbringings, or couldn't stand one of their own parents (Dewey, for instance, who had seven children, two of them adopted, didn't much care for his mother, a strict Calvinist). Some childless philosophers, like Immanuel Kant (who was also celibate), are considered among the sagest thinkers ever about human being. Even so, the long and short of it was that I started daydreaming about what it would be like to be a dad, carrying a little one on my shoulders, going to the playground, having great conversations like the ones Cali and I now have.

"Look at me, Daddy," Cali says now, interrupting my reverie. "Can't you see a big sister waiting to be born?"

I can.

"I'll make sure she grows *up*, not down," she throws in for good measure.

"What do you mean?"

She traces an arc with her hands. "Make sure her mind and heart and spirit grow upward and outward. So she won't wilt."

I study my daughter. She is "childing" me. Cali falls into my arms, knowing I'll catch her, and hugs me.

"Don't worry, Daddy. You and Mommy go ahead and have little Cybele Margarita or Christopher Amado when you're ready. Oh, and by the way, you're ready now."

Flower Children

Soon after this one-sided exchange, Ceci became pregnant again. She had a miscarriage two months later. Many a tear was shed. "I'm still here!" Cali reminded us, going out of her way to keep our spirits up even as she coped with her own sadness over the loss.

With the passage of time, I started to wonder whether we'd been ready, ideally, to add to our family. Many things considered, I concluded that I for one was not yet as ready as I'd like to be, and my age, it turns out, was the least of it. Of course, if Ceci's pregnancy had gone to term, we'd have welcomed the baby with immense joy and love, and all would have turned out well enough.

Eventually, Ceci and I did try again to conceive. Months passed, and she didn't become pregnant. After a number of heart-to-hearts, we decided we should be content as we were, a tight-knit family of three. Cali, meanwhile, continues to unfold at her own pace, in her own way, and we do our best to figure out how best to facilitate that. Resilient and strong in some ways, vulnerable and sensitive in others, it is a delicate balancing act to make sure she continues to sprout in well-adjusted fashion.

Swedish folklore distinguishes between an *orkidebarn*, or "orchid child," and a *maskrosbarn*, a "dandelion child." Like the flowers of that name, dandelion children are resilient to life's slings and arrows; they manage to thrive in just about any environment, thanks to a self-nurturing nature that's impervious to outside forces and factors that would keep them down. Orchid children, on the other hand, are fragile like the flower. They need lots of TLC from parents or caregivers if they are to blossom. But if and when they do flower, so the traditional belief goes, it is something to behold.

In recent years, developmental specialists have found that there is a scientific basis for this folklore—so much so that they have come up with an "orchid hypothesis." Bruce Ellis of the University of Arizona and W. Thomas Boyce of the University of California, Berkeley, who study genetics and child development, got the ball rolling by identifying gene sequences that can pinpoint an orchid child, whom they equate with "a flower of unusual delicacy and beauty." Other researchers have since gone on to find that the very genes that put some children most at risk of depression, alcoholism and ADHD, can, with proper nurturing, spark breathtaking flourishing. According to the psychology writer Wray Herbert, "The idea of resilient children was hardly new, nor was the related idea that some kids are especially vulnerable to the stresses of their world. What was novel was the idea that some of the vulnerable, highly reactive children—the orchid children—had the capacity for both withering and thriving." The same gene sequences can lead you to soar, or to plummet, spectacularly. This make-or-break capacity is at the center of ongoing efforts to develop strategies for nurturing children to help ensure that those of the orchid variety burgeon.

My own daughter, though, seems a mix of both the orchid and the dandelion. My wife is the dandelion in the family. When I asked her what kind of flower she thought I was, the flower enthusiast replied, after giving it some thought, that I was a late and long bloomer, like the monkshood. I suspect that down the road it will be discovered that there are many other kinds of "flower children." Maybe one day a genetic analysis will reveal whether we're likely to be early bloomers or late ones, or even whether we're apt to bloom periodically, like perennials, or maybe just once in our lifetime, like the spiky, exotic, six-foot-tall *Puya berteroniana*, which waits for nearly a century before it comes to full bloom, only to fade and die about two weeks later. Or the time might come when we'll be able to determine through a close inspection of our genes whether some of us need to experience harsh or challenging conditions that test our mettle in order for us to display our "flower power" in all its glory. Probably gene sequences will be discovered that reveal that some of us are akin to azaleas or crocuses: unlike most flowers, which wilt if there's a sudden chill, they must experience a punctuated period of harsh conditions in order to bloom. Some percentage of us may need to experience an existential deep freeze in order to unfold, sort of similar to witch hazel, which unlike most flowers blooms in the dead of winter. Even if gene sequencing becomes so refined that it makes it possible for our natures to be identified with great precision, surely there will always be those who will defy whatever their inner programming predicts their blossoming can or will amount to. Just as there will continue to be those who will rise above their genes and those who don't live up to their genes' potential, there will be those who become like any flower, or blend of flowers, they choose to be, and those who will create new types, not just hybrids, but species unto themselves.

Can we ever know when a human is blossoming fully? Perhaps it's easy to tell with an orchid child, since they flower in such a blaze. But overly rigid or simplistic criteria for what constitutes human flourishing can blind us to its more muted occurrences. For instance, some among our species are like the Japanese holly; they flower in so subtle and insignificant a way that one can miss it altogether unless one knows how to look. More to the point, if we equate human blossoming mostly with happiness, we might discount the fact that some of the most deeply unhappy people, from Freud to Nietzsche to Edith Wharton, have left us some of the most lasting and insightful works. Despair, depression, and trauma can be among the elements that lead to exceptional artistry or insight. On occasions, they can serve to liberate. While we shouldn't purposefully create conditions that cause anyone to experience life at its most negative or destructive extremes, there is also a different kind of risk in going to lengths to control conditions overmuch for one's growth, to protect and preserve in ways that seal one off to unexpected opportunities for growth. Struggle, intensity, suffering, adversity are often part of the fabric of a fully flourishing creative life, and happiness often is not.

To the much-discussed British philosopher Anthony Grayling, if one avoids life's pains—or if others try to stand in our way and be a buffer between us and life's pains—"stifling appetites and desires in order to escape the price of their fulfillment—one lives a stunted, muffled, bland life only."

It is practically tantamount to a partial death in order to minimize the electric character of existence—its pleasures, its ecstasies, its richness and color matched by its agonies, its wretchedness, its disasters and grief. To take life in armfuls, to embrace and accept it, to leap into it with energy and relish, is of course to invite trouble of all the familiar kinds. But the cost of avoiding trouble is a terrible one: it is the cost of having trodden the planet for humanity's brief allotment of less than a thousand months, without really having lived.

But so many principally experience life's agonies and know only wretchedness, disaster, and grief. It's not that they seek out trouble, but that their environs breed trouble, make it unavoidable. It's not that they live in surroundings similar to a wildflower, in which there is no human intervention at all, but rather there is constant intervention of a sort that breeds only the tragic elements of life.

Ripeness and readiness are often bedfellows. According to *Merriam-Webster*, one definition of ripe is "suitable, appropriate," as in "the time was ripe for the attempt," indicating that one is "fully prepared" and "ready." In Hamlet's case, he convinces himself that the time is as ripe as it will ever be to attempt revenge against Claudius, who killed his father so he could assume the throne. Hamlet places a much higher premium on readiness than ripeness—so much so that, as he puts it, "the readiness is all." When Laertes, who wants to avenge his father's and sister's deaths, challenges him to a duel, he accepts without hesitation. Hamlet believes his fencing skills are as honed as can be.

Ready's primary dictionary meaning is: to be prepared either mentally or physically, or both, for some experience or action, and as a consequence to be "prepared for immediate use." Hamlet was ripe and ready physically, but mentally and emotionally stunted. As the fates would have it, Laertes bests him, delivering a mortal wound—but not before Hamlet manages to slay Claudius. His mental and emotional ripeness, never any great shakes, was at an all-time ebb when he lost the duel. He was both ripe and ready to die, his mission accomplished.

In *The Iliad*, when Achilles, Greek hero of the Trojan War, knows his mortal moment is about to end, he declares, "I'm going to die, but this story will be like a beautiful flower that will never wilt." But one's story can also be like an ugly flower that will never wilt, continuing to do damage long after one is no longer of this world. How might you strive to make your life a story, in balance, one that leaves an influential imprint? Such "positive" striving, as Anthony Grayling notes, can entail great trial, can spring from wrong and even damaging turns, obstacles (including of the self-made variety), and despair. But while it can lead to dead ends, it can also be an entryway. If you're willing to examine carefully what you've wrought so far and how you've gone about it, if you invite the insights of caring others to the inquiry and put your imagination to work in order to visualize new possibilities, approaches, and strategies, this can be the recipe for kinds of self-understanding that make it possible to overcome what so far has kept you from fully blooming. It can make you ripe and ready to live at last.

How can we create conditions that make it so most everyone can be part of what Grayling calls the electric character of existence, so they can, if they choose, experience an eclectic variety of life's rich palette of colors, rather than just the most sad and sobering ones? What would our figurative soil have to be fertilized with, and how would it have to be tilled, for this to happen?

We might learn a thing or two on the subject from what is known about coffee beans. Harvesting them at just the right moment is all. Coffee must be processed from ripe beans—which are in fact a fruit called cherries—when they are at their zenith in natural sweetness, replete with floral and fruity notes. If coffee is processed from unripe cherries, the taste is bitter, thin, astringent—in a word, yucky. One of the challenges unique to harvesting coffee beans is that coffee fruit does not ripen uniformly. So it is that the same tree will contain cherries at various stages of ripeness—from ripe red cherries to unripe green ones to ones that are past their prime, dry and black and shriveled.

In many coffee-growing regions, those hired as pickers are expert at removing at a brisk clip only the ripe cherries. Throughout the harvesting season, they return again and again to the same tree, indeed the same branch, as each individual fruit becomes ripe for the picking. In other regions, where machines are used for harvesting, all coffee fruit is stripped in one swoop. Little surprise that those coffee-growing regions renowned for having the most flavorful beans are those with individual pickers who harvest with painstaking care the ripest beans. The regions that employ harvesting machines predictably have a mixed record. Their approach to extracting coffee beans mirrors the way so much of the American public educational system "harvests" young minds. Such an approach yields poor fruit for society.

In America today, the emphasis for public school students in particular is on achieving uniform standards demonstrable through regular testing. The problem isn't with standardized tests per se, but lies more with the fact that we have devised the wrong sets of standards to be assessed. It is scandalous, for instance, that our society hasn't developed a standard bar of achievement that requires young school-aged children to master a variety of languages, tapping into their inborn ability to absorb like a sponge new tongues. Most children could easily have three or four languages under their belts by age ten or so. It would be for the greater good of society, the path to building bridges to other peoples and cultures, but also to far more expansive forms of individual self-expression. As much lip service as Americans place on celebrating individualism, it is a borderline miracle when anyone's talents are fully detected, teased out, and developed while one is young—and one big reason is because we have set such a skewed (and low) bar on the kinds of educational standards that kids are expected to meet.

Developmental specialists today are finding that very young children tend to be natural-born empathizers, scientists, reasoners, and explorers. Our colossal failure to grow such innate capacities at the time they're ripest for development makes the odds more likely that dull habits of mind, and aggressive habits of behavior, will emerge in their stead and "ripen."

Even if conditions for human growth are ideal, can you ever know when you're as good as you're going to get in an endeavor, whether parenting or writing, sympathizing or inventing? Would you want to know? If you feel you've reached the summit of achievement, would you become lax, ease off in your striving, miss out on opportunities for further advancement and discovery? One of the best-ever playwrights, the ancient Greek trage-dian Sophocles (496 BC–406 BC), wrote his masterpiece, the three-part Oedipus cycle, when he was nearly ninety. The novelist Harriet Doerr (1910–2002) published her first book, *Stones for Ibarra*, when she was seventy-four. Her lean, spare tales, wrought with a generous dollop of magical realism, are a marvel. A confluence of factors in her latter years led to her being a late bloomer. Thank heavens these two writers hadn't decided they'd passed their prime, or they would have never made the attempt to craft works in their final years, when it turns out their gifts were at their most exceptional. Our world would have been poorer for it.

When Greek civilization was at its crest, its citizens loved nothing better than getting together in the *agora*, the public marketplace, where they not only bartered goods, but exchanged ideas and ideals, usually over a shared bottle of wine. They knew a lot about grapes, one of their most important agricultural crops. For instance, they knew that grapes have three stages of ripeness—immature, ripe, and raisin. The ripe and raisin stages represent two different peak points: as a mature grape, it is at its moistest and tasti-est; as a shriveled raisin, it is at its driest and tastiest. The potential lesson for humans? We might have more than one peak point, or more likely, a variety of peak points, at different junctures in our lives.

Great Expectations

I'm gathered with a goodly number of people at a cozy corner café that I frequent a few short blocks from my home in downtown Philadelphia. I'd mentioned my latest Socratic project to the café owners, who were intrigued enough to close off their café one evening to regular customer traffic and turn over their space entirely to my philosophical pursuit. All it took to bring in a sizable crowd was the owners' announcements on the store chalkboard, and on their Twitter and Facebook sites. Many on hand are expecting a child in the near future. Maybe they're here because the eye-catching announcement says I'm investigating "philosophies of childing."

Before I even think about soliciting a question for exploration from those on hand, Phoebe, forty-one, stands up and says to us, "I'd never planned to be a parent. No one who knows me well would consider me 'maternal.'" The entrepreneur, who runs a website that provides advice for social media startups, places her hands on her round abdomen. "I became pregnant quite by accident. Not with someone I love. I have no plans to inform the person. I went through an agonizing process before I decided that I want to be a parent. I was never one to believe that becoming a parent was the ultimate in personal fulfillment, though the self-help gurus these days claim parenting—and after that, to add insult to injury, mate acquisition and mate retention—to be the pinnacle of what makes life worth living. They even place it above self-actualization, which had long been the holy grail of human motivation."

She then says, "My nearest and dearest assure me that my maternal instinct will come to the fore when my baby boy is born. Meanwhile, I've been taking all sorts of classes in preparation for parenthood, and I've been reading lots of books about how to raise a healthy and happy child—*Bringing Up Bébé, No Regrets Parenting, The New Basics: A-to-Z Baby & Child Care for the Modern Parent*. Maybe my pregnancy wasn't planned, maybe I'm not naturally warm and fuzzy with other people's kids, but I will be a loving and caring parent, and I want my parenting skills to be at a high level from the start."

Phoebe holds up dog-eared copies of those perennial favorites, *What to Expect When You're Expecting* and *What to Expect the First Year*. "They're great sources for informing newbie parents what they're in store for. I'm wondering, though, what should our newborns expect from us?"

Marco, twenty-eight, who owns a graphics design studio in the city, is the first to reply. "A child's expectations for someone they look to as a parent or parental figure is for you to be there for them. I'm not talking just about being there financially and providing the basic necessities, but being a constant presence, no matter your economic status, no matter the ups or downs in your life.

"I fathered a child when I was twenty-three," he says next. "I wanted nothing to do with parenthood. I wasn't at a place in my life—not at a place in my mind or heart—to be a parent. The woman I was with told me she understood my feelings, but that she was going to have the baby. Legally, she could have demanded my financial support. She asked for nothing from me, though she didn't earn a good income.

"I'm ashamed to say that over two years passed before I got back in touch. She'd had a boy, Federico. She asked me if I'd like to see him. I said I would. She must have known that's why I'd called. They were living in modest circumstances. Her extended family helped care for Federico so she could keep working without paying exorbitant bills for childcare. He was surrounded by people who doted on him. He's an amazing child, so full of joy. I spent all day with him that day. Call it what you will, paternal instinct, paternal pull, whatever, but from that time on I wanted to be part of his life."

Bertrand Russell (1872–1970) writes in his autobiography that "the paternal feeling, as I have experienced it, is very complex. There is, first and foremost, sheer animal affection. . . . Next, there is a sense of inescapable responsibility, providing a purpose for daily activities. . . . Then there is an egoistic element . . . the hope that one's children may succeed where one has failed."

"Over time, Federico came to understand that I'm his biological father. That loving, exuberant child accepted me into his circle. That was three years ago. He now expects to see me regularly. He gets anxious when we part company. He says, 'You're coming back?' I assure him I am, and of course I now help with the expenses of raising him. He gave me a card for Father's Day last week—a handmade card in the shape of a heart. It says in bright letters of varying sizes, 'Happy Daddy's Day.'" He takes a moment to regain his composure. "I'm getting far more from Federico than I have a right to expect."

Marco then says, "I used to think that if you didn't have sufficient economic resources, you had no business bringing a child into the world. Yet many parents who earn good incomes have little to do with their children. I myself was a latchkey child. I had every material possession a child could want. But both my parents were emotionally distant, from me and one another. Their expectation of me was that I shouldn't expect more from them than a nice roof over my head and nice belongings. I had no siblings, no friends close by, no relatives to bond with. I've come to see that those who may not have much in the way of material resources can be exceptional parents, and provide 'essentials' that every child should expect—love, attention, a sense of belonging."

"Expectant parents themselves need certain essentials if they're to be able to provide to their offspring the ones that Marco speaks of," says Janan, thirty-four, soon afterward. Several months pregnant, she and her husband own the café. "They need to have some tranquility and nurturing of their own—the mother especially—in order to be able fully to meet a child's basic expectations. She needs to be in a life situation in which she can have a peaceful pregnancy. I read a study about how the fetus's brain development is totally connected to its experience in the womb. If, during pregnancy, you're experiencing extreme stress, anxiety, or depression, the fetus will too, because you're emitting stress hormones straight to the womb, where the fetus feels emotions and recognizes stress elevation patterns in the mother's voice.

"For most pregnant women, a peaceful pregnancy isn't a possibility," she goes on. "In the US for working women, taking extra time off to care for yourself while pregnant is almost unheard of. And maternity leave policies are barbaric compared to other developed countries, many of which also give the father ample time off. This is happening on our watch. We should expect more of our society, and ourselves, and the developing fetus should expect more of us."

"Should these particular expectations be rights?" I ask.

"Among others," says Phoebe. "The baby also has a right to be conceived by parents who are drug-free, so it can develop in a uterus that has no toxicity. I've been reading about the great increase in the number of infants born with toxic amounts of alcohol or drugs. When pregnant mothers drink or take drugs, they go straight to the babies' system.

A newborn won't be able to develop a great set of expectations for herself if the environment she developed in is a damaging one."

After a pause, Janan's husband, Kushal, thirty-six, says to Phoebe, "It sounded strange to me at first when you asked what newborns should expect. They'll just have entered the world, so I was thinking, they have no idea what to expect, no idea what the word 'expectation' means. Now it's occurred to me, they may not know the word 'expectation,' but they know when they're hungry, and they expect to be fed. They know when they're cold, and expect someone to make them warm. They know when they're tired, and expect help falling asleep. Newborns are, and should be, a bundle of expectations—of us, and of the world we're bringing them into. Even before they're born, they should expect us to be giving a lot of thought to their present, and their future."

"How do you best do that?" I ask. "I want more than ever to do my bit to make the world a more life-affirming place. Since my daughter, Cali, was born, a big part of that is being present for her. Before she started attending school, she and Ceci could usually travel with me. More and more, I go alone to hold dialogues, and I'm as miserable as they are when I'm away for any great length of time. On the other hand, I'm miserable in another sense when I'm not giving my all to my calling. Many of the 'world changers' I most admire are lousy parents, and their children suffered. How do you strike an 'expectations balance,' where you meet your own expectations and the expectations of those you bring into the world?"

To which Phoebe says after a pause, "Some parents are too intent on saving the world, making their mark in a big way. They do so at the expense of their own children. Your children aren't a footnote. A newborn should expect to be at the center of your life. My father looked for meaning in grand acts, big gestures. He was an important scholar and activist. He was showered with honors and awards. He was always away at a lecture or a conference or some sort of demonstration. He even missed my birth. Family came second. When I decided I wanted to be a parent, I also decided I wanted to be remembered by my child most of all as a loving and attentive parent, even if no one else in the world ever knows much about me."

"Should that be the child's expectation starting as a newborn?" I ask.

"I would like to think so. When my father died of a heart attack at sixty-two, I mourned someone I didn't know nearly as well as I'd longed to. Yet the memorial service was attended by hundreds who revered the ground he walked on. Maybe I was selfish in my expectations of him as a father. He did make a huge difference to so many others." She then tells us, "I'm naming my son after him. Whenever I look at my Albert, I will think the best thoughts of my father." And then: "I hope my son will think the best thoughts of me as he grows up. But maybe he'll set such a high bar of expectations, as maybe I did for my father, that I won't be able to meet it."

"Should the newborn expect you to have expectations of him or her?" I ask.

"Eventually, but not as a newborn," says Janan. "That is something to instill in them over time. Kushal and I will raise our child to have a social conscience. But a newborn should expect to be very much at the center of our world." She contemplates some more. "On the other hand, we do her a disservice if she's so much the center that we forget about the world at large. We make our newborn's world better by doing our part to make the world better for all newborns.

"My husband and I focus our own energies on our own backyard. Because of draconian budget cuts in child protective services, in medical care and mental health care, the system often isn't intervening in time. And the number of homeless children is at the highest rate since the Great Depression. The message to poor children is: 'leave your expectations at the door.' The growing divide between the haves and the have-nots is also an expectations divide."

Emily, who works as a barista at the café, and is in the seventh month of her pregnancy, says after an engrossed silence, "I would like to say that a newborn should, when raised by a couple, expect as one of 'the basics' that both of those who made the commitment to bring her into the world and raise her to always be there for her. But she shouldn't expect that we will always be together as a couple. I love my boyfriend, love having a baby with him. However, we don't know what the future holds for us as a couple. We're honest about that. But we'll be committed to our child, no matter what. If our child can't expect that from us, we'd have no business bringing her into the world."[7]

"My commitment to Jessica is part of my commitment to our child," says Teresa. A staff sergeant in the army, her partner became pregnant through artificial insemination. "Our child should expect that of us. I don't say that to be holier-than-thou. I know things can go wrong in the best of relationships. And I know about growing up in unhealthy circumstances. My father abandoned me and my mother when I was five. I'm grateful that a loving aunt took me in and raised me after my mother became too mentally ill to care for herself, much less for me.

"So what I'm expressing is an ideal expectation. The moment our newborn enters this world, he or she will sense that there is no separating the love Jessica and I have for one another from the love we have for her."

"Even so," says Jessica, "our child should never expect that she has to meet any of our needs. We do bring children into the world because their presence in our lives gives us so much fulfillment, but they should add to our full lives, not fill a void. Yet when my mother became incapacitated, I was there for her gladly. Unlike the Jewish mothers in Philip Roth novels, she never raised me to feel obligated in any way to be there for her, though she sacrificed so much for me. I've had to be careful about how I care for my mother, though. She's fiercely independent. Parents in need should expect you to care for them with the same philosophy with which you'd care for a newborn—that you never put yourself above them at a time when they're at their most needy and vulnerable, and that show they're the ones doing you a favor by making you feel so needed."

To the Roman philosopher and statesman Seneca (4 BC–65 AD), when we care in the right way, we are attentive, devoted, and conscientious about figuring out and meeting the needs of those in our care. Further, it's

---

7 About five months after this dialogue took place, Emily wrote to me to say that she and her boyfriend broke up, that he moved to Seattle and is already in another relationship. She said he does not provide financial support to their baby.

paramount for those caring for others to do so in a way that those on the receiving end—no matter how testy or demanding or seemingly ungrateful—feel no sense of obligation. Martin Heidegger believes that to have a conscience is to heed "the call of care." Heidegger's view, like Seneca's, is that bona fide caring requires one to go to great lengths to determine the wants, needs, aspirations, and expectations of those being cared for. To Heidegger, the aim is to enable someone in need to live with greater dignity and self respect. His claim is that such caring for a fellow human is a principal way we become more conscientious stewards of the universe itself. It's also a way for us to gain greater well-being. As psychologist Daniel Goleman notes, brain scan studies of someone displaying compassion indicate that "the very act of concern for others' well-being . . . creates a greater state of well-being within oneself."

"Expectations by your children should be a one-way street," says Vasiliki, seventy-two, a moment later. She is seated in a far corner of the café, and we have to strain to hear her. "They didn't ask to be brought into the world. They owe us nothing in return. My oldest son is thirty-eight. He's had a lot of problems, caused a great deal of hurt and troubles for others. He's made it clear he blames his woes on my late husband and me. He has lashed out at me horribly, called me when he's drunk or stoned and said the cruelest things. He showed up at my doorstep last month. I hadn't seen or heard from him in over a year. He needed money. He made up this elaborate story about what it was for, about this great business he was starting. Even though I knew better, I gave him a good bit—not as much as he wanted, though, and he showed his disappointment. He left without so much as a hug. I don't expect to hear from him again until he needs more money.

"My husband and I recognized early on that James had a predisposition to meanness, to dishonesty, even to cruelty. Sometimes a combination of therapy and medication and parenting strategies seemed to help, but in the end no amount of nurture did much to change his nature. But my commitment to him is not quid pro quo. Parenthood is about loving your child all the way, no matter what—and to fulfill that philosophy, you may have to adjust your expectations of your child, and of yourself as a parent. No parent plans on having a problem child to any extreme degree. But things can go terribly wrong in the life of any of your children at any time. Perhaps I should practice tougher love. But when I think about James, and on the rare occasions I see him, I still see that newborn, that bundle of joy I brought into the world, and my heart melts. He surely knows this, and exploits it. So be it."

Vasiliki pauses, staring at her hands folded on her lap. "I fell in love with James the moment he entered the world. It was a difficult labor, but as soon as I saw him and held him, all of that was forgotten. He was a big baby, nearly nine pounds, healthy and gorgeous. Perfect in my eyes. There was already such a deep connection between us. I had visions of all the milestones to come in his life—the first time he would say a word, his first time crawling, then walking, his first day in kindergarten, his graduation day from high school, then embarking on his college years, then getting his diploma and taking on the world."

Her smile is sad as she looks around at us. "Tomorrow is his birthday. I have no idea where he is, or how to reach him, or if he's okay. But I am going to celebrate the day with all my heart. I love my precious child, no matter what."

Ripe Choices

The distinguished feminist philosopher and social activist Martha Nussbaum believes that among our greatest expectations should be the right to realize our version of the good life. To this end, she identifies a set of "central human capabilities" that she maintains "are implicit in the idea of a life worthy of human dignity." These include political autonomy, bodily integrity (which for a woman includes having complete reproductive choice), a quality education, an array of good nutritional choices, adequate housing, and health care. Nussbaum considers these capabilities "core human entitlements that should be respected and implemented by the governments of all nations, as a bare minimum of what respect for human identity requires."

If a government grants such entitlements, is this all we need to become the dignified "maker of choices" that Nussbaum envisions? Or do we also need certain kinds of caring communities to go along with such entitlements? Noted sociobiologist Sarah Hrdy believes that society itself at its most foundational level needs to be organized in a certain way if we are fully to tap into our basic nurturing instincts and meet one another's most cherished expectations. In *Mother Nature: Maternal Instincts and How They Shape the Human Species,* Hrdy contends that if parents and caregivers are to provide the abundance of loving care needed by infants if they are to prosper, and if adults, in their own right, are to be all they can be, they need to take their cue from the primates species and extant primitive human cultures she's been observing for over three decades. Hrdy asserts that first and foremost we must look to "allomothers"—relatives and others who care for their child as if she were their own. Her claim is that all such caregivers "become the emotional equivalents of kin."

> While the mother is uniquely equipped to meet that need, with her physical contact, her scent, her milk, she's not the only one who can answer when an infant seeks the meeting eyes of love. . . . Any (committed) caretaker is capable of communicating the message infants desperately seek—'You are wanted and will not be set aside.'"

Hrdy is convinced that long-prevalent conceptions of the maternal instinct in human mothers are distorted at best, and contribute to the long-standing custom of putting the primary burden to care for children squarely but unfairly on mothers. This isn't to say that mothers today can't fulfill this role; they so often do, often with little or no emotional or financial support. But it's done at the expense of the full flowering both of child and mother, and of society as a whole, since this goes against the natural state of things. What Hrdy contends *is* natural is for mother and child to be plugged into a wider network—fathers, grandparents, nannies, neighbors, among others. Likewise, Bertrand Russell asserted decades earlier, in *Marriage and Morals*, that there is "in either a man or a woman a tendency to feel affection for any child whom he or she has to attend."

To Hrdy, this network in modern times should extend into the workplace and schools.

I can speak to the benefits of cooperative education. My wife and I enrolled our daughter, Cali, starting at age two, in a preschool co-op. Dads and moms made a periodic commitment throughout the school year to spend the day helping with their child's class. This freed up teachers to do a greater range of educational enrichment activities, while it made us an essential part of the classroom community. An additional bonus for me was that, by looking after other children, I learned how to better to care for my own daughter. In turn, Cali became used to other trusted adults besides her mother and father pitching in and caring for her. What's more, whenever any of us in the co-op community needed a sitter in a pinch, we turned to one another, thanks to the almost familial-type bond developed among many of us. Many families, alas, that would love to be part of a co-op school can't because their workplaces don't allow the kind of flexible hours necessary so they can commit periodically as volunteer helpers. It's nearly impossible to resuscitate the kinds of caring communities Hrdy calls for when there are such fixed boundaries between the world of adult work and of child-aged education. This is to the detriment of us all since, according to Hrdy, when we make child-rearing a cooperative affair, our deep-rooted altruistic inclinations emerge. Generalizing from her observations in the field, Hrdy asserts that we humans have an ingrained capacity to "voluntarily do things that benefit others." She's not speaking only of adults, but of infants as well: "Right from an early age, even before they can talk, people find that helping others is inherently rewarding."

The rationalist philosopher Baruch Spinoza (1632–1677), whose works served as the springboard for the eighteenth-century Enlightenment, posited in his *Ethnics* that we are conditioned to cooperate. John Dewey, who was influenced by Spinoza at an early stage in his career, believed such conditioning is true mainly when we're young. He singled out kids, who are "marvelously endowed with power to enlist the cooperative attention of others." He attributes this to their "flexible and sensitive ability . . . to vibrate sympathetically with the attitudes and doings of those about them." It turns out that babies are the most flexible and sensitive of us all. Recent cognitive studies show that the youngest are hardwired to exert themselves above and beyond the call of duty to be helpful. Felix Warneken of Harvard and Michael Tomasello of the Max Planck Institute, who explore the origins of social cognition and the roots of our capacities for altruism and cooperation, conducted a series of studies that show that even those as young as fourteen months will go out of their way to help others achieve their goals. Infants demonstrated this in a variety of ways. For instance, those in the study went to great lengths—even crawling over heaps of cushions—to fetch for the adults conducting the experiment objects such as pens that looked to be out of their reach, or to help them open cabinets that the adults feigned they couldn't open on their own. The infants did this without expectation of an external reward of any kind. In fact, amazingly, rewards proved to be counterproductive, a disincentive to this ingrained capacity of theirs to help because helping is reward in itself. If this is so, then our entire system of carrot-and-stick incentives is out of whack and needs to be radically changed.

Not only are babies cooperative and helpful in their way, but they're bundles of empathy. Babies cry in response to the wails of other babies, "and not just because it's a sound that upsets them," according Carolyn Zahn-Waxler, a leading developmental psychologist who studies the development of empathy. "They cry more in response to human cries than to other aversive sounds. Somehow, there's a built-in capacity to respond to the needs of others."

What might be called the "infantile instinct" to care is in its way every bit as formidable and bond-creating as that of adults. Infants somehow know that a profound sense of helplessness and vulnerability is not their exclusive domain, but rather, that adults can be just as susceptible to such feelings. They feel the pain of the significant others in their lives, and are determined to share with them their healing powers. It is what infants innately expect of themselves.

Rights and Wrongs

It's a sweltering Sunday afternoon in Phoenix, Arizona, but you wouldn't know it inside an ice-cold Panera Bread, where fifteen or so parents are gathered with me around a long rectangular table with a Formica-like top. Most, though not all, belong to the same church. They've left their kids with babysitters or in the safekeeping of older siblings, as they do at least one Sunday each month. One among us, Stefan, I'd come to know at the Socrates Café I'd established in the greater Phoenix glop after moving here in 1999, relocating from the too-pricey Bay Area of California, when Ceci landed a job as a bilingual literacy instructor at an elementary school. I'd told Stefan, forty-three, an information technology specialist with the state government and father of two, of my latest Socratic quest. He let me know that those with whom he gathers at Panera usually have a give-and-take that touches on parenting themes, and invited me to join them. When I found myself back in the area to give a presentation at a university, I made sure to carve out time to attend their latest Panera get-together.

"At our sermon this morning, our pastor quoted from that beautiful passage in Ecclesiastes 3:1, 'to every thing there is a season,'" Jasmine says in due time, after I tell the group about the theme I'm investigating. The thirty-four-year-old mother of two sets of fraternal twins from two marriages is in pharmaceutical sales, working out of her home. "I'm wondering now: is there a season when it's most ripe for learning right from wrong?"

"The lines between right and wrong have become so blurred," she goes on. "Take the academic cheating scandals that have come to light across the country. Teachers and professors and administrators often seem more upset over getting caught than over what they did and the example they're setting for young people. The attitude is, 'Everybody else is "breaking bad," so why not me?' I read that they even experience a 'cheater's high,' how going against established morals gives them a positive self-image.[8]

---

8 See "The Cheater's High: The Unexpected Affective Benefits of Unethical Behavior," October 2013 issue of the *Journal of Personality and Social Psychology*.

"We could talk forever about how we've gotten to the point that so many associate right with whatever works in getting what they want, and wrong with whatever stands in their way. But I'm interested in understanding how we can make conditions ripe for learning that right is doing good of some kind, and wrong with the opposite."

The lull is not uncomfortable as everyone, engrossed in thought, tries to think of a reply. Finally Edmond, forty-one, a local developer, says, "One condition—necessary but not sufficient—is that it has to be the 'season of reason' in your life. Only then can you 'listen to reason' and understand why some forms of behavior aren't appropriate. And only then can you consider the consequences of your behavior." The father of two children and three stepchildren looks at Jasmine as he goes on to say, "But also, only then can you understand why the lines between right and wrong are sometimes blurred, for good reason. I've taught my kids that lying is wrong, stealing is wrong, cheating is wrong. Yet I flat out lied when I was my oldest kid's age. Once, my father asked me point-blank if my little sister had broken a vase in the dining room. I knew if I told him the truth, he'd whip her. I decided it was more right than wrong to lie. Only by lying could I prevent my father from committing what I felt was a great wrong. My lie was the result of my reasoning through the consequences of the possible replies I could have given."

The British ethicist Elizabeth Anscombe (1919–2001), one of the most important philosophers of the twentieth century, is the originator of the philosophy of "consequentialism," which maintains that the morality—the rightness or wrongness—of any given action hinges on its outcome, or consequences.

Then Patty, forty-three, a financial advisor with four children between ages three and seventeen, says to us, "From all I've read, there's still a lot of disagreement among developmental experts about when someone is first able to distinguish right from wrong, or as Santa would say, to tell nice from naughty. Some say you can understand the difference as early as three or four, while others say you have to be a good deal older. My experience with my own kids is that it varies. My second-to-oldest is the most challenging to reason with. He still isn't totally with the program on lessons of right and wrong, no matter how gentle or how assertive I am, regardless of whether I punish or am permissive, no matter the lengths I go to try and reason with him. If there's a recipe for creating ripe conditions for him so he can learn right from wrong, I haven't discovered it."

She reflects some more. "The most important condition for ripe learning about right and wrong is conscience. Jiminy Cricket says, 'Let your conscience be your guide.' But for that to be so, first you have to have a well-developed conscience. Otherwise, you don't respect others and don't care about how your actions affect them. My second-oldest lacks this conscience to some extent. My oldest, on the other hand, has such an extreme conscience that I almost wish sometimes it was less developed. One time he was given too much change at a WaWa, and he didn't discover it until he got home. He couldn't sleep at night, because he felt he'd cheated them. Nothing was right with his world until we returned to the store the next day and handed over the change. This is the same WaWa where, years earlier, my second-oldest once was caught stealing a loaf of bread on a dare from his friends. To this day, even though he was punished, I don't think he regrets it, except for being caught. We continue to have behavior issues with him. He may listen to reason, but he doesn't go along with it. Now, my youngest has the ideal balance of conscience and reasoning ability. He is such a gentle and kind nature that I've rarely had to say a thing about right or wrong. Conditions within him are ripe in a way that he seems instinctively to understand the difference."

Jasmine, who has been nursing her mug of coffee as she listens intently, now says, "But I think we can all agree that a one- or two-year-old isn't yet capable of knowing the difference between right and wrong, good or bad. If that's so, then the season can't be ripe for teaching moral lessons to someone of that age, because they don't yet have a moral sense."

Then she says, "I was on a plane flight last month. A woman seated catercornered to me had her child, maybe eighteen months old at most, on her lap. He was a little unruly. He sometimes kicked the seat in front of him or pulled down the seatback tray to drum his hands on it. It was a short flight, yet she must have said to him 'bad' or 'you're bad' at least fifty times—at times referring to what he was doing, at others referring directly to him. Directing that kind of language at a young child isn't appropriate, because they don't yet know what 'bad' means. It's okay to instruct them in some general way that what they're doing isn't appropriate. You can tell them that behaving in a way that bothers someone else is 'a no-no,' something like that. Even better, you can just channel their energies and movements elsewhere. But for heaven's sake, leave 'bad' out of it. All you'll be doing is shaming them, teaching them to feel guilty, and that could make them resistant to learning about right and wrong when the time finally does become ripe.

"At some point, the little boy looked over at me," she goes on to say to us. "He smiled and waved. I did the same, and I told him, 'You're a good little boy, not bad at all.'"

"When you told the little boy that he was 'good,' that he was 'not bad at all,' do you think he understood what you were trying to convey?" I ask.

"I must have," she says in due time. "But no, he no more understood my 'good' and my 'not bad' than he did his mother's 'bad.' What I believe he *did* understand was the kindness and gentleness of my voice and the kind expression on my face."

"It's okay—good, even—to use positive words of reinforcement, even with kids at that young age," says Stefan. "They may not understand the terms per se, but they can tell whether there is affirmation behind them because of your tone of voice and the look on your face."

Jasmine considers what Stefan has said. "Even if that little boy had been older, and able to understand the difference between good and bad, it would have bothered me that the mother made no distinction between the person or the act. Good people can misbehave, can do wrong things. But that doesn't make them bad."

Aristotle was one of the earliest Western philosophers to point out that someone may act wrongly and yet in no way be a bad person. In his

Nicomachean Ethics, he opines that when a man "acts with knowledge but not after deliberation, it is an act of injustice," since such acts are "due to anger or to other passions necessary or natural to man; for when men do such harmful and mistaken acts they act unjustly." However, Aristotle stresses, "this does not imply that the doers are unjust or wicked; for the injury is not due to vice." On the other hand, by Aristotle's yardstick, when someone acts after careful deliberation, and he nonetheless winds up doing harm, "he is an unjust man," no matter how honorable his intentions.

I eventually say, "Even if a young child isn't ripe to learn hard and fast lessons about right and wrong, she can still teach them. Once, when my daughter, Cali, was about three, I was carrying her on my shoulders on our way home from a park near where we were living in Mexico at the time. She was sipping juice from a carton. A good bit of it spilled on my head. I was not happy. I took her to task for doing it deliberately. She was silent as we continued to make our way home. Finally, she said to me from her perch above, 'Daddy, sometimes accidents happen, even when you're careful.' Cali knew the difference between doing something on purpose and by accident, as well as the difference between an accident that happens from carelessness and one that happens no matter how careful you are. Her unspoken message was that what happened had nothing to do with right or wrong. She conveyed it to me in a way that made me see the error of my ways without putting me on the defensive. I apologized. I had wronged her, and she righted the situation—and our relationship. Cali knew the nuances of right and wrong better than I did in that situation."

"Your children, even at very young ages, feel awful when they've done something wrong *in your eyes,*" says Aisha, a stay-at-home mom who's been silent until now. "Even if they don't totally grasp what the concepts of right and wrong are all about, they do grasp whether their parents approve or disapprove of their actions. When they detect disapproval, they can punish themselves. I've committed the very offenses I've scolded my children for—talking about others behind their backs, not picking up after myself, acting as if two wrongs make a right. I can be temperamental and fault-finding and defensive when I'm under a lot of stress or I'm sleep deprived. But I don't always give my kids a break when they're feeling likewise. The time can't be ripe for imparting lessons of right and wrong if we're lacking in self-honesty about our own faults. It's always so much easier to see others' shortcomings than our own."

Jasmine looks troubled. "I didn't give the mother of that child on the plane an equal break. I didn't know a thing about her and the kinds of things she might be dealing with in her life, yet I was going to teach her a lesson about when and whether to use the term 'bad,' whether she liked it or not. She could have lashed out at me, and who would have blamed her? I know when adults try to let me know that they don't think I'm parenting my child properly, I can get steamed. Yet she just gave me what I'd call a pissed-off look, and then returned her attention to her son—though she didn't use the word 'bad' again."

The face of Zoe, a single mother, has been impossible to decipher as she listens intently. Now she decides to say something. "Even when you're an adolescent or adult, you might lack the ability to reason. Whenever that's so, then ripe conditions for learning right from wrong aren't possible.

"As some here know, my seventeen-year-old daughter is a drug addict," she tells us. "Ainsley uses and sells. I've gone to numerous support groups seeking guidance about how to get her the help she needs. No matter how I tried to intervene, it did no good. I threatened to call the law on her myself when I caught her selling at home. I tried explaining to her that we would get evicted by the home association if she's caught. But she wouldn't listen to reason. She kept using and selling. I felt I had no choice but to carry through with what she thought was an idle threat. I called the police. She was arrested. She's now in a residential substance abuse treatment facility.

"In Ainsley's eyes, I've committed an unforgiveable act of betrayal. All I care about is to help my baby overcome her addiction. She lies, cheats, steals, because of it. It's beyond her control. Learning right from wrong?

I pray that the day arrives when she's ready to do so—I should say, do so again. Through most of her growing-up years, she was the most upbeat and honest and reflective child you could hope to have. She was well-behaved by anyone's standards, and far more open to criticism than most I know, of any age. I never had to put to use any of the strategies for curbing 'bad' behavior that most other parents had to employ. But Ainsley changed noticeably during tenth grade. That was the year her father, with whom she was close, left us. She became defiant and withdrawn. She's told me drugs are the only thing that give her pleasure. Yet I see them masking a brokenhearted soul. They're keeping her from confronting the issues that keep her from being the naturally happy person she is."

The British utilitarian philosopher Jeremy Bentham (1748–1832) believed that right and wrong can be determined by evaluating the "pleasures" and "pains" of any given action. By the calculus of Bentham—who was considered at age three a prodigy, and who went on to become a jurist and reformer who advocated for the abolition of slavery and of the death penalty for children—action that gives someone intense pleasure, but only over a short duration, is not morally right if all it does is cover up an underlying mental and emotional anguish. To Bentham, a course of action that holds out the probability of giving someone greater well-being over the longer term can be considered right, even if over the short haul it creates heightened turmoil.

Zoe pauses before going on to say to us, "I ask myself all the time if I did the right thing in a world in which there are no perfect choices. The best I can say is that my intentions were honorable."

According to Immanuel Kant, we all have it within ourselves to do the right thing. By this he means that as long as our intentions are principled, we have "done right." To Kant, rightness and wrongness hinges on the goodness or badness of one's intentions. Even if a particular course of action goes awry, what matters to Kant in assessing right or wrong is whether one's intentions were right-minded—meaning that, before acting, one must deliberate carefully over the best course, with the end of doing some good (which to him is helping someone else gain more dignity and independence). Whenever we do this, come what may, Kant contends that our act is "something that sparkles like a jewel all by itself, something that has full worth in itself," with its own "usefulness or fruitfulness."

"There are no absolutes when it comes to ripe moments for learning and teaching matters of right and wrong," says Patty after awhile. "I would like to say that one key is consistency, to not send mixed messages. It's confusing to your kids if the parents of their friends have different sets of consequences for the same 'bad' behaviors—or if they don't consider behaviors to be 'bad' that other parents do. Some parents don't care if their adolescent kids smoke pot, while others consider it grounds for severe punishment. Some are lax with their children for arriving home later than agreed on, yet children of other parents can find themselves grounded for a long time. Even when both parents share the same notions of right and wrong, their children can learn early on that justice isn't always meted out fairly. Even within the same family—I'm speaking of my family—one child might be let off for committing a wrong with a slap on the wrist, and another might be dealt with much more strictly for committing the exact same transgression. Instead of learning lessons of right and wrong, conditions are ripe for them to learn about hypocrisy, to learn 'do as I say, not as I do.'"

"But sometimes, part of consistency is teaching that there are exceptions to every moral rule," says Jasmine. "I believe in the commandment 'thou shalt not kill,' but I used to serve in the army reserve, and I would kill to defend my country. Or, for that matter, my family. I'm also an avid hunter. My husband wouldn't kill even a spider on purpose. He and I both have convincing reasons for why we think hunting is right, and wrong, as the case may be. Each of our children is going to have to decide what is right and wrong. All we can do is thoughtfully present our points of view. Sometimes there are no easy answers. There can be exceptions to almost any situation that demands a moral response and can be judged right or wrong."

As the French existentialist and feminist philosopher Simone de Beauvoir (1908–1986) says in her noted work *The Ethics of Ambiguity*,

"Ethics does not furnish recipes any more than do science or art." Rather, every ethical response has to be tailored to the situation.

A pensive Aisha soon says to us, "I've been thinking about this question on a larger scale. If you're a social activist and have the courage of your convictions, if you see wrongs that you feel need to be righted, don't you sometimes have to force the time to be ripe and exercise civil disobedience to bring about change? Martin Luther King Jr. said that there is no such thing as waiting for the time to be ripe for taking direct action against the wrongs you see in the world. He believed that you have to force the issue, even if you have to put your personal well-being on the line. If he and so many other people of conscience hadn't acted on this belief, our society today probably would be far more backward about treating all people equally."

"Our society's notions about right and wrong are still backward in many ways," says Jasmine. "The US is the only Western nation that doesn't consider corporal punishment morally wrong, much less a punishable offense. The fact is that a parent—or, here in this state and twenty others, a principal or a school teacher—can resort to corporal punishment whenever he sees fit. When a child learns right from wrong by being physically punished, so many studies have concluded that he is way more likely to practice corporal punishment himself when an adult, or commit some other wrongful and violent act. I'm part of an organization working to ban corporal punishment in Arizona. No matter how angry an adult gets, no matter what a child does, the time is never ripe to discipline a child physically—or the time will never be ripe for that child to absorb lessons of right and wrong."

Time passes before Edmond says, after some hesitation, "Several years ago, at the height of the recession, I was in a heated talk on the phone with a bank manager about my mortgage. With the economy in the dregs, my business revenue was down dramatically. I was behind on payments for the first time in my life. I was holding my then-four-year-old son Hank in one arm, and he kept slapping me. He was in a slapping phase. One of his slaps stung. I should have simply put him down. Instead, quicker than thought, I slapped his cheek with force. I said for good measure, 'How does that feel?' Hank was stunned. He started wailing. I hurt my son. I wronged him. Just as my father had done to me on many occasions, and that I'd vowed never to do to my own children.

"I sought help. Thankfully, Hank forgave me. No matter our infractions, kids that age are quick to forgive their parents. We wrong them, and they know we've wronged them, even if they're too young to put it in exactly those words—and they forgive. We adults can learn a lot from their example."

"Matthew 7:1, says 'judge not, lest ye be judged,'" he says next. "But we all judge. What we need to do, for lack of a better way of putting it, is learn to judge 'ripely,' if we're to expect anyone to learn lessons of right and wrong from us. To me, that means to judge yourself more severely than you would anyone else. Plenty of parents who live lives of tremendous stress would never harm one of their children. Yet I'm one of the parents who did. I condemn more, not less, anyone who would ever harm a child, even as I'm more understanding and forgiving, including of my own father. I will punish myself forever for what I did. I pray my son will always be a 'better person' than me on his worst day than I was on mine."

Edmond attempts a smile but it wavers as he goes on to say, "I'd thought, after a couple years had passed, that Hank not only had forgiven me, but that he'd forgotten the incident. But last month, while *he* was on the phone, with one of his school friends, I playfully picked him up unawares. He turned to me . . . and with a knowing look, he gently slapped my cheek."

Survival of the Ripest

The conservative British philosopher Herbert Spencer (1820–1903) coined the term "survival of the fittest" in applying Darwin's theory of natural selection to human society. Spencer argues that it is the way of the human world that the weakest among us will be elbowed out and the more ascendant will prevail. Spencer's hypothesis, however, is more

hopeful than is evident at first glance, since he holds that this more domi-
nant lot will be of the virtuous variety. According to Spencer, "the fittest"
are a voluntarily cooperative and morally progressive lot who will produce
a progeny of goods for one and all. If so, then it would follow that eventually most everyone will be of the ascendant variety.

Does the world scene today resemble what Spencer predicted it would
come to be? Have we reached a state of peak moral ripeness? Or is it the
case that while, as the existentialist titan Jean-Paul Sartre (1905–1980)
insists famously, we are "condemned to be free"? Do too many exercise
such freedom in ways that imprison others, that constrict their possibilities
for development? Does our world have more than its fair share of Oberons
(albeit sans fairy powers) who will resort to most any means—cheat,
deceive, or worse—to get what they want, who feel a sense of entitlement,
no matter how undeserved, and could care less about the damage they do
to anyone and anything standing in their way? Is self-improvement these
days mostly about selfish improvement? If so, is that okay, as long as most
people are okay with it and equate it with moral ripeness?

It wouldn't be okay to Immanuel Kant, one of the most regarded philosophical figures in the realm of morals, who notably advocated that we
should treat others as ends in themselves, rather than as means to serve our
own ends. To Kant, if we act with a sense of impunity against any common good, we are puny people, no matter how we try to puff ourselves up.
For Kant, the $64,000 question today would be, how do we "child" one
another in ways that increase the odds we'll act in a manner that elevates
others—and see this as self-elevation as well? Even if history reveals that
we humans as a lot are more in the grip of destructive tendencies than
constructive ones, we've had rare periods of unprecedented flourishing on
broad scales. This indicates that we have it in us to overcome those inclinations that would keep others down out of the belief that this is how we
best prop ourselves up.

Maybe so, but a bevy of polls show that Americans believe our moral
fabric is unraveling. In particular, there is incessant hand-wringing about
the dismal moral state of our children. Often this is attributed to the

break-up of the "traditional" family. The typical argument is that its dissolution has triggered faulty emotional maturing, which breeds a host of ills in our young, from distrust to jadedness, low self-esteem to lack of moral sense, and that this in turn erodes kids' capacity to grow into caring, responsible, idealistic, compassionate adults. To be sure, what the typical American family constitutes these days is far different than that of yesteryear. But has there ever been any such thing as a typical American family unit?

Children today surely face an unprecedented array of challenges to developing optimally. It's all the more admirable then that they are founts of vital kinds of wisdom and insight and experience for how we might arrive at new answers for how to go about shepherding human development in all its dimensions.

Tell that, though, to the British political philosopher and moral theorist John Stuart Mill who argues in his classic *On Liberty* that we should be free to behave as we please, regardless of whether our actions are considered right or wrong by others, even if we do ourselves harm, as long as we don't hurt anyone else:

> . . .the only purpose for which power can be rightfully exercised over any member of a civilized community, against his will, is to prevent harm to others. His own good, either physical or moral, is not a sufficient warrant. . . . Over his own body-mind, the individual is sovereign.

Mill makes one exception to this otherwise hard and fast doctrine: "It is, perhaps, hardly necessary to say that this doctrine is meant to apply only to human beings in the maturity of their faculties." So it is that he is "not speaking of children. . . . Those who are still in a state to require being taken care of by others, must be protected against their own actions as well as against external injury." Yet all of us, throughout our lives, need to be taken care of by others to one degree or another (whether we care to admit it or not). What's more, who among us is ever totally sovereign over our minds and bodies? Everything we say, do, and make is to some degree the prisoner of custom, convention, education, and laws of nature.

Are most adults in the maturity of their faculties? Can one's faculties always stand more maturation, no matter one's age? Is it possible that one can have more mature faculties in many respects when young, and that these faculties can become less mature as we age? Was Mill's own father mature in his faculties when it came to raising his son? James Mill forbid his son from associating with other children so he could focus solely on his studies; he was determined to make of his son a genius. By age eight, John Stuart Mill could read all of Plato's works in the original Hellenic Greek, and then he learned Latin, Euclid, and algebra. But he paid a price; he suffered a mental breakdown at age twenty.

Because of his father, did John Stuart Mill have an excess of maturity, making him overripe intellectually, to the detriment of his all-around development? What if Mill had had a more normal upbringing? Might other opportunities for genius have presented themselves, without the cost to his mental health? Clearly Mill's father never catechized himself with such questions. He was a predecessor of today's Tiger Parent.

Is it quite a different matter to be mature in one's faculties as a child than it is to be in such a state as an adult? Are there different benchmarks for deciding what constitutes having mature faculties as a child versus as an adult? At whatever age we find ourselves, how do we best go about further maturing our mental faculties? John Stuart Mill maintains that practice makes more perfect.

> The human faculties of perception, judgment, discriminative feeling, mental activity, and even moral preference, are exercised only in making a choice. . . . The mental and moral, like the muscular powers, are improved only by being used.

But the mere repetitive act of making a choice can be tantamount to exercising such faculties in the most immature way. Choices of any serious nature must whenever possible be made with considerable and at times agonizing deliberation as one weighs the pros and cons of alternatives. Our skills in perception, judgment, discriminative feeling, mental activity, and moral preference may flatline and even diminish, no matter how great the tally of times we've made choices. Many world leaders make decisions that impact millions, with little if any reflective deliberation beforehand about courses of action. They often fail to recognize nuance and complexity, make snap judgments based on stark black-and-white moral sensibilities and narrow perceptions, and lose not a moment's sleep in the aftermath, no matter how disastrously the choices they make go wrong. The sheer quantity of times a person—whether a president or a parent—makes a choice is by no means enough. One must strive to hone one's deliberative powers in a conscientious way to stand a good chance of developing a moral code that more and more manifests a social conscience and intellectual integrity.

Ain't Misbehavin'

The American psychologist Lawrence Kohlberg (1927–1987) believed that we're ripest in our adolescent and adult years for learning about right and wrong. To Kohlberg, children not only pass through successive cognitive stages, as his hero Jean Piaget had earlier surmised, but they advance (or potentially advance) through parallel stages of moral reasoning. Kohlberg's research, highly influential to this day, centered around a series of moral quandaries that those participating in his study were asked to puzzle over. Their responses led him to elaborate a moral stage theory. In *The Philosophy of Moral Development*, Kohlberg shares his conclusion that younger children are at a "pre-conventional" level of morality, and so are not yet capable (much less well-enough versed) to act in accordance with society's mores. As a result, they look to adults, particularly their parents or caregivers, as guides. What's more, he claims that children at this "pre-moral" stage are so self-involved that if left to their own devices, their actions in the moral sphere would be guided by the question, "What's in it for me?" Kohlberg characterizes the second moral level as "conventional." Those at this stage—some older children, adolescents, adults—can internalize society's values, and have a desire to conform. His third and highest stage is a "post-conventional" morality. Those rare adolescents and adults who manage to achieve completely this level demonstrate a considerable degree of moral autonomy, and are capable of acting in ways that transcend strict self-interest. When need be, they are spurred to act against prevailing societal norms if they believe doing so will achieve a higher good.

Kohlberg's notion that one progresses through the moral stages as one ages is questionable at best. He hails from a long line of developmental theorists who operate from the Aristotelian premise that our youngest are by far our most egocentric, and essentially start out in life as amoral beings, and that only as they become adults can they become capable of acting with any acute moral sense.[9] Mounting evidence, however, indicates that we start out with a predisposition to be moral, and that one reason Kohlberg found otherwise is that (as with Piaget) his preconceived pejorative notions of children, and the leading (or misleading) questions he posed to them, overly prejudiced his studies from the outset.

Ongoing research today by child development specialists like psychologist William Damon of Stanford University and his colleagues indicates that moral life begins in infancy, even before language, and so a keen sense of right and wrong is part and parcel of our lives early on. "All children are born with a running start on the path to moral development," Damon asserts.

> A number of inborn responses predispose them to act in ethical ways. For example, empathy—the capacity to experience another person's pleasure or pain vicariously—is part of our native endowment as humans. Newborns cry when they hear others cry and show signs of pleasure at happy sounds such as cooing and laughter. By the second year of life, children commonly console peers or parents in distress.

Damon finds that by the time they are two-and-a-half, children have taken significant strides in their moral development, contrary to the stance of Piaget and Kohlberg, who insist that they are not capable of true moral knowledge until they are of adolescent age. In her own

---

9 Even Shakespeare, in *Troilus and Cressida*, makes it a point to note that "Aristotle thought [them] unfit to hear moral philosophy." The young weren't even capable of hearing moral matters, much less weighing in on them.

comprehensive study of young children, developmental psychologist Judith Smetana found that they are quite morally attuned, and practice a form of empathic reasoning that is alien to many adults. Children in her study were presented with scenarios about daycare rules. One involves picking up after oneself, and the consequences of failing to do so. The children agreed that it's okay if a preschool teacher changes the rules about whether they have to keep things neat and tidy. So, for instance, if a teacher about-faces and decides messy is fine, that's fine with the children, too. On the other hand, they believe it's absolutely wrong for a teacher ever to change the rules in a way that would make it okay to physically punish or harshly berate a preschool child for failing to pick up after himself. To them, that would be tantamount to doing harm, and in their worldview, intentionally harming someone is always a moral no-no.

Long before such studies were undertaken, Karl Jaspers staked the claim that all indications are that our moral sense doesn't necessarily become more refined as we grow older. He insisted that "with the years we seem to enter into a prison of conventions and opinions, concealments and unquestioned acceptance." To Jaspers, it is a rare and wonderful occurrence when people (Socrates among them) managed to "preserve their candor and independence" with age. Dewey also parted from mainstream views that adults are kids' moral guideposts, but not the other way around, in asserting in *Reconstruction in Philosophy* that people of all ages need one another—the adult with the child every bit as much as the other way around—if we are to continue our moral ripening over the years:

> If the moral business of the adult as well as the young is a growing and develop-
> ing experience, then the instruction that comes from social dependencies and
> interdependencies are as important for the adult as for the child.

Yet it remains the inclination of adults to "exaggerate the intellectual dependence of childhood so that children are too much kept in leading strings, and then we exaggerate the independence of adult life from intimacy of contacts and communication with others." Children can help us upend those routines of custom that keep us from further sculpting our moral selves, so we can continue "to set free and to develop the capacities of human individuals without respect to race, class, or economic status"— or, for that matter, of age.

Another principal roadblock to such liberation is that adults too often assume that moral development can only be had with a highly refined sense of guilt and shame. When it comes to matters of teaching and learning right from wrong, Walter Kaufmann (1921–1980), the rare academic philosopher whose piercing scholarly works are just as much addressed to general readers as to his peers, provocatively posits in *Without Guilt and Justice* that we must no longer "depend on guilt and fear, as our fathers and mothers did."

> The person who cares deeply about the opinion of his peers and about the expectations they have concerning his performance is likely to feel deep shame when he lets them down. Guilt feelings are much more likely to arise vis-à-vis one's parents, especially if one feels that they have made great sacrifices and that they therefore deserved better—even if they themselves do not feel that way.

Conversely, parents who feel they've let their kids down can equally feel great guilt. A friend of mine, a college professor, had to move across the country to land a tenured job. He related to me with palpable anguish how his teenage daughter continues to mourn over being thousands of miles away from her boyfriend and her clique of friends at her former high school. He told me that one of his colleagues turned down a tenured job so his family could stay put, even though it has left them in financial jeopardy. He questions whether his own decision was "more wrong than right."

What about harsh criticism that is driven by our own exacting yard-sticks? According to Kaufmann, "Those who have fallen short of their own high standards in painting, writing, or sports"—or for that matter, parenting—"are clearly sensible when they do not feel guilty, nor need they feel shame."

> It is reasonable for them to try to criticize their own performance carefully, to ask themselves what went wrong, and to map strategies for doing better next time. And if there is no next time and the failure is somehow irrevocable, they may well feel keen regret, but they would be unreasonable and neurotic if they felt guilty.

Kaufmann's assessment might apply to cases in which our actions impact only ourselves (if there is such a thing). But what about when one's actions do lasting damage to others? There is no "next time" when it comes to raising a child, no dress rehearsal. What would be an appropriate response if one fails in critical aspects of parenting? What if such failure is irrevocable, and there is no next time to map out new strategies for doing better? Is it sufficient to feel keen regret? Or is it far more likely that such a parent would no more experience regret than guilt in the first place, much less take the time to evaluate critically his conduct as a parent?

Are there times when one's behavior should be immune to considerations of right and wrong? Many adults believe one should be appropriately solemn at funerals. Yet children often carry on otherwise. My own daughter, at the funeral of my wife's father, Armando Chapa de Zambrano, went to the space in front of the casket during the viewing. She danced and twirled a series of steps with an invisible partner. She was remembering the many times she danced the day away with her grandfather. At six feet, two inches, he towered over her. He'd gently lift her in the air, tuck an arm around her waist, wrap his fingers around her tiny hand, and they would dance the tango, salsa, merengue, or some new invention of their own. Cali was in seventh heaven, as she was at the funeral "dancing with his spirit," as she later described it to me. Judging from some of the glares directed her way from adults, this was not considered appropriate behavior. Yet it was the most fitting gesture of mourning imaginable, for her, and the most moving for her mother and me. Her last dance with her grandfather did great honor to his memory.

The Good, the Bad, and the Ugly

After the Boston Marathon bombings, the writer Dennis Lehane, in an essay in the *New York Times*, relates how he "went home and tried to explain to my four-year-old daughter that the reason Mommy and Daddy were upset was because bad people had done some bad things."

I'm not used to feeling so limited when it comes to expressing myself, but trying to explain an act of mass murder to a 4-year-old rendered me . . . speechless. . . . My daughter asked if the bad men were like the bad woman who hit her on the head with a suitcase last time we were on a plane and then didn't apologize. I assured her the bad men were worse, and my daughter asked if they would hit her on the head when she was on the street. I promised her they wouldn't, but really, what do I know?

Even if the bad men were far worse than the bad woman, are there some disturbing similarities? Recently I witnessed a man who looked to be in his thirties, absorbed in sending a text on his smartphone, bump hard into a little boy while walking along the sidewalk, causing him to stumble. The boy called out as he rubbed his shin, "You didn't say excuse me." Without so much as looking back, the man replied, "That's right, I didn't." He brings to mind the woman who struck Lehane's daughter, and also a woman whose enormous dog scared my child when she was five and it approached her without warning. Instead of trying to comfort Cali, instead of trying to assure her that the dog was friendly, the dog's owner said to her, "That's right, stay away, it's a big bad wolf." The ancient Chinese philosopher Mencius (371 BC–289 BC) opined that "no man is devoid of a heart sensitive to the suffering of others," and he felt certain that this holds particularly true for adults' sentiments toward children. Skip forward a couple of thousand years and the acclaimed cognitive scientist Steven Pinker is sure that "if a child has been frightened by a barking dog and is howling in terror," adults like himself will step forward and provide a "sympathetic response" and "comfort and protect her." Yet this woman set back a great deal my daughter's attempts to overcome her fear of dogs, and even took some delight in frightening her. Though to a dramatically different degree than the Boston bombers, these everyday adults, in failing to acknowledge the equal humanity of younger others, showed a chilling ugliness in their lack of compassion toward them. Is such a glaring lack of compassion still the exception among adults, or is it increasingly the rule today?

The German idealist philosopher Georg Wilhelm Friedrich Hegel (1770–1831) asserts in *The Philosophy of History* that we become more tolerant and understanding as we grow older—"the result of the ripeness of judgment" that comes from being "more deeply taught by the grave experience of life." Yet it seems to me that what Hegel ascribes mostly to youth—"the ripeness of indifference"—is in fact largely the province of adults.

The German philosopher Arthur Schopenhauer (1788–1860) argues in his acclaimed *The Basis of Morality* that morality is based on "the everyday phenomenon of *compassion*, . . . the immediate *participation*, independent of all ulterior considerations, primarily in the *suffering* of another, and thus in the prevention or elimination of it." For Schopenhauer, compassion, or *mitleid* (fellow-feeling), is intuitively rather than rationally based, and so it supersedes rationality. In his view, all the world's great religions represent attempts to express this notion of compassion, and what connects all is the shared recognition that human life consists of endless suffering. To Schopenhauer, an act of compassion is no more egoistic than altruistic; rather, one who demonstrates compassion puts himself on a completely equal plane to the suffering person: "I . . . *feel it with him, feel it as my own*. . . . This presupposes that . . . I have identified myself with the other man, and in consequence the barrier between the ego and the non-ego is for the moment abolished."

Friedrich Nietzsche, both revered and reviled for his penetrating critiques of prevalent moralities, was deeply influenced by Schopenhauer. Nietzsche nonetheless parts company with him on this matter and asserts that compassion is a weakness, indeed a vice, rather than a virtue, and as such is nothing more than our demonstration of pity for another person—and to show pity for another, he believes, is the same as showing contempt. Nelson Mandela, for one, could not disagree more with Nietzsche (or agree more with Schopenhauer). "Our human compassion," he maintains, "binds us the one to the other—not in pity or patronizingly, but as human beings who have learnt how to turn our common suffering into hope for the future." His perspective springs from the Southern African humanist philosophy of *ubuntu*, which translates as "humanity toward others." *Ubuntu* is based on the notion that all people are equal—of no greater, but no lesser, importance or value, and that it is only through practicing compassionate acts that we become more fully human.

In times past, when callousness and indifference have prevailed, it has proved the tipping point to some of the darkest times in human history. What would a "compassion index" reveal about the US today? Would it show that, by and large, we exhibit lots of fellow-feeling? What if such an index included economic indicators as a key measure of our collective compassion? The proportion of Americans living in poverty is higher than it's been in half a century. While those in the upper economic echelons have enjoyed a dramatic increase in personal wealth, there has been a commensurate decline in personal income among the middle and lower classes, along with cuts to the marrow in budgets for social welfare services and assistance for the neediest, children and the elderly in particular. Yet there has been little hue and cry to create a more level playing field, or to create a system with safeguards that assure that the most vulnerable are protected. Cases of elderly abuse are increasing significantly,[10] as are cases of workplace discrimination against the elderly, at the same time as funding for protective and preventive services continues its dramatic decline. "A population that does not take care of the elderly and of children and youth has no future," maintains Pope Francis, "because it abuses both its memory and its promise."

If compassion in the US these days is missing in action toward our most vulnerable, how might this be remedied?

In *Nicomachean Ethics*, Aristotle asserts that it is imperative for us to be raised from our "very youth . . . so as both to delight in and to be pained by the things that we ought." Who are those with the most highly attuned sense of compassion, altruism, and empathy, and as a consequence most adept at determining what we ought to delight in, and what to be pained by? Many cognitive scientists and developmental specialists today believe the evidence points to children, hands down. Alison Gopnik's disturbing, important question is, "If children are so good, if empathy and altruism are such a deeply rooted part of human nature, then why are adults so

---

10 The *New York Times* notes that a study by the federal Government Accountability Offices reports that a "rising number of elder abuse threatens to overwhelm inadequately staffed adult protective service agencies in many states."

bad?" Is it because, as she speculates, that "the impulse to evil seems to be as deeply rooted as the will to do good"? If so, why is it, as she claims, that the impulse to do good is so much at the fore when we're young, and how is it that it is so often supplanted by the impulse to do evil as we grow older? To Gopnik, it is indisputable that "early empathy and altruism emerge in the close face-to-face intimate encounters between babies and their caregivers—the most intimate relationships we ever have." If this most intimate relation we ever have is getting less and less intimate, then it almost goes without saying that it will lead to an ever earlier development of less healthy—or more harmful—impulses. Even when parents are with their kids these days, they're often not with them. Rather, they're ensconced in their home media centers or are absorbed in their smartphones or tablets—when they're not sharing them with their babies and toddlers, quite often to distract or calm them so they aren't disruptive.[11] Studies also indicate that the predictable outcome when parents spend scads of time on their potpourri of electronic devices rather than engaging with their infants is that the their language development takes a huge hit. Same goes, in even more abysmal scales, for parents who allow kids to use these devices, even when parents are in their close company. Surely, it will soon be found that this decrease in genuine intimacy not only impacts language development, but spills over to hinder or stunt the development of empathy and altruism. Surely, the dearth of kinds of intimate encounters between child and parent or caregiver also severs kids' deep empathic and altruistic roots, which are pushed aside by darker impulses that otherwise would never have taken firm root. This is a tragic outcome, needless to say. As Gopnik recognizes, "for genuine global morality we need to extend those feelings beyond our intimates to the six billion other human beings out there." First, though, we need to nurture those feelings for our intimates. When intimacy is stillborn during one's youngest years, we never develop much of a local morality, making the prospect of realizing a more

---

11 See, for instance, this NPR segment on the subject: http://www.npr.org/blogs/health/2011/10/22/141591126/will-smartphones-and-ipads-mush-my-toddlers-brain.

global morality a pipedream. If we lose the innate ability to empathize with our nearest and dearest, we can't come to feel the pain and suffering of those we don't know nearly as well, or don't know at all.

Erik Erikson (1902–1994) intriguingly asserts that each of us harbors a tug-of-war proclivity between "generativity" and "rejectivity." He posited that if generativity—the will to care for others—is properly nurtured, then over time it's something we will be inspired to practice not only with those in our immediate circle, but ever farther afield, and as a consequence exhibit that we "advocate a more universal principle of care." It isn't easy to put this into practice, though, because we have another impulse, rejectivity, which makes us predisposed against caring for others and inclined to only care for ourselves. What we must do, according to Erikson, is bend our will toward nurturing our generative impulses. In particular, adults must do so, since they are charged with "the generational task of cultivating strength in the next generation" and so must master "the impulse to cherish" our young.

The quintessential practitioner of generativity, according to Erikson, was Gandhi, "father and mother, brother and sister, son and daughter, to all creation." Erikson fails to acknowledge that our youngest can be most adept at practicing generativity. Even those children and youth living in the most demeaning circumstances demonstrate a decided capacity for doing so. National Book Award–winning journalist Katherine Boo attests to this in *Behind the Beautiful Forevers*, which chronicles the lives of slum-dwellers in Mumbai, India. She relates how she was "continually struck by the ethical imaginations of young people, even in circumstances so desperate that selfishness would be an asset." If such children ostensibly lose this capacity as they grow older, Boo believes it's because they "have little power to act on those imaginations." But she stresses that this does not in any way indicate that they have in fact become uncaring. Rather, they still "felt the loss of life acutely. . . . What appeared to be indifference to other people's suffering . . . had a good deal to do with conditions that had sabotaged their innate capacity for moral action." They cannot do what comes naturally to them, cannot reach out to others and alleviate their suffering, any more than they can ease their own. This sense of impotence runs up hard against their inborn desire to be of service.

According to Martha Nussbaum, if we lose our "tragic sense of compassion for people who unequally suffer the misfortunes of life—including both those who remain good and those who turn to the bad—we are in danger of losing our own humanity." What the children Katherine Boo encountered show, though, is that those who suffer unequally the misfortunes of life themselves never lose their own tragic sense of compassion for others, no matter how rotten their lives are made by unspeakable wrongs. Yet they refuse to allow their own moral sense to be corrupted or defined by what they witness, or be victimized by the world. They remain good in a world turned, if not altogether bad, then upside down.

Anne Frank was given a diary shortly after her thirteenth birthday. She began making entries three weeks before her family went into hiding, on July 6, 1942, and kept it until August 1944 when she and seven others were captured by the Nazis. In one of her final diary entries she wrote, "It's really a wonder that I haven't dropped all my ideals, because they seem so absurd and impossible to carry out. Yet I keep them, because in spite of everything, I still believe that people are really good at heart." Anne Frank must have wondered: how is it that a Nazi could take part in the worst atrocities, yet go home at night and be a loving father and spouse? How can some be ripe for both good, and evil? In the midst of the systematic attempt to eliminate Jews, as well as the Romani and people with disabilities, and in the midst of her own helplessness to act on her ideals, she nonetheless concluded that people were essentially good at heart. Is this childlike naïveté, a refusal or inability to see things as they are? Or is it that the way things were did not keep her from being able to tell the difference between a person and his acts, even of the most heinous kind?

Right, Wrong, and Plastic Brains

The Harvard neuroscientist Joshua Greene has made it his forte to scan people's brains while they consider moral dilemmas. In *Moral Tribes*, he shares his findings that when we agonize over matters of right and wrong, our brains' "standard-issue moral machinery" equips us with "automated behavioral programs that motivate and stabilize cooperation within personal relationships and groups. These include capacities for empathy, vengefulness, honor, guilt, embarrassment, tribalism, and righteous indignation." On the other hand, our so-called moral brains fail us when "our" group is vying against other ones. In such instances, our better angels are "thwarted by tribalism . . . , disagreement over the proper terms of cooperation, . . . a biased sense of fairness, and a biased perception of facts." Greene believes our ability to reason morally boils down to how well we wage the struggle between our atavistic gut instincts—which drive us toward more combative and selfish behavior—and our more advanced rational capacities that enable and inspire us to bridge differences. He concludes that our tendency toward tribalism is driven by older parts of our brain, while our will to cooperate and empathize stems from our more recently evolved neocortex. Greene maintains that we can override our more destructive impulses because our brains endow us with "a general capacity for conscious, explicit, practical reasoning that makes human decision *flexible*."

If this is so, who is by far the most flexible among us in this regard?

An array of studies makes clear that adolescents have unrivaled brain plasticity, and that when this is properly tapped into, it allows them to learn and adapt far more quickly and adeptly than adults.[12] What if we older folks exploited this capacity of theirs? To do so, we'd have to see this highly transitional stage as a window of opportunity. We might learn how best to evolve this capacity for conscious, explicit, practical reasoning, so that it stays with us and progresses over time. The problem is that those of us in the best position to realize this happen to be those with the least plasticity. We're not inclined to reach out to adolescents, no matter how much insight we might gain about how to remain more malleable, adaptive, and responsive to rapid changes.

---

12 One among many articles on the subject is "The Teen Brain: Primed to Learn, Primed to Take Risks," by Jay N. Giedd of the National Institute of Mental Health. A child and adolescent psychiatrist, Giedd specializes in brain imaging. https://www.dana.org/Cerebrum/Default.aspx?id=39411.

Neuroscience didn't exist as a field in John Keats's day, but the early nineteenth–century romantic poet (1795–1821) offered a prescient paean to plasticity with his coinage "negative capability," which denotes our capacity to transcend preconceived limitations, and hence rewrite the story of our lives. To Keats, the most standout thinkers and doers demonstrate negative capability to an unsurpassed degree. They are at home with a world of "uncertainties, mysteries, doubts, without any irritable reaching after fact and reason." Exemplars of negative capability (he considers Shakespeare the foremost among them) embrace paradox, dissonance, ambiguity, the unpredictable, and the unknown, and unhesitatingly venture into existential terrain where others fear to tread. It's not that fact and reason don't have a place in their seeking. Rather, it's not the be-all and end-all. Sense and imagination also are equal partners.

Keats's coinage has been appropriated in modern times by the progressive Brazilian philosopher, social theorist, and progressive politician Roberto Mangabeira Unger, who equates negative capability with that element in our nature that enables us to overcome the most daunting cultural, socioeconomic, and institutionally imposed barriers to healthy human flowering. In *The Self Awakened*, Unger (one of Barack Obama's professors while a student at Harvard) insists that

> we are not exhausted by the social and cultural worlds we inhabit and build. They are finite. We, in comparison to them, are not. We can see, think, feel, build, and connect in more ways than they can allow.

Adolescents in particular should take this as a clarion call. Unger's take is that it is up to adolescent, to take the bull by the horns, rather than passively waiting for the unlikely time when adults will treat them as equals. Many adolescents today are doing just that, putting their negative capability on grand display. Through social entrepreneurial initiatives like Do Something, Be the Change, and Youth Venture,[13] adolescents are showing just what innovative, active agents for change they can be. They are making

---

13 For more information see DoSomething.org, BeTheChangeInc.org, and www.genv.net.

real the vision they have of themselves and of their rightful role in fashioning a world of their liking and making.

Unger's progressive Brazilian predecessor, philosopher Paolo Freire (1921–1997), one of the most influential educators of the twentieth century, made it his life's work to equip the marginalized to become more protean selves who could mold and dictate their own destinies. Freire's revolutionary work *Pedagogy of the Oppressed* elaborates how he wed literacy education with communal dialogue as a principal means for problem-solving and practical action. His outreach focused in particular on his nation's poorest adults. To Freire, a literate person is one who can reach her full potential, and hence achieve "human completion." Learning to read is not sufficient. One needs other capabilities in order to overcome an existing power structure designed to keep the disenfranchised in their place. By Freire's yardstick, many who cannot read are nonetheless literate in other ways. For instance, many of the poor know how to grow crops in the most severe environments or how to engage in complex negotiations for what they produce, and these are kinds of literacy. In teaching them how to read, his aim was give them the tools to "read the word as well as the world"—in other words, for literacy to be a key means for making them better able to advocate for themselves, so they could write their own life story.

Given Freire's focus on poor adults, he clearly believed that even the most deprived are plenty "plastic enough" in their capacities to give their lives a radical makeover. Current neuroscience research indicates that he is right. Studies reveal that adults who engage in certain kinds of learning—such as mastering new languages, playing a musical instrument, becoming more schooled in math, or learning to read and write for the first time—catalyze the creation of new connections in the region of the brain involved in learning.[14] This makes adults' brains more malleable and adaptable[15] and catalyzes changes in the brain's structure and

---

14 I look forward to the study that will one day show that adults who care for children—from parents to professionals—and who genuinely nurture them experience gray matter growth.

15 See, for instance, the article "Brain Plasticity in Older Adults," in the April 27, 2013 issue of *Psychology Today*.

function because the brain is prompted to grow more gray matter.[16] The more gray matter we have, the more cerebrally equipped we are to exploit our negative capability.[17]

The adults with whom Freire worked typically had faced severe neglect since infancy. In recent studies, MRI scans of the brains of infants who suffer from deprivation show that their brains are smaller than those of infants who receive ample care.[18] They have less gray matter. This can lead to "faulty wiring" in the regions of the brain that stimulate development in language, vision, and emotion. Yet as long as these infants receive proper care by age two, researchers hold that these negative effects often can be reversed.[19] Even those who continue to encounter privation in their adult years at times can show a phenomenal capacity to recover. Freire's successes with marginalized adults would seem proof positive of this remarkable recuperative ability. Perhaps it is due to the fact that they are at last being shown a kind of care and compassion that is based on the belief that they matter and count as much as anyone else, and are as capable and deserving as anyone else.

Freire's literacy project, which remains a mainstay in Brazil and has expanded to other impoverished regions around the globe, surely challenges and stimulates the brain in a way that makes it possible for adults who have been deliberately left out to join their younger counterparts in

---

16 Neuroscientist Michael Merzenich at the University of California, San Francisco, has been at the vanguard of those demonstrating that the adult brain can continue to grow and develop. See also "Research Shows Adult Brains Capable of Rapid New Growth," http://phys.org/news/2011-04-adult-brains-capable-rapid-growth.html A paper titled "Proceedings of National Academy of Sciences" presents findings that show that the adult brain can experience rapid growth when introduced to the kinds of stimuli babies are exposed to when familiarizing themselves with their environment.

17 As one, for instance, in 2012, researchers from the University of Zurich found that people with more gray matter at the junction between the parietal and temporal lobe are more altruistic than those with less.

18 See, for instance, "The effects of early life adversity on brain and behavioral development," at https://www.dana.org/Publications/ReportOnProgress/The_effects_of_early_life_adversity_on_brain_and_behav-ioral_development/; "HMS Professor Studies Orphanage Impact on Brain Development," at http://www.thecrimson.com/article/2011/11/9/hms-prof-brain/; and "Kids whose bond with mother was disrupted early in life show changes in brain" at http://www.sciencedaily.com/releases/2013/12/ 131202134852.htm.

19 See NPR's feature "Orphans' Lonely Beginnings Reveal How Parents Shape A Child's Brain" at http://www.npr.org/blogs/health/2014/02/20/280237833/orphans-lonely-beginnings-reveal-how-parents-shape-a-childs-brain.

challenging and changing the status quo structure and function of their immediate world. The result is their endowing of the world itself with a greater plasticity.

A Tale of Two Extremes

In *As You Like It*, after opining that "all is mortal in nature," the wise fool Touchstone observes, "from hour to hour we ripe, and ripe, and then from hour to hour we rot. And thereby hangs a tale." Can it be, though, that from hour to hour many of us ripe *and* rot at one and the same time? Can it be, for others, that their lives move back and forth between moments of ripeness and rottenness, of a variety of sorts? Periods of growth can be punctuated by, or intermingled with, periods of decline or regression or stasis. Often these processes can take place simultaneously within the same person.

Can pure rottenness ever transmute to pure ripeness?

Elwin Wilson, a former Ku Klux Klan member, was in his physical prime when he was at his most morally bankrupt. In 2009, his health in decline, he saw the error of his ways and asked forgiveness from a person he'd mercilessly beaten during the civil rights unrest a half century earlier. His victim, Congressman John L. Lewis, forgave Wilson without hesitation. Lewis explained that the brand of civil rights activism to which he'd subscribed was based on tenets of nonviolence, love, and forgiveness. If he hadn't forgiven Wilson, he would have been betraying his own values. Lewis's moral ripeness had remained in a steady state of "peakness," making Wilson's act of contrition all those decades later even fuller.

Rare though such occurrences may be, Wilson's example shows that how we act in the present can transform our past, and touch future generations. But it also shows that sometimes a human core that has been presumed to be corrupted beyond repair in fact still has dormant goodness that is able to bloom late in life.

Kierkegaard almost gets it right when he opines that "life must be lived forward, but can only be understood backward." Rather, by living life in a forward-looking way, with a vision of who we might still be and what we might still accomplish, we can give new meaning to the past, and in a sense recreate it. As Walter Kaufmann puts it in *Discovering the Mind*, "We are unfinished as long as we live and work and can add a few lines" to the story of our lives. To Kaufmann, "what is still coming could change the apparent meaning" of all that we have done up to this point—at least, if we add a few audacious lines that demonstrate our transformed sense of humanity, as Elwin Wilson did, that could recast our entire story.

All is mortal in nature, Touchstone claims; but all is immortal in nature, too. Our words and deeds have a ripple effect long after we are gone. And thereby hangs the tale.

Ripe to the Core

Is ripeness the main ingredient for peak human being-ing?

In *King Lear*, Edgar hides his blind father, Gloucester, one of the most powerful men in Lear's kingdom, under leaves in a forest while he goes to survey the battle scene. The news he has to share upon his return is bleak: Lear's troops have lost the battle; the king and his youngest daughter, Cordelia, have been taken and now are held in custody. Edgar and Gloucester must move quickly if they're to escape capture. But the news has sapped Gloucester's spirit; he'd prefer to end his life than go on: "No further, sir, a man may rot even here." His son will have none of it. Edgar insists that Gloucester, who at this point of the tale doesn't know that Edgar's his son, get a grip on himself and come along with him:

> Men must endure
> Their going hence even as their coming hither.
> Ripeness is all. Come on.

Edgar insists that no one has the right to choose one's time of death, no more than one can choose when or whether one is born. What we must do is keep on keeping on until our time is up. Gloucester is moved to reply: "And that's true too."

Socrates chose not to endure—he killed himself rather than go into exile, upon his scandalous conviction for committing treason—even though his spirit was at its peak. Or more correctly, his spirit was at its peak, but so was his despair—not for himself; he had no regrets about the way he lived—but for his venerated Athens. Unlike Edgar, Socrates believed that man could choose his time and way of death. He died of a full heart, and a broken heart.

In Joseph Heller's classic *Catch 22*, the protagonist, John Joseph Yossarian, captain of a World War II air force squadron, "felt goose pimples clacking all over him as he gazed down despondently at the grim secret Snowden had spilled all over the messy floor." As Snowden, a member of his flight squadron, lay dying, Yossarian studied the gaping wound in his stomach. For Yossarian,

> it was easy to read the message in his entrails. Man was matter, that was Snowden's secret. Drop him out a window and he'll fall. Set fire to him and he'll burn. Bury him and he'll rot, like other kinds of garbage. The spirit gone, man is garbage. That was Snowden's secret. Ripeness was all.

Ripeness here is equated with man's spirit. Yossarian fails to recognize, though, that it is Snowden's death that resuscitates his own hibernating spirit. Studying Snowden's corpse, he discovers the will to live a certain kind of life. In risking it all to do so, he abandons his life-rotting ways and becomes the picture of human autonomy. Yossarian refuses to fly any further missions in a war he no longer believes in, though he could be executed for treason for failing to obey the direct orders of his commanding officers. He embarks on a do-or-die escape from the military. He makes it. Even if he hadn't, what matters is that he has at last become his own man.

Yossarian's path to ripeness was the precise opposite of that of Socrates. Yossarian risked life and limb to escape his circumstances, and this revived his spirit. Socrates refused to escape his circumstances, assuring that his spirit would never become rotten. His beloved polis had taken a wrong turn; incurable societal rottenness was all around him. By dying as he did, he set his spirit free of strictures of time and space, and ever since has touched people across the ages who share his determination to arrest destructive developments in their society so that one and all could develop in a progressive way. Both Socrates's and Yossarian's actions were, in the end, consummate acts of autonomy, for a greater good. The real secret is that man's life is garbage unless he lives a certain way, true to himself, no matter the outcome. In the case of Yossarian and Socrates, their spirits beckoned: come on.

Chapter 4

Play's the Thing

Players

Above the main entrance to The Globe Theatre, built by Shakespeare's playing company in 1599, was a crest engraved with the motto *Totus mundus agit histrionem*—Latin for "The whole world is a playhouse." The Dutch cultural historian Johan Huizinga (1872–1945) would find apropos this philosophy of the world. In his estimation, we humans, at our core, are playful beings—so much so that our species, if he had his way, wouldn't be called *Homo sapiens*, wise guys and gals, but instead, *Homo ludens*, playful people. In his masterwork *Homo Ludens* (literally "Man the Player"), Huizinga, a founder of modern cultural history (which combines the approaches of history and anthropology to study cultural traditions), stresses that "civilization [itself] arises and unfolds in and as play." This is as if to say that if we fail to play, the fall of civilization is nigh.

The word "play" has always been connected to the world of make-believe. At its origins, though, this word, and the world it's connected to, was as much the province of adults as it was of children. In England of old, playing was a special occasion for one and all. As the poet and scholar John Milton (1608–1674) put it in 1638, "young and old come forth to play on a sunshine holiday." Today, the kind of unfettered play in which you let your imagination loose of all strictures is associated mostly with children.

The United Nations High Commissioner for Human Rights recognizes play as the right of every child. Should play also be the right of every adult, of every human being, if we are to continue growing a sound mind and body? What kinds of play make for a happy and healthy child? How about a happy and healthy adult? If we don't tend to our playful side, can we continue to "child" in as rich and manifold a way as we otherwise might?

All Play and No Work

I'm holding a cyber-dialogue with millennial youth. Everyone on hand besides me entered this world sometime around the mid-1990s. They go by a variety of tags: Generation Next, Generation Y, the Net Generation, and Generation We. Those taking part, seven in all, started a weekly Socrates Café via Google Hangout about a year ago. Two of the founding members are in the final year of high school international baccalaureate programs and had read my *Socrates Café* in their theory of knowledge class. I'm taking them up on a standing invitation to join them. I've told them ahead of time that I'd like to hold a dialogue that explores some aspect of "humans and play."

Our cyber-exchange gets off to a low-tech start when Emerson, eighteen, from Portland, Maine, holds up to his computer camera a well-worn copy of Dickens's *Great Expectations*, which he'd been reading to his kid sister Desi, who I can see in the background, in a beanbag chair, talking animatedly to the dolls she's dressing and primping. He strikes upon the page he's looking for. "Miss Havisham says she has 'a sick fancy that I want to see some play,' and so 'with an impatient movement of the fingers of her right hand' she orders Pip and her adopted daughter Estella: 'play, play play!' Pip has to play cards on demand. It's one of his favorite things to play, but on this occasion it's making him self-conscious, intimidated, miserable."

As Emerson runs his hands through two mops' worth of curly blond hair, he says next, "My question is: Can play ever be play if it's forced on you?"

His precocious sister is the first to respond. "It can't be *pure* play, even if you end up playing, because, just like you said, it's forced. If my mom or dad tells me to go outside and play, it's more like having to do a chore or homework," says Desi. "But usually, after a while, I start playing and forget that it wasn't my idea. Then it becomes fun, even if forced fun. Until then, it can't be play, and it will never be play all the way.

"Same goes with Pip. As long as he's playing something against his will, it can't be pure play. Because pure play makes you feel free of everything— of time, of your parents, of space, of work." Likewise, to Aristotle, when you're playing, the moment is all that matters, because you're so wrapped up in what you're doing, with no other end in mind than the activity itself.

"Maybe Pip can't be said to be playing at all," Emerson says now. "After all, Miss Havisham pays Pip's uncle, Joe Gargery, twenty five guineas for Pip's services. When you get paid to play, you're not only working, but it's a job. Your time is not your own, even if you're enjoying the activity."

"It can still be play, even pure play, if it's that thing you do that makes you the most joyful," says Matako, eighteen. The accomplished pianist from the other Portland, in Oregon, reflects on this some more. "There are many days when I have to force myself to practice, when I wish I could just snap my fingers and play brilliantly, perfectly. But as my parents taught me, anything worth accomplishing probably requires a lot more hard work than you realize—even some of the best and most freeing kinds of playing. Once, whether I'm practicing or performing, I cross that threshold into the world of music, everything else disappears. I've entered a world free of all limits."

Then he says, "A lot of well-paid performers—musicians, actors, athletes—lose the joy that was a big reason behind their decision to excel at what they do. They may still perform at a high level, but when the pleasure and delight—the euphoria—is gone, no amount of money can make it play again."

Similar to Matako's philosophy of play, the writer and naturalist Diane Ackerman characterizes as deep play "the ecstatic form of play. In its thrall, all the play elements are visible, but they're taken to intense and transcendent heights. Thus, deep play should really be classified by mood, not activity. It testifies to *how* something happens, not *what* happens." To Friedrich Nietzsche, on the other hand, while we humans may be play-things of the forces of nature, we can channel these forces and bend them to our will, through creative pursuits like art and music and dance and activism and thinking itself. He considers human play at its most exalted an unselfconscious happening in its how and its what, a manifestation of human freedom showing itself off. To Nietzsche, play is a kind of inquiry that might be driven by a theatre of feelings that run the gamut from ecstasy to agony.

Soon afterward, Levi, from St. Paul, Minnesota, says to us, "More and more sports stars are walking away from the game they once loved, and from their lucrative contracts." A college dropout, at age twenty Levi started his own software company, which develops interactive learning platforms for middle and high school educators. His company now has upward of twenty-five employees, and has been featured in magazines that celebrate entrepreneurship by Millennials. "One of my favorite Minnesota Vikings' players, Christian Ballard, quit the game before this season officially started. He said football wasn't fun anymore."

Levi takes a moment to dig up the online article announcing Ballard's retirement. "Ballard is quoted as saying, 'Making that much money—that was fun. But money is still a material thing. You can always make money. You can't make that time that you lose with your friends and your loved ones. Time is something that you can never get back.'"

"But once you're an adult, your time is never totally your own, unless you're crazy rich," says Hajera, an eleventh grader from Fremont, California. "You have to make ends meet, and that means you have to work. That makes play time all the sweeter, because you're choosing to carve out time for it. And once you're doing it, you lose track of time." She muses for a good while before then saying, "Work is a 'material thing' that, depending on the kind of work you do, is made more tolerable for some, even more enjoyable for others, by the immaterial thing of pure play."

"I need to play like I need to breathe air," says Emerson. "Without play, I'd be a dull boy in my work life, whether at school or after school in my job as a barista. I'm into all kinds of recreational play—camping, mountain-biking, hiking. I play the drums, I play sports. Like Matako, I don't always enjoy the time I have to put into the practicing, but when it's show time or game time, it's pure playtime for me. Yet for my father, play is what makes him a dull boy. If he's not working, he's not happy. He'd prefer not to have to take time to play with us. When my sister or I corral him into playing, he's counting the minutes."

"It's not because other kinds of play are the ones that have an unforced quality to him?" I ask. "For instance, my dad used to accompany me on father-and-son Boy Scout outings where we'd go camping, hiking, fishing. He didn't hide the fact that he was miserable, that these were things he'd never do if he was deciding what kinds of outings the Boy Scouts should go on. Raised on the Florida coast, his idea of play was limited mainly to going to the beach, lying in the sun and sweating, or body surfing the waves."

I think some more. "I'm talking more about leisure activities. These aren't anything like the pure play activities of the kind Desi described."

After considerable thought, Emerson says, "Yeah, we're talking about likes and dislikes for leisure activities. They can be great escape from work and also from pure play. They're in the twilight zone between the two. You relax your mind and body so that when you get back to work or play, you have even more energy. My dad's preferred leisure toys are an RV and a houseboat. He had both, couldn't afford either, and had to sell them."

Emerson says next, "My dad has never made it financially, but he loves work. He's had many jobs, but whatever it happens to be, he gives all of himself to it. These days he makes routine work rounds giving sales strategy seminars. But anyone who sees him in action would consider them anything but routine. I've sat in on a couple of them. He's like an actor performing on a stage. Those taking part in his seminars usually clap at the end. If you've ever had to sit through a seminar, you know how rare that is.

"My dad has had so many disappointments," he goes on, "but he says to me that disappointment keeps him motivated. He encourages me to pursue whatever activities I'm most passionate about and tells me that I shouldn't let his own setbacks discourage me when it's time for me to take on a profession. But he says I need to realize that success in any worthwhile occupation will probably take a lot more hard work than I realize. His attitude, though, is succeed or fail, you should live out your days with a playful, never say die attitude. He basically tries to live according to Mark Twain's philosophy of work. He has this quote from Twain's memoir in a frame on his office wall. It says, 'What I have done I have done, because it has been play. If it had been work I shouldn't have done it.'"

"This has me thinking that my dad's work is in many ways his play," Hajera says. "He's an investment analyst. When he's working, he's doing something he truly wants to be doing, even if it's a material thing."

"But he wouldn't do it for free, one of the criterion that we agreed makes play what it is. I don't know any investment analyst who would," says Levi.

"I'm not so sure," she says. "His work is the supreme statement of who he is. Even in years when the market has clobbered him, he thrives on the pressure, the sport of it. He revels so much in his work that maybe he would do it even for free, if it came to that. It defines him. He loves the material reward, but even if his clients were the only ones who made money and he didn't, I swear he'd do it at least as a hobby and figure out some other way to support the family. While to me is work his dull, to him it's as creative as it gets. When he's really had an exceptional day, he's so full of himself that he's compared himself to da Vinci."

"My *yaya* was a prolific poet," I'm moved to tell the group. "It made worth living what was otherwise a hardscrabble life. She drilled into me that I should always strive for what the Greeks call *meraki*. When you're doing something that is the essence of yourself, to her that is an expression of *meraki*—the soul, creativity, and love that you put into something, whether work or play."

Then Levi says, "When you're putting all of yourself into something, do words like work or play do justice in describing what you're doing?"

"I tried to make work at my company too fun, too unforced," he goes on to say. "It had the opposite effect. I wanted work to be a playground. I tried 'fungineering.' The team leaders did everything from wear costumes to dress up as French waiters to bring in catered cuisine. I tried gamification, turning work projects into games, with competition and even prizes. Productivity actually decreased. My colleagues didn't have the heart at first to tell me that they work best—with the most intensity and creativity and playfulness—when there are no 'outside stimulants.' They consider the work itself playful, creative. They're really like artists, all working on the same canvas to make a thing of beauty. When they're in their zone, words like work and play aren't even necessary."

Levi says to us next, "Two years ago, on Holocaust Remembrance Day, I traveled to Poland with my father to visit Auschwitz, made into a museum in 1947. Over a million people died there when it was a concentration camp. There is still the sign at the entrance, '*Arbeit mach frei*,' that was there when my great-grandfather was imprisoned in the concentration camp. 'Work will set you free.' The Nazis made a mockery of real work. If the prisoners in concentration camps couldn't do the meaningless back-breaking labor forced on them, they were put to death."

"I visited the area at the camp that was converted into a football field each Sunday," he then says. "My great-grandfather Joshua, ninety-six now, on one of the few occasions he's talked about his experience there, said that Sundays were the one day of the week they had free time. They'd play football. There were several teams. The games were very competitive, and they were so popular that everyone else in the camp—including the guards—would attend and cheer on their favorite team. The Red Cross was even given permission to donate uniforms and equipment. My great-grandfather had been a standout high school quarterback. He told me that at times during the game, he was so caught up in the action and the joy of playing that he would actually forget he was at the camp. He said those Sunday games kept everyone's spirits up, made them feel human again."

The German philosopher, playwright, and poet Friedrich Schiller (1759–1805) had this to say of play: "Man only plays when he is in the fullest sense of the word a human being, and he is only fully a human being when he plays." To Schiller, when we play, we do so out of "sheer plentitude for vitality," making us like the gods in that we are freed from all constraint, severed "from the bonds inseparable from every purpose, every duty, every care."

"I'm fortunate that he lived with us all through my growing-up years," Levi then says. "Because of my great-grandfather, I learned the value of creative work, of doing something that was productive that also was a statement of who you are. He'd often repeat a quote to me from Aldous Huxley, whom he'd read as a boy. Huxley called 'creative work, of however humble a kind, . . . the source of man's most solid, least transitory development.'

"He was an old-school clothes tailor and cutter. He had several long-time customers who came to our house. He took a lot of pride in creating new patterns. He was sad that most everything done by tailors these days is so cookie-cutter, like it all came off the same assembly line. To him, it's like people are deciding to take away choice and freedom. He thinks people no longer value true craftsmanship, even though to him, it's what pure play is all about—expressive, inventive, and creative."

After an absorbed silence, Matako says to us, "In the movie *Life Is Beautiful*, a Jewish bookstore owner, Guido, is sent with his three-year-old son, Joshua, to a concentration camp. He convinces his son that they're participants in a competition, and that the first to earn one thousand points wins a real tank. Even when Guido is engaged in degrading labor, like carrying anvils to a furnace, he makes Joshua believe it's all part of the competition. Guido managed in that horrific setting to create an alternative world, a space of pure play for his son."

"Did he create it for himself as well?" I ask.

She considers. "He did not. But in creating it, it kept his own spirit strong, kept him from giving in to despair. Like Levi's great-grandfather, his nature was playful to begin with, so in doing what he did for his son,

Guido was able to keep alive that pure, playful part of his nature." She thinks some more. "So then, yes, you could say that he did it for himself too, even if that was not his primary intention."

Matako's nine-year-old sister, Ciera, pokes her head in front of his computer camera. He turns to her and asks, "If you could, would you just play all the time?"

Ciera is incredulous. "*Just* play? Just? Play is . . . it's everything. You put a lot of yourself into play. It's a lot of *work*." She looks at her brother, and then out at the rest of us in the Google Hangout universe. "When I make a castle in the backyard for me and my prince, I put a lot of myself into it. I forget all about myself, about time, just like my brother does when he's playing the drums."

The psychologist Mihaly Csikszentmihalyi famously described as "flow" that state of being in which you're in an effortless state of intense concentration and immersion in a creative undertaking from which you gain a sublime sense of joy and satisfaction.

This brings Matako to say, "Before I learned to play the piano for real, my dad and I would have make-believe concerts. Each of us would take turns pretending we were playing all the musical instruments of an orchestra. We'd spend hours doing that, having so much fun with instruments made out of thin air as we hummed real music of our own making. Now we do that with real instruments, me with the piano, him with the violin, which he learned on his own as a boy. We even create our own music out of thin air."

The provocative British-American anthropologist and humanist Ashley Montagu (1905–1999) claims that unlike children, few adults can "content themselves with simple playthings enriched by their imagination." Yet Ciera's dad is an exception to this. My mom was too. Though shouldered with adult responsibilities at a tender age, her playful nature would not be suppressed. No matter how oppressive the surroundings, she always found a way to make them playful to her five brothers and sisters under her care. She worked the same magic on me. She immersed herself in my childhood world of play and imagination, spent hours on end with me as I created on a toy printing press a neighborhood newspaper filled with interviews, articles on local happenings, stories and poems of my own—even a few philosophical meanderings. (Like, "If all the world was brown, would we need a color called brown?") I was painfully shy, but my role as publisher and reporter brought me out of my shell. I became downright conversant with people of all ages, my curiosity about them getting the best of me. Little wonder that I started out my adult life as a journalist, then went on to have poems and short stories published before I became a maverick philosopher. The American moral and social "street philosopher" Eric Hoffer (1898–1983), a role model for me whose works were popular with both scholars and lay readers, said "the creative mind is the playful mind," and that "philosophy is the play and dance of ideas." Thanks to my mom, the play and dance of ideas has always been at the center of my life.

My reverie is interrupted when I feel a tugging on my shirtsleeve. The other Google Hangout participants are all smiles. I look down and there is my daughter, Cali, who's just returned from ice-skating with her mom. My doe-eyed child looks up at me: "Daddy, I want to play. I want to make an ice-skating rink in the family room. With you. Now."

Culture of Play

For Johan Huizinga, the Renaissance era's impact is so memorable and lasting because it was imbued with a playful element:

> We can scarcely conceive of minds more serious than Leonardo and Michelangelo. And yet the whole mental attitude of the Renaissance was one of play. This striving, at once sophisticated and spontaneous, for beauty and nobility of form is an instance of culture at play.

This culture of play, which reached an incomparable zenith in fifteenth and sixteenth century Florence, also peaked for a time in ancient Athens, giving rise to exceptional philosophers, poets, and playwrights, and mathematicians and scientists (often all rolled into one). To Huizinga, such a milieu can only emerge in a society in which play is "pure," an end in itself. Huizinga claims that "true play knows no propaganda." As such, play's purpose isn't utilitarian; rather, "its aim is in itself, and its familiar spirit is happy inspiration." Given the fact that Huizinga lived in an era of the most pernicious propaganda—he himself was held in detention by the Nazis for his outspokenness against their occupation of his homeland and died from declining health while in captivity—this leading cultural historian's notions of pure play pack an even more powerful punch.

One of our greatest philosophers of all time, Plato, would agree with Huizinga that it is our core nature to play. Yet all the more reason, in Plato's estimation, to make sure that adults guide and channel that core nature in kids. To him, play must be sensible, responsible, bounded, serious—not at all pure, an end in itself. While Plato insisted that all work and no play would make Jack—or Aristotle, his one-time pupil, not to mention Socrates, his principal mentor—a dull boy, he argued that play must be properly packaged at all times. Plato recognized, as he put it in his *Republic*, that the lessons developed for educating children "must not be given the aspect of a compulsion to learn," because "no forced study abides in the soul." His foremost commandment for instructing our young is: "Don't use force in training children in the subjects, but rather play." But Plato's play-based approach had big strings attached. In his estimation, "if from earliest childhood [one's] play isn't noble," it isn't a form of play worth playing. By "noble," Plato meant practical and purposeful. In his estimation, play should be geared toward teaching children and youth how "to fight a war and run a house and administer a state," as if this is all that nobility can amount to. Even learning to play a musical instrument, to Plato, should not be aimed mostly at nurturing a child's creative side, but rather at instilling the value of order and laws.

Play Plato's way should help "elevate" kids over time to adult status. Any play activity should help reveal to adult educators which of three classes of society the children under their tutelage should be groomed: the producers (e.g., craftsmen, farmers, artisans) who provide essential goods for a citizenry; the warriors, who are at the front lines defending the state; or the guardians, who make up the ruling class and are groomed for the highest government and military positions. Plato's applied philosophy of play was aimed at realizing his utopian vision of a republic. His fear was that if children and youth ever got the idea into their heads that unregulated play was permissible, much less something to be encouraged, they would come to believe that they could operate by their own playbook, even make new rules for society itself—a turn of events, he was sure, that would lead to the republic's unraveling. It wouldn't have occurred to him that children and youth might, if given some free reign, change the rules for the better in matters of governance.[20] No more than it would have occurred to him that his version of play would lead to the very problem— of ossification, stasis, and instability—that he was seeking to prevent. Plato was blind to the fact that he himself would never have flourished under the type of play-based educational system he elaborated. It would have deprived him of the freedom and spontaneity to create such a playful and imaginative body of work.

Plato's mentor Socrates also would have suffocated under such a system, and surely would have met with a tragic fate at the hands of a paternalistic society at a far younger age. Surely Socrates's progressive parents—his father was a sculptor, his mother a midwife—had much to do with his creative approach to inquiry and being in the world. If Plato had had his way, parents' nurturing roles would play second fiddle to the state. As the philosophical polymath Bertrand Russell put it, "Plato would have us . . . put the State not only in place of the father but in that of the mother also."

---

20 In the Philosophers' Club dialogue groups establish in elementary schools, the young participants come up with their own protocol for engagement and how to govern themselves. For instance, those in a group I inaugurated in Phoenix decided that they should have to raise their hands and wait to speak until called on—unless they were just bursting to say something right away, and then, they came up with the caveat that each had one "free pass," and so on one occasion could speak out of turn. When they didn't engage one another according to their protocol, they came up with a set of "penalties." The first time someone spoke out of turn after using her free pass, she's given a warning. The second time, her cup of juice—we found you philosophize much better while drinking juice—is taken away. With the third offense, she doesn't get any juice at the next Philosophers' Club—only water. If someone really gets out of hand and keeps breaking the rules, she can't say a word for an entire dialogue and instead has to write a poem or a report or draw a picture about the dialogue taking place. "Justice" was meted out equitably to each and every member. Transgressors found it impossible to get upset when they were penalized for an infraction, since they themselves had unanimously crafted and agreed to the consequences stipulated. Their rules-based protocol showed how much they cared about the dialogue itself, and cared about making sure it was as participatory, inclusive, and thoughtful as it could be.

In *How We Think*, John Dewey argued that the difference between play and work in their more exalted forms is that play at its purest is an activity undertaken for its own sake, while when we work, we're aiming for a particular outcome. Other than that, though, both should be conduits for discovering one's talents and passions, all should be expressions of our creative, inquisitive, wondering selves. The role of schools, in his estimation, was to create a setting in which the transformation from play to work was seamless, transitionless. Schools should create an environment of play and work with the aim of "facilitating desirable mental and moral growth." To him, that meant tapping into kids' innate sense of wonder and desire to know and understand, and direct these inclinations toward kinds of problem-solving that were good if not excellent works, beneficial both to societal and individual prospering. Dewey was dismayed that our schools thwarted this objective. In launching his laboratory school of experiential education in the late nineteenth century, he developed a combined play- and work-based approach that was the opposite of that of Plato. His philosophy was that teachers and students alike were learners one and all, engaged in a collective problem-solving enterprise, each with talents to discover, develop, and lend to it.

More than anyone, Dewey made distinctions among kinds of work and play—between self-indulgent and self-absorbed kinds that lead to narcissistic and even damaging pursuits, and those kinds that lead us to feel more connected to one another. Dewey's aim was for learners to discover and master those talents and potentials that lead to the pursuit of avocations in which you're constantly challenged and rewarded by using your expertise to confront problems that affect many or most of us. Dewey's ideal for work was that it was an outgrowth of ideal play. It would lead people to take on pursuits in which they engage in creative work that is meaningful not just to themselves but also to others. It is work that requires a philosophy of human flourishing based on the premise that we best expand our own horizons by not only taking others into account, but enabling their talents to be optimized as well. He believed the best worlds are ones in which we all get our hands dirty cultivating the human garden, and in which we all have the resources to do so.

Counter to Dewey, the accomplished conservative English philosopher and political theorist Michael Oakeshott (1901–1990) contends that education proper enables young students to enter a conversation about our "historic inheritance or 'culture.'" Education is "above all else . . ."

> an initiation into the art of this conversation in which we learn to recognize the voices, to distinguish the different modes of utterance, to acquire the intellectual and moral habits appropriate to this conversational relationship, and thus to make our debut *dans la vie humaine* [in the human life].

In Oakeshott's view, an ideal education is tantamount to an initiation into the art of *adult* conversation, and as such sets our young on the road to becoming inculcated with adult habits. In his noted lecture, "A Place for Learning," Oakeshott made clear his contempt for Dewey's educational philosophy and its "design to substitute 'socialization' for education." He called Dewey's approach "the momentous occurrence of this century, the greatest of the adversaries to have overtaken our culture, the beginning of a dark age devoted to barbaric affluence." Learning, Oakeshott contended, must take place strictly under "conditions of direction and restraint designed to provoke habits of attention, concentration, exactness, courage, patience, and discrimination." This was the remedy to the "childish self-indulgence" that he claimed characterized Dewey's approach to education.

If you want to put a fellow adult down, call what he's doing childish; and if you *really* want to put him down, then go a step further and characterize it as a childish self-indulgence. Yet Dewey's educational ethos does not at all promote mere socialization, and certainly it is not childish in the way Oakeshott wields the term. Rather, it is education for social conscience, for intellectual autonomy and integrity, education of a kind in which the subject matter explored often emerges from life experience—if that's childish, then it is a most excellent sort.

To Dewey, if and when the type of education that Oakeshott advocates is fully realized, it will create an educated elite, with the vast majority of citizens relegated to the margins. Which is pretty much what we have. As Dewey puts it, "the result is that which we see about us everywhere—the division into 'cultured' people and 'workers.'" A Platonic society realized, in other words.

Dewey wouldn't disagree with Oakeshott's view that "every human being is born into an inheritance of human achievement and an education is the initiation into that inheritance." But he would be the first to point out that Oakeshott looks only at the bright side of that inheritance, putting on blinders to its seamier sides. One can look at the flourishing culture of the Weimar Republic, made up of a highly educated citizenry, as a cautionary tale for how one can be educated to be fully conversant in and about one's culture, yet deliberately deny this "initiation into the art of this conversation" to huge segments of society. As Walter Kaufmann notes, it is "unfortunately quite false that students trained by great scholars generally learn on their own to apply to morals, politics, and other vital issues the critical thinking they have been taught to apply to academic questions.

> During the first third of [the twentieth] century the German universities could boast of a galaxy of distinguished scholars who applied the highest standards in their specialties and won a large number of Nobel Prizes. But their students did not learn to apply similar standards of rationality to moral and political questions, and Hitler was as popular with students and university-trained people as with less educated Germans.

What Kaufmann neglects to address is why many among this galaxy of distinguished scholars themselves failed to apply standards of rationality to moral and political questions. For instance, the revered philosopher Martin Heidegger became part of one of the most pernicious mass movements in human history when he joined the Nazi party. In 1933, when Heidegger became the Nazi rector of the University of Freiberg, he not only turned his back on his four most stellar students, with whom he'd had close personal relationships, at their time of greatest need, he went to lengths to make his existential notions serviceable to and compatible with Nazi ends.

Four of our most celebrated modern philosophers were students of Heidegger's. All were of Jewish descent, and all overcame his betrayal to become exemplary moral models: Hans Jonas (1903–1993) made his mark as a philosopher of the environment, his works serving as the intellectual foundation for Germany's Green Party and much of the environmental movement that later spawned. Karl Löwith (1897–1973) became one of the renowned German philosophers of the twentieth century, gaining particular acclaim for his works on the problematic relationship between Christianity and Western history, and on modern historical conscious- ness. Herbert Marcuse (1898–1979) was anointed the standard-bearer of the New Left, his philosophical oeuvre examining the dehumanizing effects of modern technology and naked capitalism. Hannah Arendt, who at age eighteen began a tumultuous three-year romantic relationship with Heidegger, went on to become one of the premier political theorists of all time. It was up to these "children" of Heidegger to take the most humanizing elements of his philosophy of caring and employ them for a greater good. They put into practice principles that Heidegger preached about and betrayed. As the intellectual historian Richard Wolin puts it in *Heidegger's Children*, these students of his strove to confront and combat the "obscene uses" to which the rich intellectual traditions from which they hailed were put by Heidegger and others. In the aftermath of Hitler's seizure of power and Heidegger's complicity with the regime, his "'chil- dren' sought to philosophize *with Heidegger against Heidegger*, thereby hoping to save what could be saved, all the while trying to cast off their mentor's long and powerful shadow"—lest, "like a Greek tragedy, . . . the sins of the father will be visited upon the daughters and the sons."

To Walter Kaufmann, who lost loved ones in the Holocaust, the central question of any applied philosophy of education worth its salt is: What kinds of men and women should we try to develop? "This was very clearly understood by Plato," he observes. "And though I do not accept his answer to this question, he also understood that types of men are corollaries of types of societies, or vice versa." The triumvirate of social-emotional-intellectual learning that Dewey espoused was aimed at developing kinds of men and women in which all were important participants not only in the conversation, but in the actual crafting of their culture. While many are employing today an array of progressive approaches to promote this type of learning in schools and at home, typically the adults "coach" the children to develop what Daniel Goleman famously calls "emotional intelligence"—a term less rich and multifaceted than Dewey's coinage of "passionate intelligence," which is "as ardor in behalf of light shining into the murky places of social existence, and as zeal for its refreshing and purifying effect."[21] Goleman insists that "parents need to make the best use of the golden moments they have with their children, taking a purposeful and active role in coaching their children in key human skills like understanding and handling troubling feelings, controlling impulses, and empathy." Wise counsel, to be sure, but those are also golden moments for parents to learn from children. Adults, in their way, can be just as in need of guidance with handling feelings, controlling impulses, and developing empathy.

The work of Russian social psychologist and philosopher Lev Vygotsky (1896–1934) has come into vogue in educational and parenting spheres. Vygotsky's principle of the Zone of Proximal Development holds that children will become more independent learners in the many dimensions of what learning can constitute if they have the continual guidance, starting from very early on, of adults—"more knowledgeable others"—more skilled in what they're trying to achieve. The premise is that if a child can first observe and emulate a task undertaken by an adult, he then can more readily attempt it, with success, on his own.

This learning technique that Vygotsky sets forth, called "scaffolding," is based on the premise that by partnering with adults when learning something

---

21 The same day I attended a forum that included scores of the most well-known educational progressives with programs in tens of thousands of schools nationwide aimed at inculcating youth empowerment of varying sorts, a few hundred feet away there was a parallel gathering of hundreds of kid activists in a separate enclave. I look forward to the day when the notion that kids and adults sitting around the same tables, brainstorming as equals about their shared passions, will no longer seem alien but will become the norm—and that those of us implementing educational programs will include as one critical outcome measure the growth and development of the adults involved.

new, children are best equipped to build on knowledge they already have, from hands-on skills to social and emotional capacities. However, while adults are more knowledgeable and skillful in some ways, children are in their own ways, too. A child who demonstrates inordinate empathy, or exceptional self-control over impulses, or a remarkable gift in forgiveness, a child who shows a stick-to-it-iveness in fixing a broken toy that a parent has given up on mending, is a child from whom much might be learned. Children and adults need one another in their respective Zones of Proximal Development, or better yet, such zones need to overlap.

Game On

I'm taking part in a Monopoly tourney in an Atlantic City casino. I became a die-hard player when I was a kid. My family played almost every Sunday evening. It's not an exaggeration to say that in some ways it was the glue that kept us just this side of functional. Monopoly fed our competitive natures, but also brought out our playful sides. The board was a medium for healthy verbal back-and-forths. As we played, we could rib one another about serious things in a way that wasn't possible any other time. While I managed to enjoy open lines of communication with the other individual members of my family, we found it difficult to the point of painful to talk things out as a group. Except when we had Monopoly to offset and temper our exchanges. Looking back, I'm sure that a big reason I had such a desire to hold meaningful dialogues with intimates and strangers alike in my adults years was in part driven by my inability to foment this in my own family when I was a child.

For me, Sunday nights could not arrive soon enough. I had the board set up in the family room and the play money distributed hours before game time. I made the popcorn and poured our drinks. We each had our favorite pieces—my mom's was the thimble, my brother's the race car, my dad's the ocean liner, and mine the Scottie dog (a pet I'd always wanted in real life). As I got older, I became a player to be reckoned with. The board game brought out my inner mogul. It also gave me my first exposure to the free market and to the spills and thrills of real estate speculation. As most everyone knows, the aim in Monopoly is to bankrupt your opponents by buying up so much real estate that when they land on it, they have to pay you a bundle. While what the political philosopher Thomas Hobbes (1588–1679) said of the world at large—that "there is no other goal, no other garland, other than being foremost"—is arguable, it definitely applies to Monopoly.

Over the years, I became even more of a Monopoly enthusiast, maybe because, as in my childhood days, it afforded me the opportunity to try to be someone—a tycoon—I'd only enjoy being in the world of pretend. These days, besides playing Monopoly routinely with my wife and daughter, I also feed my addiction to the game by taking part in tournaments. During a break in play at the Atlantic City event, as ten of us sit around a large round table and partake in an embarrassment of delicacies from a buffet, we talk about Monopoly's decision, after keeping the rules unchanged for more than eighty years, to release a new version that gives its official blessing to its fans' ten most popular "house rules"—rules that thousands of players use, even though they clash against the official rules.

"It was bound to happen," Patricia, sixty-eight, one of my long-time playing antagonists and a fellow Socrates Café stalwart, tells us. "I'm a Monopoly purist, but the rest of my family isn't. When I feel the need to operate outside traditional rules, I play esoteric card games. My oldest daughter turned me on to them. In one of them, called Eleusis, one player gets to make a rule in secret: he decides which cards can be played on top of each other. The rest of the players then have to use deductive logic to figure out what the secret rule is. Then there's Mao, a card game in which the first person to get rid of all his cards wins. Those taking part are forbidden from explaining the rules to newbies. All you can say to them is, "The only rule I can tell you is this: I can't tell you the rules." They have to figure the rest out on their own. Not only that, the winner of a round adds a new secret rule of her choice to the rounds coming up."

"If it were up to my daughter, she'd make Monopoly as esoteric as those games," I say. "I let her bend or break the rules, or make them up as we go along. She gets so much joy out of winning that I don't have the heart to make her stay true to the rules. I try to tell her that it's best to win fair and square, and hopefully that will sink in one day. But for right now, I let her do whatever. I hope I'm not sowing the seeds of a future cheater by allowing her to do whatever."

Of late, I've been exploring how the games we play impact our possibilities for childing. I'm now prompted to wonder out loud, "Is 'doing whatever' the same as playing without rules? Is it possible to play a game with no rules whatsoever?"

"Without any rules at all, there would be chaos, pandemonium," says Allan, nineteen, one of a sizeable contingent of young people taking part in the tournament. "You could say, 'bridge is poker, and poker is bridge.' No one could dispute your claim, since rules wouldn't be subject to debate. Legitimate or illegitimate play wouldn't enter the picture, because there'd be no rule against any move of any kind."

"Rules are a fact of human life, not just in the games people play, but in all our dealings," says his girlfriend, Eliza, also nineteen. "Rules keep us civilized. As Jack said in [William] Golding's *Lord of the Flies*, 'We've got to have rules and obey them. After all, we're not savages.'"

"Even if you say, 'Okay, there are no rules today,' that's a rule!" says Blake, seventy-four. "The rule is that anything goes."

"We can't invent 'The Ruleless Game'?" I say.

"You might as well call it 'The Gameless Game,'" says Oshila, seventy-seven, who last week celebrated with Blake, two years her junior, their fiftieth wedding anniversary. "Because whenever you play a legitimate game, those playing agree on the rules beforehand. Even if the rules are changed in the middle of the game, or even if some of them are secret, or you make them up as you go, there has to be agreement about this among all those involved, or there'll be conflict."

"We wouldn't be able to have this conversation without rules," says Blake. "There would be no rules for language, grammar, syntax, so we wouldn't be able to understand each other. In a world without 'language rules,' each of us right now would be gibberishing in whatever language we made up on the spot. It'd be a Tower of Babel."

"Even if we could make ourselves understood with gestures," says Osh-ila, "it would be chaotic, since there'd be no rules for social courtesies like speaking in turn or paying attention to one another. Our society would sink to an even lower state, because there would be no rules of professional conduct like Robert's Rules of Order, or moral rules like the Golden Rule. Rules rule not only in games, but all human dealings."

"We're reading in my book club Khaled Hosseini's *The Kite Runner*," Patricia tells us. "It revolves around a kite-fighting tournament, an old-time winter event held throughout Afghanistan. The tournament doesn't end until only one kite fighter is left with a kite in the air, with his opponents, their kite lines cut, vanquished." She fires up her Kindle and accesses the book. "Amir, the story's protagonist, relates that 'a bratty Hindi kid who moved into the neighborhood told us that where he came from kite fighting had strict rules and regulations.' Amir says the kid 'would soon learn what the British learned earlier in the century, and what the Russians would eventually learn by the late 1980s: that Afghans . . . cherish customs but abhor rules. And so it was with kite fighting. The rules were simple: no rules.'"

"The thing is, though, kite fighting isn't really a ruleless game," says Blake, who has also read the bestselling book. "It takes amazing skill to be the last kite fighter standing. The one who wins has outplayed all the others and weathered all their attempts to bring down his kite. If it was genuinely without rules, then no one could be declared a winner, because there would be no rule for determining who comes out on top."

Soon afterward, Allan says, "Those who come out on top either pretend there are no rules or bend them to their advantage. I binge-watched the Netflix series *House of Cards*. As most of you know, it centers around a character, Frank Underwood, the House Majority Whip. Underwood says on the last episode, 'Of all the things I hold in high regard, rules are not one of them.' Underwood—the public servant in charge of the most august assembly, where rules are everything if our democracy is to function—thumbs his nose at rules. But he wouldn't want anyone else to. He can only get away with what he does because others abide by rules of morality. They'd never do to him what he does to them."

Then he says, "My dad is Underwood's opposite. He's a stickler for playing by the rules. He's an accountant. The rules for accounting change, but whatever they are, he adheres to them. The colleagues at his firm who are on the fast track are the ones willing to break or skirt the rules in ways that benefit their clients. He's told me and my mom that he almost wishes he could 'learn to play the game' like others in his firm, but he has to live with himself. He complained to his firm's directors when one of his colleagues 'cooked the books' to cover up malfeasance by a client. Ever since, he's only been given make-work. He's being punished for playing by the rules."

Eliza says soon afterward, "My dad loves to quote Don Draper from *Mad Men*—'you're born alone and you die alone and this world just drops a bunch of rules on top of you to make you forget those facts.' Then there are those, like my sister, who don't break the rules, but to whom rules don't apply, no matter how many rules the world drops on you. She reminds me of Pearl in [Nathaniel] Hawthorne's *The Scarlet Letter*." She retrieves the book on her e-reader. "Hawthorne said of Hester Prim's daughter Pearl—an 'imp' with 'sprite-like intelligence'—that 'the child could not be made amenable to rules.'" She goes on to read, "'In giving her existence, a great law had been broken; and the result was a being whose elements were perhaps beautiful and brilliant, but all in disorder; or with an order peculiar to themselves.'"

She says now, "Hawthorne was speaking of the laws of nature—kinds of rules that can't be broken. But he's saying that when Pearl came into being, somehow these laws broke down. Pearl's nature was alien to them."

Natural law philosophers, from Aristotle to the Stoics to John Locke, believe that the laws of nature are key to figuring out how humans should conduct themselves. To them, by putting our reasoning powers to use analyzing the nature of individual humans, over time we can work out binding universal rules for our moral behavior.

"Did Pearl still live by rules, even if of her own making?" I ask.

"As Hawthorne goes on to say, while to everyone else the elements that Pearl was made of seemed 'all in disorder,' they really had 'an order peculiar to themselves.' That's what rules do, create order of some kind."

"But they can create order of the wrong kind," says Oshila. "I recently read the first in the *Hunger Games* series." She's speaking of the popular science-fiction trilogy set in a post-apocalyptic nation. The plot centers around the battle to the finish between 'tributes'—twelve- to eighteen-year-olds chosen by lottery to participate. "The tribute Peeta reveals his unrequited love to his fellow tribute Katniss before a worldwide audience. They're so moved that they begin showering Peeta with gifts—food, medicine, tools—that he'll need to survive. But if Peeta's hopes for a lasting relationship with Katniss are to come true, the rules of the Hunger Games have to be changed, since the existing rules dictate that only one person can survive, and that person is then declared the winner.

"The game's millions of followers have become attached to Peeta and Katniss. Katniss is admired for her bravery, and even more for her compassion. This leads the powers that be, the Gamemakers, to enact a rules change halfway through the games. From then on, two tributes from the same district are allowed to win. This means that both Katniss and Peeta have a chance of surviving. Katniss searches for Peeta and finds him in hiding, wounded. She tends to him until he's healed. It looks like it's going to be 'happily ever after.' But then the Gamemakers reverse this change, because, one, they're sadistic, and two, they want a sensational ending, because they think that's what their audience really wants.

"But Katniss refuses to go along. She and Peeta plan to commit suicide by taking poisonous berries. When the Gamemakers discover what they're up to, they sense disaster for their contest. So they again reverse course, and announce that both will be declared the winners of the seventy-fourth Hunger Games.

"I admire Katniss," she then says, "because she didn't defy or break the rules to gain an advantage. She did it because the rules imposed by the Gamemakers went against everything she believed in and valued as a human being. She was willing to end her life rather than live by their rules."

"She's a modern version of Antigone," Eliza says, speaking of the heroine of Sophocles's tragedy. "Antigone stood up to Cleon, the ruler of

Thebes, who forbid a burial for her brother Polynices. She saw to it that Polynices had a proper burial, though Cleon decreed it would be against society's laws, which are enforced rules. Antigone was willing to break the rules if they take away someone's dignity."

In an essay published in *Words Without Borders*, Vaishali Raode, a transgender-rights activist in India and a *hijra*, a term for someone who is transgender, relates how at first he observed all the intricate rules imposed by his community, including one forbidding him to speak to the media. But Raode eventually rebelled: "I began to give interviews to the media. I appeared on television. . . . The community fined me for these transgressions. I paid the fine and committed the 'offenses' again. I was all but ostracized from the community." But Raode remained unbowed: "I was educated and had a mind of my own. So what if I broke all the rules?"—especially if doing so shatters stereotypes in ways that might enable an excluded group to emerge from the shadows.

Allan says after a thoughtful lull, "I'd like to think that, no matter what, I'll be like those who live by their own rules if they're 'higher' than the ones imposed on us. But I wonder if I should first play the game as it's played, even if the main rule is to break the rules. That's the only way I'll be able to get to the top in whatever field I pursue. Then I'll be in a position to be a game-changer."

He gives us a searching look. "If I go that route, would I even care any more about changing the rules for the better?"

Rules for Living

Are there rules in life that all should live by? Bertrand Russell, to whom a life spent studying philosophy was the way of life that best enabled you to explore and understand the inner and outer cosmos, came up with ten of them. One of them is, "when you meet with opposition, even if it should be from your husband or your children, endeavor to overcome it by argument and not by authority, for a victory dependent upon authority is unreal and illusory." Yet Russell's only daughter, Katherine Tait, writes in *My Father, Bertrand Russell*, that he did not model what he preached. "In practice, . . . 'making up our own minds' usually meant agreeing with my father, because he knew so much more and could argue so much better."

Russell's principle-based rules were at times aimed at upsetting conventional rules for living. In *Marriage and Morals*, he developed a set of rules to support his liberal view of marital relations. Among them were that betrothed couples were free to have relations with others, should never show jealousy, and should never have spats over how to bring up their kids. "My parents' marriage was founded on these principles," Katherine Tait recounts, "but it turned out that the new morality was no easier and no more natural than the ideal of rigorous life-long monogamy it was intended to replace."

> We had imagined our parents to be superior in every way to the conventional: our parents would never quarrel sordidly over conjugal rights or the way to bring up children; they were far too generous and intelligent. Yet there they were, not only doing these things, but even trying to involve us in their disagreements. . . . It was at that time that I came to regard progress, like Santa Claus and the Easter bunny, as a myth of childhood, and I have never since believed in any utopian project of any kind.

Should she be so jaded and discouraged? Is one principle rule about humans since the beginning of time that we often don't live up to our lofty rules for living, even though our claim is that they would lead us and others to a more enlightened or good life? Do we often suspend the rules we swear by when they conflict with other impulses or objectives? Even so, does that make our attempts at creating particular, peculiar, or universal sets of rules that reflect our ideals, values, and aspirations any less worthwhile and necessary?

How about when it comes to dialoguing with others? Are there ideal rules of engagement? The beloved humanist Stringfellow Barr (1897–1982), in his popular essay "Notes on Dialogue," thinks you can't go wrong in following the "rules of thumb" established by Socrates. They include close and careful listening, but also encourage spontaneous offerings by participants—the opposite of dinner party conversation, "where interrupting a speaker and . . . a quick question" is verboten.

> These thumb-rules may seem guaranteed to produce bedlam. And, indeed, when they are first tried, they generally do produce it. But inexperienced dancers on a ballroom floor and inexperienced skaters on an ice rink also collide. Experience brings a sixth sense in Socratic dialectic too. The will of self-insistence gives way to the will to learn.

To Barr, the foremost rule of thumb for meaningful dialectic "was laid down by Socrates: that we should follow the argument wherever it leads." But not follow it in a ponderous way, as in a court pleading. Rather, "the name of the game is not instructing one's fellows, or even persuading them, but thinking with them and trusting the argument to lead to understanding, sometimes to very unexpected understandings."

A peculiar kind of playfulness is at work in such inquiry, one that spawns "the imaginative and the unexpected." It's often overlooked how playful Socrates was in his dialogues, not just in his persona, but in the way he examined—imaginatively yet rationally, methodically yet open-ended—questions and answers from a variety of vantage points, showing that one can accomplish important things, gain profound insights, without being deadly earnest. The twentieth-century German philosopher Hans-Georg Gadamer (1900–2002), heralded for his magnum opus *Truth and Method*, regularly harped on the fact that dialogue at its best was a form of play, a dance marathon of questions and answers. The Socratic method itself, when practiced correctly, oozes such playfulness. Socrates showed that you can arrive at profound insights when you are serious yet at your most playful. According to Friedrich Nietzsche, "A man's maturity consists in having found again the seriousness one had as a child, at play."

The Game of Life

If you could ask Martin Heidegger which comes first in the human experience, play or games, his answer, hands down, would be play. "We play not because there are games, but rather, the reverse. There are games, because we play."[22] Games are a kind of play, but play can be so much more than games, fun or otherwise, rules-bound or otherwise.

Johan Huizinga maintains that play in all its forms is a purely social activity bounded within a specified set of manmade rules. Yet Heidegger's intriguing view is that the fabric of the universe itself is playful. To Heidegger, human existence can be described as "the game of life" because the universe itself is imbued with a "play character" in which hard and fast rules do not necessarily apply, or at least, are bendable. Heidegger intuitively grasped what physicists have since confirmed, namely, that there exist "singularities" in our universe in which the laws of nature break down. The universe is not merely mechanical, but has a creative element, what one might call a playful element.

Heidegger considers children our most excellent practitioners of rule-less play. While adults insist on rules for every activity in which they engage, children do not, and that's why, Heidegger feels sure, adults find children so inscrutable. To Heidegger, as noted in *The Heidegger Dictionary*, this makes of the child "in a metaphysical sense something that we adults can no longer comprehend at all." Heidegger was influenced in this perspective by the pre-Socratic Greek philosopher Heraclitus (535–475 BC), famous for his pronouncement that change was the only constant in life. Heraclitus called the universe itself "a child," and maintained that if there is such a thing as a transcendental eternity—if there is not the eternity of some religious faiths—but only one of a sort that makes of the universe itself an entity with no beginning or end, then "eternity is a child playing, playing checkers; the kingdom belongs to a child."

Language Games

Ludwig Wittgenstein (1889–1951), galvanizer of the linguistic philosophy movement in Britain and the United States, famously coined the term "language-game." The term is meant, as he writes in *Philosophical Investigations*,

---

22   From *Heidegger and Practical Philosophy*, Eds. Francois Raffoul and David Pettigrew, Albany NY: State University of New York Press, p. 109.

"to bring into prominence the fact that the *speaking* of language is part of an activity, or of a form of life"—namely, the human form. Wittgenstein asserts that language functions by an agreed-upon "network of rules," and that words derive their meaning from public agreement about what they mean. His contention is that the "rules" of grammar are not mere technical instructions that dictate the protocol of correct language usage; rather, they express the existing norms by which people use language to make themselves understood to one another. Hence, he maintains, every language is contingent—subject to the influence of culture, context, and public agreement. This leaves room for the invention of new words, of new meanings for old words, and new ways of stringing words together into sentences. What is not subject to change is its rules-bound nature. Wittgenstein is at odds with most analytic philosophers, who maintain with a religious zeal that language is the direct portal to reality—that it describes existence "as it really is." To Wittgenstein, language is nothing of the sort, and as language changes—which it often does, given that it is contingent on culture, context, era, and discipline—so does the reality it describes. Wittgenstein notes that learning to speak a language has a game-like element to it, and that when children are first taught to speak, they learn the rules of a language somewhat like they do the rules of a game.

But who is most talented at "playing" this language game?

It is well established that children are by far the most adept among us at learning new languages. It's a game to them, child's play. What is equally well known but far less appreciated is how playful they are with their mother tongue (or tongues). Their attempts to create new words, new usages or meanings for old words, and new twists on coinages, all too often are soundly quelled by adults, well meaning and otherwise. It is just as well established that as we get older, we lose our facility for learning new languages. It is no longer fun and games, but instead a lot of hard work. Do we also often lose our capacity to express ourselves, even in our native tongue, as we grow older? Once upon a time, I made a pretty penny as an editorial consultant, "translating" the gobbledygook of bureaucrats, academics, and other professionals with post-graduate degrees into intelligible English. In my own scholarly discipline of communications, in which I earned a PhD, typical academic journals, especially those considered the most prestigious, are impenetrable, indecipherable. More than one university colleague has confided to me that he's not sure of the meaning of much of the forbidding jargon he wields in his academic writing. The only thing he's sure of is that it must be used if his work is to stand a chance of passing muster in the ruthless anonymous peer review process. If this is so, then it breaks a fundamental rule of Wittgenstein's language game, namely, that shared agreement within a group on what a concept means precedes its actual usage. If there is agreement among the overseers of academic journals that there must be shared use of certain pedantic jargon, but few who use it have any earthly idea what it means, then genuine communication—not to mention knowledge acquisition and diffusion—cannot happen. To the extent that any of us loses our ability to communicate our thoughts intelligibly, are we a bit less human?

It is highly probable that children were the originators of human language—and just as likely that they are the principal creators of new languages. Consider the development of a form of *creole* in Hawaii after the explosive growth of sugar plantations on the islands in the late 1900s brought with it a tremendous influx of laborers from places like China, Japan, Korea, Puerto Rico, and the United States. While adults among the different groups made scant and halting progress in communicating with one another, the children made comparatively fast work inventing a nuanced pidgin language. They soon were able to converse with one another, while their parents couldn't make heads or tails of what their children were saying.

How did the children do it? The regarded linguist Derek Bickerton concludes in *Adam's Tongue* that children not only have an inherent ability to invent grammar, but that they have an inherent grammar hardwired in their brains. This gives them the capacity to create a fragmented pidgin language that, with practice, evolves in short order into a genuinely new language. Bickerton further posits that early members of the human species first began communicating with protolanguage, which is a language without any syntactical or word-construction rules. When this protolanguage first came into existence more than two million years ago, it was lawless. But as humans became more practiced at speaking with one another, language gradually came to be interwoven with rules. From this linguistic organization, Bickerton theorizes, complex thoughts became possible, and this spawned modern humankind. Who did he pinpoint as those most adept with this protolanguage? Kids.

Bickerton's theory is supported by how Nicaraguan Sign Language emerged. Until the 1970s, deaf children in Nicaragua couldn't communicate with one another because a sign language had never been developed for them. So the children set about inventing their own language. Those younger than age ten proved to be the most expert at fashioning a language for themselves. According to a *New York Times* article on this phenomenon, cognitive scientists who observed what was transpiring concluded that kids' brains have "a dedicated neural machinery for language." While there have been other instances, such as that in Hawaii, of the creation of a new language through the pidgin-creole route, "the Nicaraguan situation is unique . . . because its starting point was not a complex language but ordinary gestures. From this raw material, the deaf children appear to be spontaneously fabricating the elements of language." The language fashioned by the Nicaraguan children does follow the basic rules of language usage common to all tongues, yet amazingly, "the children were not taught any of these basic rules—indicating that they had an inborn protolanguage ability." Dr. Ann Senghas, a cognitive scientist at Columbia University who observed the children in Nicaragua, notes that while we adults "lose the ability to break information into discrete elements as we age," kids have it in spades: "It is not just that children *can* do it, but adults *can't* do it."

If this is so, then why are adults the language "gamemakers"? What might the world, our world, reality itself, be like, look like, if children were allowed to take the lead in articulating it? To Johan Huizinga, "the great archetypal activities of human society are all permeated with play from the start"—and no such activity is more imbued with this play element than language itself, "that first and supreme instrument which man shapes in order to communicate, to teach, to command." He contends that "behind every abstract expression there lies the boldest of metaphors, and every metaphor is a play upon words. Thus in giving expression to life man creates a second, poetic world alongside the world of nature." Yet this world is not alongside of nature, as Huizinga's reductionist perspective would have it; rather, it is nature itself, captured in poetic words. Are children—and those adults with a well-developed childlike sensibility—most capable of expanding our horizons about the world of nature?

The Italian political philosopher, rhetorician, and historian Giambattista Vico (1668–1744) asserted in *The New Science* that "in the world's childhood men were by nature sublime poets." According to the Enlightenment iconoclast, little appreciated in his own time but now considered one of the greatest thinkers of the eighteenth century, it was second nature to those at the dawning of human consciousness to communicate "in poetic characters." As a consequence, when the discipline of philosophy was in its infancy in the West, the pantheon of pre-Socratics philosophers—Anaxagoras, Empedocles, Parmenides, and Heraclitus—put into words their explorations of the inner and outer cosmos by way of poetic aphorisms. In Vico's view, they reasoned metaphorically, imaginatively; theirs was a "poetic wisdom."

Justus Buchler (1914–1991), a standout philosopher at Columbia University who specialized in metaphysics, agrees with Vico. As Buchler writes in his luminous work *The Main of Light: On the Concept of Poetry*, "in the beginning all language . . . was metaphorical, . . . the linking of things according to their similitudes . . . the expression of the imagination." This begs the question: Which human group was most capable of making such linkings? Lewis Thomas (1913–1993) did some etymological sleuthing to come up with an answer. He examined, among others, the word "pupil," and its dual meanings—a pupil in the eye, and a child who is a pupil at school.

Every language derived from Indo-European has the same connection, and for the same reason: when someone looks very closely into someone else's eye, he sees the reflection of himself, or part of himself. But why call that part of the eye a pupil? The same duplication, using identical terms for the pupil of the eye and a child, occurs in totally unrelated languages, including Swahili, Lapp, Chinese, and Samoan. Who would most likely have made such a connection, and then decided to use the same word for a child and the center of the eye? Most likely . . . a child. Who else but a child would go around peering into someone else's eye and seeing there the reflection of a child, and then naming that part of the eye a pupil? Surely not, I should think, any of the members of a committee of tribal elders charged with piecing together a language; it would never cross their minds. The pupil-eye connection must have turned up first in children's talk.

Thomas is convinced that language first evolved through the mouth of babes, and further speculates that poetry, with its roots in childhood, at its origins was the exclusive domain of children.

Has language itself evolved? Is it better than ever at serving as a conduit for expression? The use of metaphor has fallen out of favor, or at least, is relegated to second fiddle at best. Those who use language as a means to directly describe reality are considered to have evolved it. If Shakespeare was alive today, he'd likely be a pariah, what with literalness all the rage. His capacity for poetic expression reached unequaled heights in his adult years. He coined well over five hundred words. Not only that, he used a wide range of existing words in new ways. He didn't just play with words, didn't engage in mere wordplay for the sake of it, but rather employed words in ways that presented new functional usages as well as metaphorical leaps that astonish and delight to this day. Somehow, Shakespeare made it to adulthood with his facility to work magic with language intact. While there are few hard facts about his own upbringing, it *is* known that the children of Elizabethan England as a lot displayed a precociously witty and eloquent facility for wielding language. In his day, as Shakespeare scholar Ann Blake points out in "Children and Suffering in Shakespeare's Plays," this facility of children for layered and nuanced language was mirrored in his plays. Shakespeare, then, came by his inventiveness honestly, since it mirrored that of your everyday Elizabethan child of his time.

Children are not little Shakespeares per se, but they are potential Shakespeares. Unlike jargonists, whose awkward and off-putting linguistic spins limit, constrict, and intimidate, the terms they come up with often expand our possibilities for knowing and our sensibilities for feeling the world—not to mention serving as the grounds for bringing into creation new things. As a child, Lord Byron's daughter Ada Lovelace (1815–1852) cooked up a new branch of science called "Flyology"—a field dedicated to figuring out how to make it possible for humans to fly. She later went on to write the first algorithm for a computer—called a "thinking machine"—developed by Charles Babbage, making her the world's first computer programmer. Language was part of the wellspring for her inventiveness.

Even when kids are not coming up with new terms, they use existing language à la Shakespeare to make connections, to make visible what was blind to the naked eye. Metaphor is a big part of who and what children are. Once, when I was philosophizing with a group of three- and four-year-olds at a daycare center, I blew a bubble into the air. We watched as it made a brief zigzag trajectory and then popped. I asked the kids, "What happens to the bubble after it pops?" Some talked about all the little "bubble pieces" that now were scattered everywhere and wondered whether it was possible to put them back together. Then one tow-headed boy said, "The same thing happened to the bubble that happened to my grandmother. When she died, her soul popped."

Far more often than not, kids' inventiveness with language, their inborn expertise at using metaphor to reveal hidden likeness between what had been thought to be unlike things, gets wrung out of them. The same goes with their genius at wordplay: no sooner do they come up with a fascinating coinage than they have to put a lid on it. "That is not a word," they are told. It never gets a chance to take hold far and wide and become part of our lexicon.

What if we celebrated their mastery of the language game? What if we honored their gift and encouraged their playfulness with words? The reality that language, among other forms of expression, attempts to articulate and convey would be that much richer and more variegated. Researchers in cognitive science are discovering that those of any age with the capacity to speak more than one tongue have more means to sculpt their view of the world and how they process life—and hence to fashion life itself.

What if we brought together on a regular basis children from around the world who did not speak the same tongue? They would come up with altogether new languages, all sorts of novel combinations for expression. This would set the stage for the creation of entirely new and dazzling realities. It would provide them (and all the rest of us, by extension) a greater arsenal for articulating our emotions. As a consequence, it would endow us with new possibilities for human flowering.

Dispatch from Imagine Nation

Speaking of bringing together, I never met anyone more virtuosic at wielding to full effect the myriad elements of reasoning—discursive, analytical, imaginative, and empathic—than some of the earliest members of the Philosophers' Club, the name for my Socratic inquiry groups for kids. Starting in 1997, while living in the far west of the United States, first in the Bay Area of California and then in the greater Phoenix, Arizona area, I started a number of groups for kids (and wrote two children's books—*The Philosophers' Club* and *Ceci Ann's Day of Why*—based on my experiences). Many of those who took part had recently immigrated. In some cases, their families risked a great deal to escape hopeless poverty in their native countries in Central America and Mexico.

When I first started the Philosophers' Club as a during-school club at elementary schools and an after-school club at libraries, many of these young thinkers, most between ages eight and twelve, had at best a tenuous grasp of the traditional three R's: reading, writing, and arithmetic. But as they became enamored with the joys of Socratic inquiry, many were inspired to master these learning staples. In some instances, teachers remarked to me how students became far more motivated, enthused, and diligent learners. A couple even asked me how I'd sparked such a transformation, as if I possessed some sort of educational elixir. My role was minimal: all I did was create the setting in which they could introduce them to the "fourth R"—reasoning—which the young catch onto and employ like no one else. They could hold their own with Socrates himself.

I was able to learn the whereabouts of some charter Philosophers' Club members, all now in their mid- to upper twenties. Several are now living in the South Bay region, ranging from San Jose to the more sprawling reaches of Silicon Valley. Those I contacted said they still had vivid and pleasant memories of our Philosophers' Club days, and they were happy to reunite with me and former club members. On an Indian summer afternoon that never delivered on its threat to rain, five of us gather once more, at a picnic area within an untended park close to twelve-lane Highway 101. Our gathering place bisects well-to-do Palo Alto, home of Stanford University, where even modest homes sell on average for over $2 million, and far less well-off East Palo Alto, populated by those who work low-paying service jobs that in most cases support the high-tech industry.

"One of the first questions we ever examined all those years back at Philosophers' Club was one I asked, about whether the things we imagine are 'real,'" says Emilio, twenty-six, whose wife, Socorro, twenty-seven, and son Nano, seven, accompanied him but are too shy to do more than murmur a barely audible greeting. Emilio remains disarmingly handsome, though the years by all appearances have not been easy ones.

"Like, I asked: If I can picture a unicorn in my mind, is it real? Or is it just a figment of my imagination unless I draw a picture of it or write a story about it and make it 'real' for others? Or would it still be unreal, because it doesn't exist in the real world?"

"Of course it's real, as soon as you form a picture of it in your mind. It exists as an imagined object, " says Yessica, twenty-five. The once-spindly girl, now a lithe and striking young woman who sports contacts instead of wire-rimmed glasses, has the same no-nonsense manner.

Emilio smiles. "That's the exact same position you held when we discussed the question in our club." It's also the position first staked out by Aristotle, who held in his work *de Anima* that "the soul never thinks without mental images"—what cognitive theorists today would call mental representations.

Then Emilio says, "The Philosophers' Club was an oasis for imagining. It was a great escape from my real-world life in San Francisco's Mission District. I used to imagine me and my family living someplace swanky, light-years away from gangs and drugs and poverty. But those imaginings depressed me, because they were impossible to make come true. I sometimes wished I didn't have an imagination, so I wouldn't picture such things."

While the Scottish philosopher David Hume (1711–1776), whose stock in trade was empiricism and skepticism, argued in *A Treatise on Human Nature* that imagination is that faculty that most sets us free, to Emilio, that would depend on your circumstances. Emilio's wish for an imagination-free existence is one that the British philosopher Gilbert Ryle (1900–1976) believes could be made real. Ryle argues in his influential *The Concept of Mind* that "there is no special faculty of imagination," and so there is no distinct mental activity of imagining that can be pinpointed. If so, imagination only exists among those who believe in it and then imagine it into existence.

Emilio looks at me. "My own life these days isn't much better. I'm still imagining my great escape. I work at a taqueria as manager, Socorro works double shifts at a hotel. We work hard, man, and still hardly make ends meet. I have trouble seeing things ever getting any better or easier for us." His gaze falls on his son, a miniature version of himself. "I don't want Nano to struggle or suffer so much. I want his life to be hope-filled. But I worry about running out of years to make that happen for him."

Emilio forgets about us for a moment, his thoughts in a dark place. Then he says to us, "Is it better not to imagine good things for yourself and your loved ones, if you can't make those good things come true?"

Leonardo, the one Philosophers' Club member I'd still recognize after all these years if I passed him on the street, looks with open affection at his elementary school friend from long ago. "You have to imagine good things for yourself, bro. No matter how impossible it might seem to achieve those good things when you first imagine them, you have to believe you deserve to make them come true, so you'll figure out a plan of action.

"I'm fortunate," he goes on, "I had someone in my younger years who could imagine good things coming true for me at a time when I couldn't. My high school guidance counselor called me into her office one day. She told me that I had the highest score of anyone in my grade in the English aptitude test. She asked me what I wanted to do when I grew up. I told her I had no big plans, that maybe I'd be a janitor, like my dad. She managed to get out of me how much I love books. I even confided that I tried my hand at writing stories of my own, that it was almost like I couldn't help doing it—like, the stories would appear in my mind, and I had to put them down on paper. I ended up sharing a couple of them with her. She gave me literature about careers in publishing and in writing. She gave me information on area colleges that had generous financial aid packages to support my studies.

"But she didn't get through to me at first. I didn't believe enough in myself to make good things happen. She had all the belief in the world in me, but if I didn't share it, it wasn't worth much. She told me I needed to see myself both as a character in a storybook, and as the book's author. Right now, she said, the ending was too predictable because I was letting the 'book of me' write itself. She said I needed to become more curious about myself, that I needed to start asking, kind of like a scientist would, 'What if?' Like, what if I do unpredictable 'x' for a change instead of predictable 'y'? She wanted me to see myself as a great experiment and begin investigating myself. Her belief in me began to rub off."

He smiles. "If anyone had told me back then I'd wind up getting a degree in library science . . . Now I'm a reference librarian at a public library. I may live paycheck to paycheck, but I'm doing something I love. I get to put my mind to good use, and in my spare time I keep writing short stories. Soon my first collection will be published. My future—no, my present—started the day I began daring to visualize the life that I wanted for myself, and to believe I could make it a reality."

Then Leonardo says directly to Emilio, "Bro, you have good things in your life that seem impossible for me to imagine for myself. You have a beautiful wife and child." He sighs. "I have 'imagination block' when it comes to believing I'll ever get married, have kids, read bedtime stories to them. I'm as socially awkward now as I was back then in elementary school."

"Scrunch your eyes shut and imagine it, bro," Emilio says. "Visualize making it come true."

Such are Emilio's persuasive powers that Leonardo does as ordered. A couple moments pass. A hint of a smile appears. He opens his eyes. "I've not only imagined it, but imagined how I'm going to make it real. Little does Susana know she's going to be my wife one day in the not too distant future."

Aristotle would have applauded Leonardo's use of his imaginative powers. To Aristotle, imagination is intimately connected with desire. His view is that anything we pursue out of desire and that we try to make come true can only be brought about by first conjuring an image of the desired object.

Leonardo gives Emilio a grateful look. "Now you need to do the same, bro. You have to visualize for yourself making good things become real for you and your family. Without the vision you can't create a plan to make it real."

Yessica squeezes Emilio's shoulder. "True that. You have to take yourself on an imagination journey. The final destination will be the reality of your dreams. The hardest part is to begin. I know what I'm speaking about."

Then she says, "The man who fathered my children, he turned out to be too much like my abusive father. He's somewhere in Nevada now. I've had to support my kids on my own. For a long time, I was beaten down. I couldn't see a way out. A lot of it had to do with feelings about whether I deserved to find a way out. I had dreams, but then I'd think, 'Who am I kidding?' Abusive relationships contribute to low self-esteem. But knowing that didn't help matters for me.

"I had to quit feeling stuck in place, quit thinking I could never set myself free. I got professional help. My therapist helped me confront and deal with the things that kept me from making much out of my life. For me, changes came in baby steps, but they came. This is my one shot at life and I became determined not to let anyone or anything keep me down." She then says, "I'm close to earning a bachelor's degree in non-profit administration through a low-residency degree program."

Fixing her gaze on Leonardo, she says, "My goal is to do for adolescents what your guidance counselor did for you. After I earn my degree, my internship will be turned into a full-time post. I'll be made activities coordinator at the afterschool youth center. As it is, I do the 'good imagining' for the kids I work with until it becomes contagious and they can do it on their own."

Yessica is silent for some time, then says to us, "I used to try to convince my older brother Marlon to imagine a better life for himself. But he was fatalistic. He'd tell me he was born to be a gangbanger and would die one. He had an amazing singing voice and a gift for playing the guitar. He could have made a career out of being a musician. I used to imagine myself as a ninja swooping in and landing between Marlon and the rest of the gangbangers. I imagined that I challenged the leader to a fight to the finish, with the one left standing deciding my brother's fate. If I won, Marlon would be out of the gang life forever and would pursue a career in music.

"I told Marlon about my dream. He thought it was touching, but naïve. He's been gone nearly eight years now. When I imagine good things for myself and my daughters, I do it on his behalf too—really, on behalf of all those who wind up like Marlon, because they couldn't imagine a better future for themselves."

A long while passes in silence. "I have to get over this pity party and get to work making my dreams real," Emilio then says. "What Leonardo and Yessica have shared makes me realize that the only good things worth imagining are ones that are not only good for you and your own loved ones, but for others, too. Like, if you imagine good things happening for yourself that can only be made real by keeping others down, then that's not a good thing. Too many with money and power imagine good things only for themselves. That's why the economic playing field in this region is more unlevel than ever. But I can't let that be an excuse for failing to execute a plan for achieving my dreams. I need to set an example for my son." Then he says with shy conviction, "I've long dreamed of opening up my own bakery. I'm going to develop a plan for making it come true."

Nelson has stayed on the sidelines of the dialogue so far. He'd been the first to arrive. He told me he almost hadn't come, but that curiosity about seeing me and his classmates from long ago got the better of him. He has listened carefully, his face registering a mixture of sympathy and concern and interest, but also something verging at times on sheepishness, at other times on beguilement. Nelson's is a genuine Horatio Alger story, a kid from dirt-poor beginnings who crossed the Sonoran Desert with his mother and six siblings in 1995 and went on to do exemplary things.

He says now, "It's important to imagine good things for yourself, especially in bleak times, or things will only get bleaker. My mother drilled into me that you have to be bold and ambitious in making good things come true—that sometimes you fall flat on your face, but you pick yourself up, learn from it, and keep moving forward."

Turning his attention to Emilio, he says, "You sell yourself short, bro. You always were the best thinker—the best imaginer—among us. You had this never-say-die attitude that I admired. You just haven't had the right opportunity. If you need an investor in your bakery, you come to me with a plan."

While Emilio attempts to digest this even as his spirits brighten noticeably, Nelson goes on, "My mom did the 'good things' imagining for me, until I could get with the program. I had an aptitude for math and logic. She enrolled me in an accelerated program for high school students at a community college. Didn't tell me about it until it was a done deal for fear I'd try to talk her out of it because I was so lacking in confidence. I earned an associates degree in computer programming and information technology a year after high school. I went on to earn a bachelor's and then a masters degree. A tech company in Silicon Valley came to my college for recruitment and hired me. I became part of a team that develops software to enhance the face-to-face cyber-chat experience. My first paycheck, even with all the taxes taken out of it, was for more money than I'd ever seen."

Then Nelson says, "When I was twelve, I wanted more than anything to go back to Mexico to see my grandparents. They were ailing. But if I went south of the border for real, I'd never make it back to the US. I imagined ways to make the impossible possible. I visualized teleporting myself to Oaxaca, going back to visit with them for the night, while the rest of my family was asleep, so they wouldn't be worried that I had run away. I imagined spending some hours with my grandparents—sharing stories, hugging them, telling them how much I loved them—and then returning home before my parents and siblings woke up the next day.

"My grandparents both died soon afterward. My grandmother passed first, and then my grandfather three months later. He couldn't imagine carrying life without her. I did get to talk to them both on the phone before they passed, but that's not nearly the same as being able to see their faces one last time. Online video-chats were still just an idea in the real world, but not the world of fiction. I'd read *Neuromancer* by William Gibson, who invented the term 'cyberspace.' He envisioned what a 'real virtual world' would be like. His imagination lit a fire with my imagination, and with that of a lot of others. Since he wrote that book, people in my field have worked to make more and more real the world he imagined."

In *A Treatise on Human Nature*, Hume claimed that it's "an established maxim [that] . . . nothing we imagine is absolutely impossible. We can form the idea of a golden mountain, and from thence conclude that such a mountain may actually exist." Those like Nelson who were inspired by Gibson's imaginings would agree that not only is the imagination the faculty that can contemplate possibilities, but that it can make them real.

"At the high-tech firm where I was first hired," Nelson goes on, "I was part of a group that worked on enhancing video cyber-chats. My role was modest, but it was still almost surreal for me, in the best sense, to actually be part of that. People use cyber-chats for all kinds of purposes, but my own purpose in working to enhance the experience came from imagining doing good things for people who were far from loved ones and couldn't physically bridge the distance."

Nelson is silent for a short time before he goes on to say, "My mom won't be happy till I'm married. I won't be, either. Like Leonardo, I'm too shy when it comes to things like that."

"You know what to do, bro," says Emilio.

Nelson closes his eyes. He is the picture of intense concentration. The smile that emerges is slow and gradual, but soon spreads from ear to ear. If I'm not mistaken, when he opens his eyes, they steal a meaningful glance at Yessica, paramour of his elementary school years.

Nurturing Lifelong Curiosity

The philosopher and essayist Plutarch (46 AD–120 AD) observed that "children are much in love with . . . whatever is curious and subtle." How do we nurture in kids a lifelong love of the curious and subtle? How do we help fire their imaginations in ways that give them the wherewithal— the passion and commitment and discipline—to discover and realize their talents?

In *Some Thoughts Concerning Education*, John Locke opines that "curiosity in children is but an appetite after knowledge, and therefore ought to be encouraged in them . . . as the great instrument nature has provided, . . . and which, without this busy inquisitiveness, will make them dull and useless creatures." Locke likens children to "travellers newly arrived in a strange country of which they know very little. And though their questions seem sometimes not very material, yet they should be seriously answered."

Locke exhorts adults "not to check or discountenance any inquiries [a child] may make, or suffer them to be laughed at; but to answer all his questions and explain the matters he desires to know." Sadly, he observed, all too many children "have found their curiosity baulked and their inquiries neglected."

> But had they been treated with more kindness and respect, and their questions answered as they should, to their satisfaction, I doubt not but they would have taken more pleasure in . . . improving their knowledge, wherein there would be still newness and variety, which is what they are delighted with, than in returning over and over to the same play and playthings.

Whenever an adult makes a heartfelt attempt to sate a child's curiosity in one realm of inquiry, Locke maintains, he is "leading them by the answers into farther questions." Just as importantly, the adult in question is also leading himself further along on a journey of discovery.

> Perhaps to a grown man such conversation will not altogether be so idle and insignificant as he may imagine. The native and untaught suggestions of inquisitive children do often offer things that may set a considering man's thoughts on work. And I think there is often more to be learnt from the unexpected questions of a child, than the discourses of men.

In *The Way to Wisdom*, Karl Jaspers seconds Locke's sentiment. Jaspers asserts that when a child "hears the story of the Creation: In the beginning, God made heaven and earth . . . and immediately asks, 'What was before the beginning?' this child has sensed that there is no end to questioning, that there is no stopping place for the mind. . . ." What would it be like for there to be a final stopping place for the mind? Why do many adults aim for just that, looking to pin down belief systems with conclusive answers?

Giambattista Vico believes we discount the prominent role played by imagination in both our personal development and in the growth of society at our peril. In *On the Study of Methods of Our Time*, Vico notes that since time immemorial "imagination has always been esteemed a most favorable omen of future development" of our youth, and so it stands to reason that "it should in no way be dulled." Vico recalls how the modus operandi of educators was to celebrate how "all arts and disciplines were connected." This enabled students to develop fully their "poetical powers," so they could bring to light connections among subject matter that on the face of it appeared to have nothing in common.

Needless to say, Vico was dismayed over the abrupt change in ethos that led to a concerted effort in his day to make imagination an unfavorable omen in educating young people. The state of educational affairs in Italy had become such that the arts and sciences were "sundered apart." The outspoken advocate for humanistic studies did not pull his punches in condemning this turn of events:

Those responsible for this separation can be compared to a tyrannical ruler who, having seized mastery of a great, populous, and opulent city, . . . in order to secure his own safety, destroy the city and scatter its inhabitants into a number of widely strewn villages. As a consequence, it is impossible for the townsmen to feel inspired.

The system of instruction put into place by his contemporaries made children and youth "unable to engage in the life of the community, to conduct themselves with sufficient wisdom and prudence." Vico's lament resonates powerfully today: in too many schools, the integration of play into learning, even at the youngest ages, is being eliminated. In the US, surely this contributes to (and is a result of) the heightening "imagination deficit" that makes it trying at best to solve our most intractable yet pressing problems on the socioeconomic, educational, environmental, and political fronts.[23] When imagination's dulling is in full force, as Vico indicates, we feel more disconnected from one another, more scattered and strewn about, and of course more alienated from ourselves.

Fancy That

Gaston Bachelard holds that a much-needed bookend to Sigmund Freud's "reality principle"—the term coined by the father of psychoanalysis to connote the ability of the mind to grasp and assess the external world—is an "un-reality principle." This would help us harness our imagination in ways that equip us to visualize and fashion new realities. His advocacy of such a principle is intended to press home the point that there is no such thing as seeing the world as it is; rather, the world is what we make it out to be and make of it. Bachelard maintains that children in particular not only have the "absolute right to imagine the world" as they see fit, but to

---

23 Read about one long-time elementary school teacher's lament about the Gradgrind approach to education—facts, facts, facts—in her stirring essay, "Kindergarten teacher: My job is now about tests and data—not children. I quit." at http://www.washingtonpost.com/blogs/answer-sheet/wp/2014/03/23/kindergarten-teacher-my-job-is-now-about-tests-and-data-not-children-i-quit/.

realize that world. He berates parents and educators for robbing a child of this right once they decide he has reached the "age of reason," whereupon they consider it their obligation "to teach him to be objective—objective in the simple way adults believe themselves to be 'objective.' He is stuffed with sociability . . . He becomes a premature man. This is the same as saying that [he] is in a state of repressed childhood." Which, Bachelard is certain, leads to a repressed adulthood.

Of course, Bachelard's powerful endorsement of giving full and free reign to one's imagination speaks only to its positive aspects. Imagination made real can just as well make the world more of a living hell, if the world one imagines, and then seeks to make come true, represses and demeans others. As Justus Buchler—one of our most exceptional, yet least known, Socratic philosophers of the twentieth century—observes in *Main of Light*, imagination is no more inherently good than it is harmless: "Imagination can be destructive, . . . contrary to the spirit of invention in any of its forms," including "the techniques of moral suppression that intimidate the living millions."

By and large, are destructive imaginings the province of adults? Alison Gopnik is convinced that it is in the DNA of children to employ their imaginations in ways that make for braver, newer, and potentially better worlds. She points to extensive ongoing studies by her and her colleagues of the workings of children's brains that reveal that they are hardwired in such a way that it is second nature for them to "create causal theories of the world, maps of how the world looks. And these theories allow children to envisage new possibilities, and to imagine and pretend that the world is different." Indeed, "even very young children can . . . imagine different ways the world might be in the future and use them to create plans."[24]

As Gopnik points out, conventional adult wisdom on the subject—namely, "that knowledge and imagination, science and fantasy,

---

24 See, among others, Gopnik, A. & Schulz L. (eds). (2007). *Causal learning: Philosophy, psychology and computation*. NY, NY: Oxford University Press, as well as Bonawitz, E. B., Ferranti, D., Saxe, R., Gopnik, A., Meltzoff, A. N., Woodward, J., et al. (2010). "Just do it? Investigating the gap between prediction and action in toddlers' causal inferences." Cognition, 115(1), 104-17.

are deeply different from one another—even opposites"—lags behind newfound insights that they are in many respects of a piece, something kids intuitively grasp. While it is old hat for kids to imagine alternate universes, cosmologists are at last starting to take their cue from them, and contemplate the possibility of parallel universes, or 'multiverses,' as they call them. While so far, such universes are not observable by even the most sophisticated instruments, this is no reason to dismiss out of hand these emerging theories. After all, new scientific theories hinge on the ability to posit and subsequently attempt to reveal hidden likenesses between disparate entities. This process hinges on a finely wrought imagination. It is one that Albert Einstein supposedly swore by: "Imagination is everything. It is the preview of life's coming attractions." Einstein's theory of relativity came to be as the result of a thought experiment. He imagined that he was riding on the end of a light beam. Thankfully he wasn't wedded to the reality principle, since then he would have convinced himself that riding on a light beam isn't possible in the real world.

The Creating Imagination

The Spanish naturalist philosopher George Santayana (1863–1952) considers the best poets those who deliberately set about, as he puts it in *The Life of Reason*, "fancying how creation might have moved upon other lines." Yet our greatest scientists not only fancy how creation might have moved upon other lines, but show that it *did* move along far different lines than those that had been widely presumed.

If ever there was a human who fully developed his imaginative-poetic and reasoning-scientific capacities in tandem, it was Johann Wolfgang von Goethe (1749–1832). Though far more renowned for his epic and lyric poetry, the author of *Faust* was an accomplished natural scientist who wrote important works on morphology (the study of the form and structure of organisms and their specific structural features) and set forth a provocative color theory that remains much talked-about to this day. Walter Kaufmann notes that Goethe's poetry "was not the frosting on an essentially dry and prosaic cake, a make-believe embellishment that covers up the way things truly are," but instead was the wellspring for his scientific reasoning. Then there is Shakespeare, who has long played a prodigious role in shaping modern Western thinking. Charles Darwin, for one, credits Shakespeare's "wonderful knowledge of the human mind" as the impetus for his own work. He dedicates the entire last chapter of *Origin of the Species*—entitled "The Expressions of the Emotions in Man and Animals"—to the bard. Shakespeare was far ahead of his contemporaries in maintaining that the universe was infinite—he even has Hamlet "count myself king of infinite space—and that the sun rather than the earth was at the center of the Milky Way."

I should say he was way ahead of most adults of his time, since children of his day must have counted themselves kings and queens of infinite space as a matter of course, just as they do now. Children transform the most dreary and confining place and space. They turn the tables on constraint. Stressed-out parents and business types rush through airports. Children bound and leap or pretend to swim (my daughter's preference) from one terminal to another, as if they are in a giant aquarium. They are on a grand adventure. Some parents drag them along at breakneck speed on leashes. The more chains put on them, the more their imaginations kick in. Children roam far afield in their minds, transforming their real-world milieu. We adults need to learn to go along with them for the ride.

In *A Midsummer Night's Dream*, Theseus soliloquizes that "the lunatic, the lover, and the poet are of imagination all compact." They possess "such seething brains, such shaping fantasies, that apprehend more than cool reason ever comprehends." Yet, some of our greatest purveyors of cool reason—including the physicist Galileo and the astronomer Copernicus—were viewed as madmen and heretics in their day. The Italian philosopher Giordano Bruno (1548–1600), a remarkable freethinker, was burned at the stake during the Roman Inquisition for shaping a new version of reality that threatened to upend the version that the powers that be endorsed and that propped up their authority.

In this memorable soliloquy, Theseus rhapsodizes,

> And as imagination bodies forth
> The forms of things unknown, the poet's pen
> Turns them to shapes and gives to airy nothing
> A local habitation and a name.

Yet eminent scientists also turn things unknown to shapes and ascribe to airy nothings a local habitation and a name. They are not so different from poets. Or kids.

"What is Imagination?" Ada Lovelace queried as a young scientist who never lost her childlike inventiveness. Her own answer: "that which penetrates into the unseen worlds around us" and "seizes points in common, between subjects having no apparent connection." By this perspective, imagination itself bodies forth the forms of things unknown.

Are kids and exceptional scientists like Lovelace that different from ordinary adults? If so, do they have to be? According to Karl Jaspers, those few souls who manage to make it to adulthood with their imaginative ingenuity intact as it was when they were children are "those great minds" like da Vinci, Socrates, Shakespeare, and the Buddha. John Dewey, on the other hand, is just as certain that while the creative mind at its most exceptional is usually "associated with people who are rare and unique, like geniuses," it is part of us all. Emerson is of like mind. He tells us in "Self-Reliance" that

> a man should learn to detect and watch that gleam of light which flashes across his mind from within, more than the lustre of the firmament of bards and sages. Yet he dismisses without notice his thought, because it is his. In every work of genius we recognize our own rejected thoughts: they come back to us with a certain alienated majesty.

We need emulate no one. Yet many of us end up as copycats, selling short our store of genius. Is it because, despite great lip service to the contrary, genuine originality is too often discouraged, devalued, and diminished in our society, even seen as anathema?

For everyday adults, Karl Jaspers claims, putting imagination to peak use is relegated to sleep hours, and so, "in awaking from sleep, [they] experience strangely revealing insights which vanish with full wakefulness, leaving behind them only the impression that they can never be recaptured." Yet there at least is one occasion during waking hours when some adults harness to the max their imaginations—when they are moved to come to the aid of an upset child. Such adults are masters of invention and creativity. They make up on the spot sounds and songs, stories and poetry; they make movements and gestures they didn't know they had it within them to make—whatever it takes to succor or give joy to a child in need.

Once, when I was on book tour in Italy, my daughter, Cali, then three and a half, had a meltdown to end all meltdowns in the solemn Sistine Chapel. I braced myself for the bevy of guards—who were having a field day scolding tourists who neglected to speak in hushed tones—to usher us out. Instead, they transformed into a bunch of soothing, cooing avuncular figures; their one and only mission in life to calm my child. They picked her up, twirled her around, pointed out all the beauties to behold as they sang in lilting voices. In two minutes flat, they'd redirected her emotions. Cali's blubbering turned to laughter. If I hadn't seen it for myself, I wouldn't have believed it.

I learned a world of lessons about raising my child in those few moments. I wish all those who consider screaming children the scourge of the universe could have seen how the security guards in Italy deftly dealt with Cali. They knew it wasn't her fault, that fault was beside the point, that her sensory world had momentarily overload. The more she screamed, the more compassionate they became. This experienced happened more than once in Italy. Italians love children. That is a sure sign that Rome has not had such a decline and fall after all.

What if we adults treated one another in a similar way? What if we gave one another the benefit of the doubt, showered one another with even more understanding, when we are at our worst? What if we went out of our way to help one another attend to and redirect our darker and more debilitating thoughts and sentiments? What if we devoted the same supply of genius we have in making a child's world brighter, or at least far less dim or forbidding, to our fellow adults? How much more might we flourish as a result? Is it that difficult to visualize such a possibility, much less take strides to make it part of the natural order of things?

Chapter 5

Through the Looking Glass

In *Through the Looking Glass*, Alice is in the great room at her home, listlessly perched in an armchair, when she fixes her attention on a full-length looking glass. She muses about what the world might be like on the other side. She gets up, approaches the looking glass, and studies her reflection. She pokes at it. Alice is amazed that her finger meets with no resistance. Next thing, she steps through. Once on the other side, Alice says, "Oh, what fun it'll be, when they see me through the glass in here, and can't get at me!"

What would it be like, for others to see your surface image, but never be able to "get at" you on the inside, to have no earthly idea what you're thinking or feeling? Is it possible to don an impenetrable façade? If you want others to see you "as you are," is it a must to wear your heart and mind on your life, your life an open book?

Are image and identity one and the same? Or is image mostly about how you're viewed by others, and identity about how you view yourself? What if identity and image have little to do with what's on the inside, and everything to do with what's on the outside? "By their fruits ye shall know them." So says the King James version of Matthew 7:16. It's as if to say that we come to know others by what they sow in the world, by their works and deeds, and that we only can assess what's on the inside of someone by looking at what they say and do and make on the outside.

Is the way that others see you—or the way you think that they see you—all-important in how you see yourself? What about when you're a parent or caregiver? How much influence do the children in your life have in how you see yourself? Does your image of yourself hinge on whether you think you're successful at raising a well-adjusted child? Or on how you best go about helping them develop an honest and thriving sense of self-worth?

Mini Me

I'm sitting on a long, curved filigreed bench with my friends Chrissie, Chandra, and Gabrielle. We've known each other since . . . well, since forever. We were schoolmates and often classmates, starting all the way back in first grade. We graduated together from Menchville High School in Newport News, Virginia, at a time when the city was in the throes of court-ordered desegregation. Since then, I've moved more than twenty times, while they've stayed put in this coastal city in southeastern Virginia that now has a population that tops out at 183,000. Our children are playing at the recently renovated playground that we enjoyed many a day when we were their age and lived in this once–middle class neighborhood.

Whenever I'm in the area—which is often, since my mom still lives here—we have a standing playdate. Like me, my friends became parents much later in life than most of our contemporaries, many of whom have grandchildren. Chrissie, a successful insurance broker, gave birth to fraternal twins at age forty-four. Gabrielle was a year older than Chrissie when her daughter entered the world; the former elementary school art teacher is now a stay-at-home mom. Chandra, the first girl I ever kissed, just a week or so after we started first grade, had almost resigned herself to being childless when she became pregnant at age forty-seven.

"Zaya and I were blowing bubbles earlier this morning," Chandra says to us as she surveys our kids, fast friends, in the distance. Tall and slender, her oval face beautiful in the extreme, Chandra seems hardly to have changed since our high school years.

"Zaya blew an especially big one and it drifted down and hovered in front of her," she goes on. "She said, 'Momma, I can see myself in the bubble! But my image is weird, like one of those trick mirrors where you look all funny and bloated.' Later, as I was holding her in my arms, she stared hard into my eyes. 'Momma, I can see myself!' After a while, she said, 'I wish I could see my own face directly, then I could decide for myself what I really look like.' Then she asked me, 'Momma, can you ever know what you really and truly look like?' What a question! My answer to her was that what she really looks like is the true beauty she is, on the inside and outside. Zaya was pleased with my answer, even if she didn't accept it. 'Momma, you say that because you see me through eyes of love.'

"I could read in my little girl's face that there still was something not quite right with her world. I waited her out. She finally said, 'Momma, I like that my image in your eyes is clear. I can't tell what color I am. It makes you and me look even more like identical twins.' And then: 'I wish everyone who looked at you and me was colorblind.'"

Chandra looks at us. "As you know, she and I are the spitting image. The only difference is my skin is dark, and Zaya's is white. Yet even in our own neighborhood playground, people have come up and asked me, 'Are you the babysitter?' Or: 'Are you the nanny?' It hurts. I can't deny that it influences how I really and truly see myself. Their words cut deep into my self-image. It was only after Zaya's revelation did I realize that they cut deep into hers too."

Chandra shakes her head, the hurt and frustration evident. "How can people be so blind? How can they refuse to see that we're nearly identical? Really, only white people say such thoughtless things to me. To them, image and color go together like peas in a pod. When people of color look at us, they can tell in an instant I'm her mother. They don't consider skin color. They sometimes say to me, 'You could be her older sister.'"

The insight by American pragmatist philosopher, sociologist, and civil rights activist W. E. B. Du Bois (1868–1963) on "double-consciousness" is still pertinent to Chandra and many other people of color in the US in the many decades that have passed since then. Du Bois asserted that it is the inescapable plight of black Americans to fashion an image of themselves through the eyes of white Americans: "It is a peculiar sensation, this double-consciousness, this sense of always looking at one's self through the eyes of others, of measuring one's soul by the tape of a world that looks on in amused contempt and pity. One ever feels his two-ness."

I soon say to my friends, as I watch my daughter show her friends a new thing or two about swinging upside down on monkey bars, "When Cali and I are out together, there are times when someone will say, 'It's so nice to see a grandfather and granddaughter enjoying one another's company.' Even though they say it out of kindness, it changes the way I see myself. It makes me aware of how old I am compared to most fathers of children Cali's age. It takes a while before I can let it go. Cali understands what they're saying, but so far it hasn't seemed to register with her—though just like with Chandra, it may, and she just hasn't shared it with me. As she gets older, and as I get older, I wonder if such remarks will affect the way she sees me, us, herself."

"I wish all of us could be the opposite of Marianne Dashwood," says Chrissie, her countenance thoughtful, speaking of the protagonist in Jane Austen's *Sense and Sensibility*. "Marianne says to her younger sister, 'But I thought it was right, Elinor, to be guided wholly by the opinion of other people.' I try to raise my daughters to form an image of themselves that's guided by their own opinions and no one else's."

"In my case, thank heavens for the opinions of others," says Gabrielle. "I'm my fiercest critic. I need others to help me soften my image of myself. I always wish I could be smarter, prettier, and most of all, shapelier. You know how nitpicky I am about my figure. I'm vain, I know it. I get angry at my husband when I tell him I'm getting on the pudgy side and need to go on a diet, and he tells me I look perfect. That's the last thing I need to hear when I know I need to get in shape."

"Is that really distortion?" I say. "He sees you as he truly sees you, even if you truly see yourself differently."

"Skinny, fat, just right, I suppose it's all in the eyes of the beholder," says Chrissie. "Since I decided I was pudgy, I've lost over twenty pounds. Now my children are on the bandwagon with my husband. They say I'm skinny as a scarecrow, and they miss when I was more 'pillowy.' On any health chart, though, for the median weight for someone of my height and age, I'm still a bit on the overweight side. But tell that to my children or my husband."

Her daughter calls out to her and asks her to watch while she traverses the monkey bars. "Now that girl of mine, Keyla," Chrissie says next, "in terms of looks, she favors her father 'really and truly.' But in terms of personality? She's a 'mini me.'"

Then she says, "Keyla showed me a pretty noticeable ink stain near the insole of her shoe. She confessed she'd put it there herself when she was doodling. She hadn't realized that the felt tip pen had insoluble ink. She was so upset that her shoe had a permanent stain. 'It'll never again look brand new.' I tried to console her. I told her that no one would ever notice, because her foot would cover the small stain.

"She mulled over what I said. I thought I'd won her over. Then she said, 'But *I'll* know!'" Chrissie's smile is wry. "There's no reasoning with or consoling someone with that point of view: 'But *I'll* know!'

"I asked myself, where had I heard that exact same response before? It hit me: I was having a conversation with nine-year-old me. I'd had a similar crisis when I was her age, only mine centered around a smallish stain on a new skirt. 'But *I'll* know,' I'd said to my mom after she said no one else would notice it in a million years. My response to Keyla could have been my own mother's.

"Once this dawned on me, I realized that, in a way, I had a chance to remake history. I didn't want to really and truly be like my mother. I didn't want to, and didn't have to, leave Keyla as inconsolable as my mother had left me. After all, young children don't reason in the same way we do. They're not miniature adults. My mother never got that. I said to Keyla, 'I can't do this every time—in fact, this will probably be the one and only time—but I'll get you a new pair.' My words worked their magic. She stopped pouting at once. She hugged me. I felt so good. I'd charted a new course for our relationship.

"Then Keyla stepped out of our hug. She said to me, 'It's okay, Mommy. I'll keep wearing these shoes. I'll pretend that spot doesn't exist. I know we don't have money for another pair. And even if we did, like you said, no one else would ever notice.' I'll never know for sure, but I'd like to think that I'd have responded in kind if my mother had dealt with me as I did with Keyla. But for me, the most important takeaway is that I really and truly see myself differently now, as someone who can remake myself in an image that's healthier for me and my loved ones. To do this, I had to understand those traits that I'd 'inherited' from my mother that can keep me stuck, and that I can choose to disinherit them."

"There are people from our high school years who are stuck," Chandra says. "You guys didn't miss much at our thirty-fifth reunion. I hadn't gone to any of the previous ones. High school years were painful for me in that cliquish school. If it wasn't for you three here and a couple of others who were part of my support group, my self-image might have been crushed for good during those years. I almost talked myself out of going. But then I thought, I'm being silly, surely everyone has grown up by now, surely it's time to let bygones be bygones and just go and have some fun and get to know everyone as mature grownups.

"Yet no sooner do I walk into the ballroom at the resort where our reunion was held than Yvonne Westfield walks up to me and says 'How's my favorite pothead?' That's who I really and truly am to her, a pothead, because she was present at a party the one and only time I took a toke—even though, like Bill Clinton, I couldn't figure out how to inhale. In our high school days, after that party, she went from calling me 'goody two shoes'—which I hated just as much—to calling me a pothead every time she passed me in the hall. When she said that to me at the reunion, it was like all those years that had passed since then evaporated. It was all I could do to bite my lip to keep from saying, 'How's my favorite slut?' Tit for tat.

"I almost did an about-face to leave, but I decided to stick around. After all, people who say things like that to get your goat do so because they feel so insecure. As the night wore on, I talked with some others I hadn't seen in years who'd stayed in touch with Yvonne. Turns out she's had a hard life, been in abusive relationships. Her glory days were those precious high school years, when she was prom queen, cheerleader, slut to the star athletes. How she really and truly sees me now—or really, pretends to see me—is tied up with how she sees herself. Before I left, I went up to Yvonne and gave her a big hug. I gave her my card and told her to give me a ring sometime so we could meet over a cup of coffee. She was caught off guard and touched. Maybe over time, we'll really and truly see one another in a different—*better* different—light."

"Is that the goal, to see yourself and others in the best light, rather than as they really and truly are, warts and all?" I ask. "When I went out on dates in my high school years, my mother would say to me before I left, 'Be your best self.' I would think, 'I'm not going for a job interview. I'm not looking for eternal love. I'm going on a date. Can't I just be a good and entertaining self and hope to steal some kisses, maybe lose my virginity? Do I have to shoot for the highest bar and be my best self?'"

"To get those kisses, or more, they have to like you, have to see you in a good light—not a best self in a job interview light, but in a romantic light," says Chrissie, who just completed her bachelor's degree, in philosophy, at nearby Christopher Newport University—over thirty years after matriculating but then having to leave in order to care for her disabled father. "Jean-Paul Sartre said you should strive to be your authentic self, in whatever context you find yourself in. He brings up this one example, about a young woman who lets her date take her hand. By 'neither consenting nor resisting,' by being passive to her date's gesture, Sartre says she's being inauthentic, because her message to her date is, 'Whether you're being a gentleman or a cad, it's all the same with me, so do with me what you will.'"

Chandra is incredulous. "All that message just from letting her date take her hand? I used to let a guy take my hand on a first date, maybe kiss me, but if he got the idea he could get past first base, he'd wish he hadn't."

"Take it from one who knows," I say. "You were no Yvonne Westfield."

Chandra's full-throated laugh brings others in the vicinity to smile. She soon gets more serious and says to us, "An image is in part something you project. Whatever you project at any given moment is the self you really and truly are to those in your presence at the time. You have to be conscious of that, and act conscientiously. In that vein, Zaya's actions toward others, good or bad, say something about me, too. Her actions reflect on me, on who I am as a person, a mother, on what my values are, on how I've raised her. Likewise, my actions reflect on her and how she sees herself.

"Now, my ex, may I never see him again as long as I live, he was a master of masks," she says. "I didn't see his true colors until a good while after I'd walked down the aisle with him. Then the mask came off. The difference between the image my ex-husband projects in public—you'd think he was a saint—and in private—he's the devil incarnate—is astonishing."

"That makes me think of my dad," I say. "He was confident in his professional life. You could see it in his bearing. It wasn't because of any false or distorted image he was trying to project. His job gave him a great deal of self-esteem. In private life, especially at home, he was on shakier ground. When he was lagging in confidence, the lisp he'd developed as a child—from being tormented mercilessly by schoolmates for speaking with a thick Greek accent—would return. He didn't have a father to defend him—he died when my dad was seven—and his mother didn't speak much English. But it leads me to wonder whether your authentic self varies, depending on the setting, and on whether you're in your comfort zone."

"Surely it does," says Gabrielle. "If my son Crispin is comfortable in your company, he'll talk your ear off. But it can take him ages to reach that comfort zone with you. Even when he was in his fourth month of first grade, he wasn't yet talkative in class. Both are his 'authentic selves.'"

Then she says, "As you know, in October, my father died after suffering a massive heart attack. He's a widower and was staying with us while Bob is serving a tour of duty in Afghanistan. My father and Crispin were very close. When Crispin returned to school the week following my father's funeral, I received a call from the secretary, asking me to come there and meet with his teacher. Crispin's teacher told me that at lunch time, he started wailing and kept calling out for his father. She said Crispin wouldn't explain why he was so upset. I tried to explain that his dear grandfather had just passed away, and this was surely why he had this anxiety about his father.

"His teacher paid me little mind. She had her own agenda. She told me Crispin wouldn't make eye contact with her when she tried to calm him down and find out what was wrong. Then she said, 'He's never been very communicative with me. I'm convinced he has Asperger's. You should get him checked for that right away.' A teacher who'd known my son for a short while had 'diagnosed' him. Crispin was in mourning! He was experiencing incredible sorrow, and an anxiety and concern for his dad that sprang from that. Labeling him inappropriately—just because she didn't know how to handle his outpouring of grief—was a grave injustice. I've had Crispin switched to another class. His former teacher is insulted and won't acknowledge our presence any more—talk about not making eye contact. She wasn't able to deal with his deep grief, and so she saw what she really and truly—and falsely—wanted to see in him, in order to rationalize her own inadequacy in responding to him."

A while afterward, Chrissie says, "I've been guilty of projecting my own fears and insecurities onto my children. A few days ago, I came here with Madison. It looked like we had the playground to ourselves. But soon afterward, a little girl arrived with her mother and ran to join Madison in the sandbox. She whispered something in Madison's ear. I looked over at the child's mother. She'd gone off to smoke a cigarette, didn't even check to see what her daughter was doing. The little girl—her name was Mia—followed Madison wherever she went in the playground.

"After a while, Madison climbed a ladder to the top of a steep sliding board. Mia was getting ready to follow in tow. But Madison changed her mind and decided to come back down. The slide was too high for her liking. But Mia took Madison's decision to climb down to mean that she didn't want her to follow. She began sobbing and carrying on over what she felt sure was rejection. I distanced Madison from the situation at once. I picked her up and literally ran away. I couldn't deal with it. I've always run away from emotional encounters. I'm sure it has to do with my own upbringing and how my family avoided them at all costs, since it would lead to an explosion. I've transferred all that fear and anxiety to my daughter. I convinced myself that Madison wanted to run away too.

She didn't resist me when I picked her up and carried her away. When we got to the playground shelter, I asked Madison if the little girl's crying had bothered her. Not in the least, she said. So I asked why she didn't say anything when I ran off with her. She said to me, 'I knew you needed to get away.' I then asked Madison if she liked the little girl. She said, yes, she did. I asked what Mia had whispered in her ear. She said: 'I want to be your friend.' I should have let Madison take the lead in handling Mia's crying spell.

"We went back to the playground. Mia was sitting in the sandbox, sniffling. Her mother was still off in the distance, smoking and talking on her phone, oblivious to our unfolding drama. Madison went straight to the sandbox. She pulled out a hairbrush from her jacket pocket and began brushing Mia's hair. She didn't try to console her, didn't try to pull her out of her mood. It was the most loving thing. She let Mia just be, let her bask in her undivided attention and non-judgmentalism." She pauses in thought. "You know, Madison does the same with me. How many times has she brushed my hair, and I thought it was just something she was doing to occupy her time, when she was really being there for me when I was in a gloomy moment. I'm only just learning what she really and truly is like. I've let my image of her be clouded by my own shortcomings."

Just then, Madison leaps off her swing in midflight, and hits the ground running toward her mother, into whose awaiting arms she now jumps. "I look up to you," Chrissie says to her, tousling her wavy red hair. "If one day who I really am is anything like who you truly are, I'll be a happy mother, a better person."

The Looking Glass Self

What do we really and truly look like, to ourselves? Near the turn of the twentieth century, the American sociologist Charles Cooley extensively interviewed children about how they construct their self-image. He concluded that they go about it based on how they deem that others perceive them. Cooley (1864–1929) relates in his landmark *Human Nature and the Social Order* that the self we cultivate "might be called the reflected or looking glass self."

> As we see our face, figure, and dress in the glass, and are interested in them because they are ours, and pleased or otherwise with them according as they do or do not answer to what we should like them to be; so in imagination we perceive in another's mind some thought of our appearance, manners, aims, deeds, character, friends, and so on, and are variously affected by it.

Cooley goes on to contend that "the thing that moves us to pride or shame, is not the mere mechanical reflection of ourselves, but an imputed sentiment, the imagined effect of this reflection upon another's mind." He encapsulates his views in a bit of verse: "Each to each a looking-glass reflects the other that doth pass." By this perspective, we are at the tender or harsh mercies of others with whom we interact—or at least, of how we imagine these others to see us and our acts—when it comes to sculpting our selves.

Cooley's contemporary, the philosopher, psychologist, and sociologist George Herbert Mead (1863–1931), agrees with him that the self is a totally social phenomenon. To Mead, though, our self-image is wrought in a more proactive way. As he puts it in his major work, *Mind, Self and Society*, it is created by "taking on the role of the other." As we interact with others, we assume their personas as our own—effectively trying on a variety of selves for size—and see if any of them, singly or in combination, might be a good fit for us.

The young are particularly good at this. Not only do children make it a habit of taking on the roles of "real" others, but they assume the role of imagined or fictional characters as well. Janet Wilde Astington at the Institute of Child Study is among leading developmental specialists who observe that pretend play, pretense, role play, are dual exercises by children in further cultivating empathy and in creating a satisfying self-image. It enables children to step in others' shoes, experiment with alternative states of mind and well-being (or unwell-being). It hones their ability to understand different sets of beliefs, values, and feelings.

It turns out that adults can take a similar route to empathy development. A study published in the October 2013 issue of the journal *Science* reports that those who read literary fiction perform at a significantly higher level on tests that gauge empathy, emotional intelligence, and social perception. They enter age-appropriate worlds of pretense, and emerge from the experience with a keener ability to connect in a more meaningful way with others, and themselves.

Through a Glass, Darkly

"For now we see through a glass, darkly." This oft-quoted biblical passage in 1 Corinthians 13 is taken to mean that we see but a dim image of people, places, and things. The Hellenic Greek term that has long been rendered "glass" in English actually means "mirror" or "looking glass." To the Apostle Paul, to see through a looking glass darkly is to have a blurred or obscured view—of oneself, of others, of the world. It's akin to someone imprisoned in Plato's cave, where at best one can see mere shadows of real objects. Like the Apostle Paul, Plato held a dim view of the ability of children to see clearly. Both believed that only adults have that capacity. Shakespeare's Macbeth at least is an equal opportunity pessimist, and believes none of us can see very well: "Life's but a walking shadow, a poor player, that struts and frets his hour upon the stage, and then is heard no more."

How do you go about seeing yourself more clearly? Is some distortion of "the real you" inevitable, not just by others but by you, yourself?

The full passage of that famous Corinthians section goes: "For now we see through a glass, darkly; but then face to face: now I know in part; but then shall I know even as also I am known." The promise is held out that the more you know others, the more you will know yourself. Sophocles's Oedipus knew better than anyone that this is not necessarily the case. Oedipus was able to solve the vexing riddle of man in general, yet this did not help him in solving the riddle of himself, in seeing who he really and truly was. What we fail to see can be tragic. Oedipus can't see what is staring him in the face. When the truth is revealed, he is so overcome that he blinds himself. At the end of *Oedipus the King*, after Oedipus discovers that he murdered his father and married his mother, the chorus shares the cautionary tale that even if you are adept at fathoming the great riddles, it is no assurance that you know all important truths. And so it is that Oedipus, fond of describing himself as a "child of Chance" who, steered by good fortune, started out life as a foundling and wound up as king, is in fact the unfortunate and cursed son of Laius and Jocasta. We are one step away from humility, one step away from discovering a truth that can bring the arrogant and mighty and proud to their knees, or that can make the humble even humbler. Or alternatively, maybe at times we are one step away from discovering a truth that will lift us up, if we can see through the willful distortions of others who would keep us down.

Socrates experienced a life-altering moment when the Oracle of Delphi enjoined, "Know thyself!" From that point forward, he was a man with a plan. In Plato's *Alcibiades*, Socrates cogitates to himself and his interlocutor: What if the Oracle's command to him had been instead, "See thyself!" How would we understand such advice? Socrates takes a stab at answering his own question. He notes that there is "something of the nature of the mirror in our own eyes," and so when someone else looks into them, there's "a sort of image of the person looking." By this take, we each serve as a looking glass for the other.

What if Hamlet had proclaimed: "To see or not to see, that is the question." We see and we don't. We see with lenses of love, or hate, or many other emotions. We see some things, and are blind to others, based on our belief systems, values, and cultural influences. This can lead us to emphasize, exaggerate, ignore, diminish, or distort certain qualities we detect in others.

What kind of looking glass are you for others? Do you tend to despise those who have the qualities you most despise in yourself? Do you often hold in the highest esteem those who have qualities you believe that you possess, qualities you most highly prize? Do you seek to see the best in others, until convinced otherwise? Or do you aim from the outset to see them as they really and truly are, with total objectivity? If so, does this require refined judgment skills or refraining from judgment?

How about when you try to see yourself as you really are? Is this an exercise in futility, or at the heart of knowing yourself, no matter how short you may fall in the attempt? The essayist Phillip Lopate, in "Portrait of My Body," describes what he sees when he appraises himself in a mirror. The image he confronts expresses "both the strain of intellectual overachieving and the tabula rasa of immaturity . . . for it is still, underneath, a boy in the mirror. A boy with a rapidly receding hairline."

> How is it that I've remained a boy all this time . . . ? I remember, at seventeen, drawing a self-portrait of myself as I looked in the mirror. . . . I still encounter in the glass that haunted uncertainty—shielded by a bluffing shell of cynicism, perhaps, but untouched by wisdom. So I approach the mirror warily, without lighting up as much as I would for the least of my acquaintances; I go one-on-one with that frowning schmuck.

Sort of like Shakespeare's Richard III, who refuses to "court an amorous looking-glass," Lopate believes he has to take the gloves off before going toe to toe with himself, if he's to come up with any sort of honest assessment that can lead to further personal development.

Is that bluffing shell Lopate describes a mask, and if so, must it be ripped off if he's to encounter who he really is? "It takes courage to interrogate yourself," maintains Cornel West in *Hope on a Tightrope*. "It takes courage to look in the mirror and see past your reflection to who you really are when you take off the mask, when you're not performing the same old routines and social roles." West's views are inspired by Sartre, who claims that those who wear masks are being willfully inauthentic, and must "unmask" themselves.

In the period of my life between my midtwenties and midthirties, I was living the freelance journalist's version of the fast life. On those rare occasions when I took a moment to contemplate my reflection, I felt like I was looking at someone I used to know but with whom I now had only a passing acquaintanceship. I'd look away, fast. The prospect of unmasking myself was dread inducing. I didn't care to come to grips with my contradilions, how I was both an over- and underachiever, how I could act with virtue one moment and vice soon after, how I could engage in both extreme life-affirming and self-destructive acts, how I somehow managed both to mature and regress. It took a crisis—the suicide of a dear friend— for me to force that unflinching self-confrontation. It required other mirrors as well, especially those held up by caring others who would listen to me at length while withholding judgment and who helped me see in new lights the person I was and to imagine and then plan a strategy for sculpting the one I aspired to be. Without them, I wouldn't have made it through to the other side of despair. I took to heart Rainer Maria Rilke's exhortation in the final line of *Archaic Torso of Apollo*: "You must change your life." It prompted me to break out of a world of self-imposed barriers and take sublime risks, one of which was to abandon my journalism career and start Socrates Café. Ever since, I've taken a more childlike approach to self-seeking, a "process" approach, in which the seeking itself is at the core of who I am.

Say what? What is a childlike, process approach to self?

René Descartes' (1596–1650) famous claim is that the one and only thing adults know for certain is that they have a self, because only thinking creatures possess one. He puts it this way: "*Cogito ergo sum.*" I think therefore I am. Children, considered by Descartes and most others in his time to be largely unthinking creatures, were not given credit for having much if anything resembling a self. Yet children have a distinct sense of self, but it is so different from the type of self that adults have and prize that they fail to recognize it as such. The self of a child is a seeking self, not in the sense that they are seeking their "selves" as an entity, but rather, in wondering about the world and their place in it, they are demonstrating "selves in action." Their philosophy of self is, "I wonder, therefore I am."

To John Dewey, "the self is not something ready-made, but something in continuous formation through choice of action"—or inaction. Many choices we make are not conscious ones, yet can have a decisive impact on our self-formation, or self-unraveling. Can self-formation ever be "beyond choice," particularly early on in our lives? What is second nature to infants and toddlers is a kind of self in which choices are informed by an incurable sense of wonder. It is a self that thrives on interdependence and interconnectedness and that almost can't help but grow until corrupted by those older than them who would limit their possibilities for constructing a self, and as a result, also put strict limits on their range of choices.

While Karl Jaspers believes the self is a fixed entity, his stance on the matter is nonetheless Socratic because he challenges the received wisdom that a self is only something that comes to be with age. He believes that just the opposite is often the case, that our sense of self can start out clear and get fuzzier over time. Jaspers contends that children have a remarkable awareness of themselves as "selves:"

> It is not uncommon to hear from the mouths of children words which penetrate to the very depths of philosophy. A child cries out in wonderment, "I keep trying to think that I am somebody else, but I'm always myself." This boy has touched on one of the universal sources of certainty, awareness of being through awareness of self. He is perplexed at the mystery of his I, this mystery that can be apprehended through nothing else.

Charles Sanders Peirce (1839–1914), the father of the pragmatist tradition in American philosophy,[25] would surely value kids' remarkable fluidity of self, to him a sure sign of a robust self. He asserts that "man's circle of society (however widely or narrowly this phrase may be understood) is a sort of loosely compacted person, in some respects of higher rank than the person of an individual organism." In like vein, the child self is like a loosely compacted person, more open to experimentation, evolution, and sculpting. It is a self without fixed boundaries between the inner and outer world. So it is, for instance, that when another person in their orbit is in pain, they own this pain too, because they truly believe that it is just as much theirs. If such empathy without

---

25 Those in the pragmatist camp typically hold that the value of any theory or belief system hinges on its success in practical application, in particular as a tool for prediction of consequences or outcomes in the realm of action or problem-solving.

borders is a plus for matters of self-improvement and self-growth, then the child self might be looked at as one of higher rank than the more atomistic adult type.

Identity Crisis

"Who should you identify with?" The question is posed by Shir. The seventeen-year-old is sitting cross-legged on one of the comfortable couches that take up three walls in a common room. Her dark brown locks spill out of a knit cap and frame wide, intense blue-gray eyes.

I'm at a residential substance abuse treatment center that offers comprehensive services to older adolescents and young adults, many of whom have been homeless. A Los Angeles–area social worker who has read my books and who occasionally attends a Socrates Café gathering at a local library arranged for me to hold a dialogue here. She wasn't positive they'd be open to it, since some don't reveal a great deal about themselves even to staff members. I said I was investigating themes that had to do with identity and asked if they had suggestions for a question we might take a stab at delving into.

After Shir poses her question, Ravi looks at her in a quizzical way. "Don't you mean, 'Who *do* you identify with?'"

Shir shakes her head. "My mother kicked me out of the house because who I am doesn't conform with her religious values.[26] For her, the only possibility for reconciliation is if I quit being queer. I grapple with depression and anxiety. I wish I could be who she wants me to be. But who I am is who I am. Shouldn't I be able to identify with that?"

"You should," Ravi says to her now. "You should be able to say with pride, 'I am who I am,' and like Popeye, 'I yam what I yam.' If you act in a way that goes against who and what you are, just to please others, you're identifying with a false self."

---

26 Studies reveal that a third or more of homeless teens who are not heterosexual were forced to leave home.

Ravi's view is kindred to that of Sartre, who held that we must make and act on choices that are truly our own, without outside influence, if they are to reflect our "true selves." To the extent that we fail to do so, Sartre believed, we are being inauthentic, reflecting a false self because we have acted in "bad faith."

Then Ravi says, "My parents think I shouldn't identify with who and what I am, either. My gender is fluid. Some days I'm a girl, others a guy, others androgynous. I wasn't literally pushed out of my home, but I was *persona non grata*. I want to fit in. I want them to love me. But when I act only in ways that meet with their approval, I can't but hate myself.

"On any given day," he goes on to say, "I could fall in love with someone anywhere along the gender spectrum, as long as they're gentle, kind, caring—qualities we should all identify with—if I weren't down on myself. It's kept me from forming close relationships."

"That should be the beauty of humanity," says Shir, "that you should be able to be whomever you are, or whomever you want to be or experiment with being, without apology, as long as you're not infringing on someone else's person. But even with some friends, I'm made to feel uncomfortable with who I am. I've been accused of not being 'queer enough.' What does that mean? If they had their way, I'd identify with who they think I should be, and act accordingly. But there's no one way to act as a queer, no more than there is one way to act if you're straight, pansexual, asexual, gender fluid, or whatever."

The provocative post-structuralist philosopher Judith Butler goes so far as to say that we're not born with a specific gender. She considers gender a social artifice that is fluid and subject to continual shift or change. Far from being an inherent attribute, Butler believes that our culture teaches us to "perform" specific gender roles.

Adam, tall, soft-spoken, square-shouldered, has been riveted. He came to the city from the Navajo reservation several months ago and was living in an abandoned building before he was admitted here. "All of you who've spoken so far, you know who you are," he says, "and who you are is good. Like Hamlet said, 'To thine own self be true.' Being true to yourself isn't a matter of 'should,' but of 'have to.' But first you have to know who you are. I'm struggling to figure that out. There's so much drama in any adolescent's life. Multiply that by about a thousand when you're Native American.[27] The pressure to live by others' expectations—of your peers, of traditional adult Navajos, of moderns, of whites—suffocates you."

"You shouldn't *have* to identify with anyone," says Quay not long afterward. "I don't identify with a solitary soul. 'Should' doesn't enter into it. To identify means you can see something of yourself in someone, that you can relate to someone in some way. I can't relate to anyone. I feel like an alien dropped on a strange planet."

"Do you identify with others who feel the same as you do?" I ask.

Quay doesn't reply right away. Finally he says, "I may not interact with other loners, but I suppose I can relate to some others who go their own way, who are outside of groups, whether by choice or because they're rejected. But the question is, 'should I?'"

"I listen to the music of the hip-hop group Outkast," he says next. "Ruben Bailey, the group's founder, he tells you straight up in his music that going your own way isn't easy. Ruben says that the people who dig his music are, like him, not part of the normal everyday crowd. They follow a different drummer. The mainstream treats people like him and me either like we're invisible or lepers. But we outcasts should take pride in how different we are from the mainstream, and from one another. We're not different for the sake of it, but because we dare to be who we are. I'm not quite sure how to put this, but we should identify with our determination to be ourselves, even if it means we're rejected by the rest of the world."

After a short lull, Rodolfo says to us, "I lost myself in my girlfriend. I felt like a person without a face when she left me." His look is anxious and sad. "She made me feel so good, man, made me think who I was was the finest. I'd always been on the outside looking in, until we became a couple.

---

27 American Indian teens take their own lives at more than two times the rate of any other teen demographic in the US according to statistics from the Centers for Disease Control and Prevention.

When she dropped me . . . man, I went down hard. I shouldn't have identified so much with her, shouldn't have lost myself in that relationship."

What Rodolfo shares is evocative of a passage in Ford Madox Ford's *The Good Soldier*: "We are all so afraid, we are all so alone, we all so need from the outside the assurance of our own worthiness to exist." This need is especially keen in a romantic relationship, due to the "fierceness of desire" and a man's "craving for identity with the woman that he loves. He desires to see with the same eyes, to touch with the same sense of touch, to hear with the same ears, to lose his identity, to be enveloped, to be supported."

"When I was younger, I lost myself in a different way, in a gang," Rodolfo goes on to tell us. "I was faceless in that situation, too. I didn't have to take responsibility for my actions. Then I find a girlfriend, fall in love, she helps get me on the right path. Only I end up losing myself again, this time in this one person."

The others on hand hang on his every word, their brows creased with compassion, despite their own personal travails. "You have to be able to—you should, you must, be able to—have a solid identity, so you can bear being totally alone, if it comes to that," Rodolfo tells us. "Only then can you identify with others, and them with you, in the right way, from a foundation of self-esteem. If you don't take that approach, and those you identify with bail on you, you'll do anything, take anything, to keep from facing yourself."

This eventually prompts Shir to say, "I identified with Amy Winehouse. She was totally true to herself." Shir is referring to the retro soul musician, a Grammy winner with a history of drug abuse problems who died in July 2011. "She was a rebel, a songwriter, a performing artist who lived on the edge. She turned her incredibly difficult life experiences into beautiful lyrics about pain and suffering, love and loss. As an aspiring artist, I try to do the same."

Then she says, "She made that boast in her song 'Rehab' about how people tried to get her to go clean, and how she refused. That refusal on her part—no, no, no—it became an anthem for me and my friends. When she died of an overdose, it was my wake-up call. I was heading down the same path, celebrating the dark side. She said in that song that she'd always survive, always come back, no matter how many times she put herself right there on the abyss. But she didn't come back. She fell into that abyss."

Shir takes an inward turn before she brings us back into focus. "I no longer identify with Amy all the way. I've come to realize that I shouldn't. There is too much I still want to experience in this world. But you know, she did more in her twenty-seven years than most do in a long life. She rose from poor roots to achieve fame and, even better, to leave behind some special songs. Even so, I don't want my own story to have a tragic ending. While I believe I should, like Amy, pour my pain and suffering into my lyrics, I should do so without drugs or alcohol."

"I used to think I deserved to be used and abused," says Marina in due time, breaking what seems to have been her silent pledge to participate only by listening. "Drugs dulled my senses to the point that I didn't feel that I was being used and abused. Now that I'm clean, and am in counseling, I'm understanding how much my body image has to do with how I'd seen myself in a negative light, and the connection between my low image of myself and drug use. If I don't like what's on the outside of me, that effects how I feel about myself on the inside.

"My mother has told me since I was thirteen that I needed plastic surgery for my nose, my chin, my boobs," she says. "It was one of her most effective ways to make me feel bad about the way I am. I'm struggling to grasp the lesson, the truth, that I shouldn't identify with how my mother—or anyone else who looks at me as physically imperfect, or imperfect in any other way—sees me. It's how I see myself that counts."

This brings Adam to say, "I've been an exercise freak since my early teens. These last years, though, for me it hasn't been enough to have a chiseled body. I want a 'perfect' body. I became fanatical about using steroids and hormones to try to sculpt that body I see in all the magazine covers. The more perfect I tried to look—trying to fit some image of perfect that you see in film or ads—the less perfect I actually felt, because my physique didn't match up to those images. I became anorexic. I changed every healthy habit in order to look a certain way.

"You shouldn't identify with these kinds of ideal body images you see," he goes on. "The people with those images, you don't know if they really look like that. Even if they do, you'll never feel adequate if you're all the time comparing your physique with theirs. You'll make yourself feel inferior. That's never good identifying—a 'should not' when it comes to identifying."

After a moment, Quay says, "I used to be really close to my mom. She doesn't understand why I've closed myself off. I've told my mom she needs to quit worrying about me, get on with her life. But she will deny herself any kind of enjoyable life until and unless I straighten myself out. I make her miserable, put her through hell again and again. My pains and sufferings are hers.

"If you asked my mother if she should identify with me, she would think the question was crazy," he says next, "She'd reply, 'Should? I do. He's my son, my flesh and blood.' For her, it's beyond should. When she looks at me and sees me suffering, she might as well be the one suffering herself. I should try to relate more to what it's like to be in my mother's shoes, and relate to the pain she feels for me."

The philosopher, social critic and political activist Simone Weil (1909–1943) uses the term "attention" to connote the kind of caring that can only be had when you make a heartfelt attempt to identify so fully with another that their sufferings are your own. To Weil, such attention is "a way of looking at ourselves and others" at one and the same time.

Mikeia has been on the periphery, leaning against the entrance to the common room, throughout our exchange, her arms folded, posture defensive. But now she is moved to say, "Janice, who runs this program, has helped make sure my baby isn't taken away from me for good. My baby's in a foster home just a mile away. I relapsed soon after Sophia was born. Janice has seen to it that I have regular visitation rights. She advocates for me. I look up to her because she doesn't look down on me. She looks straight at me. You should only identify with those you see, and who see you, as an equal.

"If I—when I—make it to the other side, I'll work toward becoming a substance abuse counselor, like Janice. I don't have the slightest idea what her life experiences are. She's never told me, and I've never asked. But

what a world it would be if we all identified with her way of always looking straight at a person as an equal."

Mikeia comes all the way in, takes a perch on the edge of a sofa, and
passes around a picture of her adorable daughter. When the picture is
handed back, she stares at it, as if communing with her child. "I identify
with my Sophia. I don't know if 'should' is part of it. I look at her, and I
see that helpless creature in me too. But I have to be strong, for her, really
for both of us. My baby is purity and innocence. Some may think I don't
have those qualities. But we all do. We were all babies once and that baby
within will always be part of us. When Sofia looks in my eyes, her look is
one of unconditional love, and I know that's what she sees in my face too.

"I'll tell Sophia about my hard times someday, how I was shuttled
around like a beach ball from one foster home to another since I was a
little kid. I want her to know that story, of someone who basically had
to raise herself, who was wronged too many times, and who made some
mistakes out of despair—but only after I've turned the corner, so she'll
identity with the qualities of perseverance and determination that it took
for me to overcome my past."

Now that Mikeia has started speaking, the words keep pouring out.
"I identify with all others who are moms—all who are *good* moms—no
matter how different we are in other parts of our lives or in terms of our
lived experiences." Mikeia makes eye contact with each of us and then
says, "Who should each of us here identify with? With all those souls who
maybe make a million mistakes a day, but try their best to live and love
the right way."

Identity, Life, and Death

As public intellectual and Socratic gadfly Cornel West aptly notes in
Democracy Matters, identity "is often a subject of leisurely conversation
and academic banter." In contrast, for those on the margins and those
excluded altogether, "identity is a matter of life and death. Identity has
to do with who one is and how one moves from womb to tomb—the

elemental desires for protection, recognition, and association in a cold and cruel world." The message with which too many adolescents, among others, considered different in unacceptable ways are bombarded is, "you are not like us, and that is not okay." Under such circumstances, their elemental cry for protection, recognition, and association falls on deaf ears.

According to the Canadian philosopher Charles Taylor, a leading authority in identity politics, due recognition of our fellow humans is, as he puts it in *Philosophical Arguments*, "not just a courtesy we owe people. It is a vital human need." Taylor holds that we must recognize and celebrate the fact that "each of us has an original way of being human: each person has his or her own 'measure.' There is a certain way of being human that is *my* way." Yet those whose natures deviate too much from the preconceived norm are told that their way of being human is the wrong way.

Taylor notes that there is a great deal of willful *mis*recognition, that some are deliberately seen through distorted lenses, and that this leads them to create a "confining or demeaning or contemptible picture of themselves." How do those on the receiving end of misrecognition combat it? In Taylor's estimation, through dialogue: "We define our identity always in dialogue with, sometimes in struggle against, the things our significant others want to see in us" and we have to make it clear "who we are [and] 'where we're coming from.' It is the background against which our tastes and desires and opinions and aspirations makes sense." But this can only be accomplished if the significant others in one's life don't slam the door shut on dialogue. If they refuse to open themselves to the earnest and heartfelt attempts of those who want to express where they're coming from, this can cripple their capacity to form tastes, desires, opinions, and aspirations in ways that construct a healthy identity.

In *Cosmopolitanism: Ethics in a World of Strangers*, the Princeton philosopher Kwame Anthony Appiah sets forth a philosophy of recognition that stresses our obligations to one another, as individuals linked together and as fellow members of the human race. To Appiah, we should celebrate the "value not just of human life but of particular human lives." The British-born scholar, now a US citizen, whose Ghanaian father was at the forefront of his nation's fight for independence, contends that we need to resuscitate an ethos of "cosmopolitanism." First practiced by the Greek Cynics—members of an ancient school who believed that the purpose of life was to live in virtue—a guiding tenet of cosmopolitism is that while we may have a variety of differences that stem from the religious, cultural, and national identities to which we adhere, we nonetheless have fundamental "identity ties" that bind us, and that we better come to appreciate and celebrate when we see ourselves as fellow citizens of the world. Appiah asserts that whenever in human history cosmopolitanism has been widespread—such as during the Enlightenment of the late seventeenth and eighteenth centuries—it has been the springboard for unprecedented human flourishing. To revive this ethos in modern times, Appiah urges us to create a kind of self-identity of a sort that is an ongoing "life project," so that it's "not too tightly scripted," always capable of further unfolding—and of *better* unfolding, the more we open ourselves to new identity possibilities by encountering and communing with others who are not like us.

"The final responsibility for each life," Appiah asserts, "is always the responsibility of the person whose life it is." However, for this responsibility to be fully exercised, society itself must strive to create the kinds of fertile conditions that make it possible.

Hello, Stranger

One dialogue participant said he felt "like an alien dropped on a strange planet." That's par for the course, not just among adolescents but for those at any age, according to Roger Scruton, the well-regarded modern English philosopher who specializes in aesthetics and cultural issues. "We are not at home in the world, and thus homelessness is a deep truth about our condition," he posits (as quoted in Jim Holt's *Why Does the World Exist?*). So it is, to Scruton, that 'we fall' into a world where we are strangers."

Alienation may well be part of the human condition. But to whom are we most strangers? To one another? To ourselves? Are all forms of "homelessness" created equal? Some of us are fortunate enough to "fall" into a world in which we have a soft and loving landing, and then are raised in a nurturing environment. Ours is a different kind of homelessness than that of, say, youth forced to leave their homes by those who rule the roost, because they are deemed different in a shameful way. They are subjected to deep and harsh truths about how some adults condition themselves to be intolerant, even toward their own progeny, if their natures do not conform with their values—leading often to an extreme form of alienation that stunts rather than drives growth.

According to Walter Kaufmann, alienation is the price we pay for coming into our own. Alienation, which Kaufmann characterizes in *Without Guilt and Justice* as "our second childhood, . . . is part of growing up."

> Self-consciousness cannot develop without it. Not only is the world 'other' . . . but the world is also extremely strange and cruel. Hence, as perception increases, any sensitive person will feel a deep sense of estrangement. Seeing how society is riddled with dishonesty, stupidity, and brutality, he will feel estranged from society, and seeing how most of one's fellow men are not deeply troubled by all this, he will feel estranged from them.

It is too often the case, though, that adolescents are made to feel estranged from *themselves*. The ignorance, dishonesty, and stupidity practiced toward them, especially if by those who reared them, can cause a kind of self-alienation that should never be part of anyone's growing up, since it can lead to the creation of a stunted form of self-consciousness.

Hegel held a rosy view of the family unit, which he considered a cocoon against alienation. To him, only when a child leaves the family nest to fend for himself in the outside world does alienation enter into the equation. Hegel fails to acknowledge the tragic reality that the family unit can at times serve as the incubator for a harmful form of alienation that can push youth to the depths of despair. Be that as it may, in his *Lectures on the History of Philosophy*, Hegel makes it clear that he considers the bond between parent and child sacrosanct, and so "the worst thing that can happen to children . . . is that the bond . . . should be loosened or even severed, thereby causing hatred, disdain, and ill-will. Whoever does this does injury to morality."

Do those who intentionally try to make any of our youth think less of themselves, just because they are being who they are, do injury not just to morality, but to humanity? Hegel would have us believe that the bond that exists between every parent and child is "the mother's milk of morality on which man is nurtured." By this view, parents who willingly let go of their children because they do not conform to their expectations and values are doing a kind of injury that, following Hegel's metaphor, is the mother's milk of immorality.

Self-Dissatisfaction

When Socrates heeded the Oracle of Delphi's injunction, "Know thyself," it was a tacit recognition that he considered the self not to be a ready-made entity, but instead something one has to seek. His quest to know himself was spurred by a sense of dissatisfaction with how little he knew about who he was at present. Socrates's disquiet proved contagious with his fellow interlocutors, many of them adolescents and young men. When he was convicted and sentenced to death, one of the two charges against him was that he'd corrupted Athenian youth. He was the first to admit that their shared inquiries at times fanned the flames of their burgeoning discontentment both with themselves and the direction their society was taking.

One of the instigators of the trial against him was Anytus, a powerful middle-class politician. At Socrates's trial, Anytus accused him outright of sowing seeds of discord between him and his son. Socrates acknowledged that he had an "association with the son of Anytus" and that he "found him not lacking in firmness of spirit." What got Anytus's goat wasn't that there might have been physical intimacy between his son and Socrates, but that his son's relationship with the old Athenian led him to decide that he no longer wanted to follow in his father's footsteps. We have it from Xenophon (430–354 BC), the Greek historian and philosopher, that Socrates encouraged Anytus's son not to "continue in the servile occupation [tanning hides] that his father has provided for him."

History doesn't tell us what became of Anytus's son (history doesn't even tell us his name). But we do know what became of Athens after Socrates was convicted and ended his life. It is almost inconceivable, given the unparalleled heights that the Greek polis had reached, that it could so quickly plummet, yet that's what's happened after it was shanghaied by adults who practiced outright dishonesty, brutality, and stupidity. Their successful attempt to get rid of one of the last virtuous men shows just how low they'd sunk. Socrates, in his person, embodied Athenian society as it had been in its glory days. Those who convicted him were estranged from those times; they wanted no uncomfortable reminders of all that their society had been. In a similar vein, youth today are uncomfortable reminders of who we can be and tend to be treated as thorns in adults' sides. If we'd take the opposite tack and keep them in close company, we might be inspired to live more by our ideals rather than abandon them when the going gets tough.

It's a Beautiful Day in the Personhood

"Are all persons humans, and all humans persons?" asks Lawson, thirteen.

I've come to find over the years that there are few groups of human persons more accomplished at Socratic delving than those of middle-school age. I've known the students' teacher, Marith Wilkins, for more than thirty years. She and I once were colleagues at a six-room schoolhouse in Casco, Maine, where she taught social studies and I was a part-time reading and literature instructor. Instead of retiring, Marith decided to continue her calling, only in a warmer climate. Three years ago, she returned to the coastal South Carolina town where she was born and raised. When I was in the area to visit Greek relatives, I made a stopover at her classroom. I told the students, all of them between the ages of

twelve and thirteen, of my interest in investigating a question that had
something to do with what it means to "be a person." Before my visit
I'd been refreshing myself about competing perspectives offered by philosophers—from the view of the sixth-century BC philosopher Boethius
(475–524 BC) that a person is "any individual substance of a rational
nature," to Descartes's notion that a person is any creature, human or
otherwise, who has continuous consciousness. I wondered what insights
the kids here might lend to the subject that might help me further formu-
late a philosophy of childing. In short order, Lawson produces a question
that is philosophical paydirt.

"We say 'human nature,'" Lawson says now, "but never 'people nature.'
Or we say 'human race,' but never 'people race.' We say, 'he is an immoral
person,' but never, 'he is an immoral human.' Does that mean you can be
one without being the other?"

"They go together but they're not the same. To say you're a human is
to say you're part of a species," says Kate. "Like, an ultra-narcissist might
say, while surveying his physique in the mirror, 'I'm a perfect human
specimen.' He'd never say, 'I'm a perfect person specimen.' When he
makes the 'human specimen' reference, it has to do mostly with his
opinion of his physical makeup as it compares to other members of the
Homo sapiens.

"On the other hand, to say you're a person is to say something about
your individuality, about your character traits. Like, I'm a 'people person.'
I'd never say I'm a 'people human.' That would be like saying I'm a member of the human species who's peopled by many people. Or I might say
that I'm a 'good person,' that I have a decent moral code, and that you
can tell I am by the way I treat others. I wouldn't say 'I'm a good human,'
since that would be like I'm comparing myself as one brand of human to
another brand."

"The term 'human nature' is about what's basic to all of us as humans—
that we all have an inner nature of some sort," says Hyun Jin. "But when
we start zeroing in on our individual natures, then it has to do with personhood. A person's nature can be aggressive, peaceful, violent, passive,

shy, happy, gloomy, a mix. Some parts of your nature might be fixed, and you might be able to change parts of your nature, either by personal will, or by medication, or by therapy, and as a result, alter your persona."

"In my case, my ex-boyfriend helped me change my nature," says Kate. "I used to be so shy. Now I'm outgoing, assured. Even after we broke up, I've stayed that way."

"So did he help you discover your true nature?" I ask.

She thinks on this for a bit before nodding in the affirmative. "I was a shrinking violet waiting to blossom. I was lucky enough to have someone in my life who helped me do that."

Then Kelly says, "My older brother has Down syndrome. These days, when expecting parents find out through genetic tests that their baby has Down's, most choose to have an abortion. My family has to travel a long distance to meet up with other families who have a child with Down's. All the other kids at these gatherings flock around Brian. He's a natural-born leader but also a permanent child in some ways. He is honest and trusting, open and kind. I wish we all had those qualities as part of our nature."

"Kids' human nature is not the same as adults' human nature," Lawson says soon afterward. "You almost never read in real life about kids warring with other kids. You mainly read about such things in works of fiction, like *Lord of the Flies*, where the author would have us believe that if kids were left alone, far out of reach of adults, they'd behave like little savages. But our nature is basically more peaceable than adults. We have our bullies and some kids can do cruel things, but on the whole, it's the adults who acts in the ways that Golding describes."

"Doesn't that make us more human than adults?" asks Kelly, whose nature is to remain quiet, listening intently, until she's considered a number of points of view.

"Not more human, but it makes us better models of what humans should strive to be." Then she says, "I have to say, while I'm definitely peaceful by nature on most occasions, when one of my siblings is teased or hurt, watch out; I'm their fierce defender."

"My understanding is that to be a person, you have to be rational, you have to be aware of yourself, and be able to communicate in a language," Rowan says next. "In 2013, the government of India gave dolphins non-human personhood status. It was the first nation in the world to recognize that dolphins have the characteristics of persons."

The noted and controversial Australian moral philosopher Peter Singer, for one, believes a number of animals meet the criteria for personhood. For instance, he contends that "great apes are self-aware, rational beings with close personal relationships and rich emotional lives," and so should be considered to have personhood and all the legal rights that that entails— or at least, to non-infants of the species, since he does not consider infants full-fledged persons who meet these criteria. He contends in *Practical Ethics* that "characteristics like rationality, autonomy, and self-consciousness" only come to us over time. He is adamant that "infants lack these characteristics." Yet infants have a demonstrated prowess at everything from creating causal maps, to problem solving, to empathizing, abilities that require reasoning powers, a degree of autonomy, an intricate and complex consciousness—key criteria for personhood.

Kelly is now prompted to say, "You can also be a person without being a human in the world of fiction. I'm reading the *Twilight* series." She's speaking of the popular vampire series by Stephenie Meyer. "A vampire is unique; it starts out as a human *and* a person, and it remains a person, a vampire person, after it ceases to be a human. Bella, one of the main characters, was pathetic in her human life. She was socially awkward and accident prone. There's this passage"—Kelly skims an index finger over her tablet until she hits upon the passage she's looking for—"where Bella says, 'I knew a little about what I was going to be like when I wasn't human anymore. . . . For several years my biggest personality trait was going to be *thirsty*. It would take some time before I could be *me* again.'" Kelly looks around at us. "Bella is deceiving herself. She may still have personality traits, but they're no longer human ones. She'll never be 'me again,' because she isn't human any longer. The last thing she did as a human was have sex with the vampire Edward. Bella wanted to know what the experience would be like as a human. This goes to show that, deep down, she knew that once she became a vampire, she wouldn't be 'me again.' She had sex before she"—Kate reads again—"'traded in my warm, breakable, pheromone-riddled body for something beautiful, strong.' A big part of what being human is all about is being physically fragile. She'd never be that again."

"That's why vampire novels are so popular with us humans," says Lawson. "They give us the chance to fantasize about what it would be like to be immortal, to have superhuman strength so that—except for needing human blood—we're not vulnerable and needy anymore."

"If you can be a person without being a human, can you ever be a human without being a person?" I ask eventually.

"I worry how technology can steal someone's identity," Kate says after some time has passed. "My dad's digital life has taken over his person. He won't dial it back. He doesn't take the time anymore to just be, with himself, or with the rest of his family." After some more thought says, "Technology is becoming his identity. He doesn't have much of a sense anymore of who he is. Without that sense, are you still a person?"

Martin Heidegger predicted nearly ninety years ago that technology would come to rule every aspect of human existence. He didn't renounce technology, but he could foresee how it had the potential to dehumanize us. Heidegger urged us to bend this all-encompassing phenomenon—whether it's in the form of an e-reader, a wearable computer in the form of a watch or glasses, or a virtual reality headset—to the service of humankind, lest it take us over and render us and our nature obsolete.

After a contemplative pause, Hyun Jin says to us, "When do you become human, in the first place? Is it when you are also capable of becoming a person, or when you in fact are a 'feeling person'?"

She then says, "My mother's baby was stillborn at twenty-two weeks. I overheard her and my father discussing whether to have a funeral. To my mother, she'd lost her baby girl, whom she'd already named Joon. By my mother's beliefs, Joon already had a soul the moment she was conceived, and already was as much a member of the family as any of us."

In the same vein, to the Pythagoreans, a group of esoteric and meta-physical philosophers of the fifth century BC, fertilization marks the beginning of human life, because this is when they believe the soul is cre-ated. To Aristotle, on the other hand, while a soul is created upon concep-tion, it starts out in a vegetative state, and so he believed it was permissible to have abortions early in a pregnancy, before the soul progressed to other states, from the animal to the human.

"To my father," she goes on, "we'd lost a fetus, someone not yet a human, and so hadn't had a chance to become a person. My father believes a person isn't a person until he's born." Likewise, to the Stoics, the soul enters a newborn when it first takes a breath, called the *pneuma*, or "breath of life."

"My father gave in to my mother's wishes," Hyun Jin says next, "and we had a funeral service." Hyun Jin then says, "My mother carried Joon inside her all that time. About three and a half months into her pregnancy, she'd say things like, 'I feel Joon swinging around inside me at night like a little monkey on a vine. That little monkey is a night person.'"

"'Little monkey' can be a person to your mom without being one to you," says Kate. "It's all in the eye of the beholder. If you attribute to a fetus a personality, then the fetus isn't a fetus—it's a person. And if it's a person, then it's a full-fledged human, because you can't develop indi-vidual qualities of personhood without first being a human."

"Even if Hyun Jin's mother had only thought of the fetus as a fetus, it would always have been part of her own personhood," says Thaddeus. "I read this study that shows that some of the developing fetus's cells leave the uterus and make their way to the mother's brain.[28] Even if the person carrying the fetus has a miscarriage or an abortion, those cells will always be with her, mixing and mingling in her brain. That's a deep connection. It gives her new possibilities for her personhood."

"I sometimes go to the gravesite with my mother," Hyun Jin tells us. "She talks to Joon, tells her about the rest of us, what we're up to. I'm still

---

28 June 6, 2012 issue of *Biology of Reproduction*

trying to decide if I should see her as more than a developing fetus, if I should see her, like my mother does, as a bona fide person. But I'll always wonder what she would have done with her life, about the person she would have become, and how having her in my life would have influenced the person I'm becoming."

On Human Nature

Is there something called human nature?

If the American philosopher, essayist, and public intellectual Ralph Waldo Emerson (1803–1882) is to be believed, the answer is not only an emphatic yes, but our original nature is as pure as the driven snow. "Infancy is the perpetual Messiah, which comes into the arms of fallen men, and pleads with them to return to paradise," he tells us in his essay "Nature." In Pulitzer Prize–winning novelist Edith Wharton's *Age of Innocence*, the protagonist, Newland Archer, shares Emerson's view that we have a nature, but has a less rosy outlook about it. "Untrained human nature was not frank and innocent," he surmises. "It was full of the twists and defenses of an instinctive guile."

According to Sartre, we don't have a predetermined nature or essence. Rather, we are radically free to create our own nature, through the choices we make, independent of any outside influence. But Sartre stresses that we should use our freedom in ways that also enhance the freedom of everyone else. In his prominent work *Existentialism is a Humanism*, he argues that "every man realizes himself in realizing a type of humanity"—or inhumanity.

John Stuart Mill was convinced that what we take to be human nature hinges in any given time and clime on one's cultural milieu. For instance, when it comes to women's nature, he claims in his provocative 1869 work *The Subjection of Women* that "what is now called the nature of women is an eminently artificial thing." Mill considered characterizations in his day of "women's nature" to be male-driven, with the intention of keeping women in a state of subjection, so men could continue "enslav[ing] their minds." As he put it, "The subjection of women to men being a universal custom, any departure from it quite naturally appears unnatural. . . . But was there ever any domination which did not appear natural to those who possessed it?" Mill was far more progressive on the subject than most of his Western male philosophical brethren of his day; they took their cue from Aristotle, who held women in just as low regard as he did children, and who maintained that men, because of what he claimed were their superior reasoning powers, had a natural authority over them.

The English philosopher and physician John Locke, considered the father of classical liberalism, stakes the claim in *Some Thoughts Concerning Education* that we don't so much have a nature as an impulse. He believes we are born with the morally neutral impulse to pursue whatever gives us pleasure and avoid whatever causes us pain. Apart from that one natural tendency, we "are entirely devoid of any impulse whatsoever." Jean-Jacques Rousseau, on the other hand, asserted in *Emile* that each of us is born with a built-in disposition that is capable of further sculpting and perfecting throughout our lives. Rousseau considers this temperament an inherently good one, even if it reveals itself in dramatically different ways in each of us. He goes so far as to call it our "divine instinct," our "conscience to love the good, reason to know it and freedom to choose it." If so, how is it that so many of us lose this nature of ours over time? Rousseau fingers adults as the culprit. He claims that the kinds of societies they construct leads to the cultivation of an every-man-for-himself mindset that deforms our original natures. What he doesn't adequately address is: If our nature is so good—indeed, divine—to begin with, why would we grow up to be adults who create societies that aren't reflective of it?

To José Ortega y Gasset, this question would make no sense, because "man, in a word, has no nature." Rather, he has a "history," made up of his works and deeds. Ortega y Gasset argues in *History as a System* that man is "unique in the universe" because he is "an entity whose being consists not in what it is already, but in what it is not yet." By this perspective, each of us is in the process of becoming more, or less, or other, than who we are at any given moment. Each of us represents "diverse possibilities: I can do this or that. . . . Man is the entity that makes itself." As such, man's weightiest task "is to determine *what* he is going to be." In going about this task, the French philosopher and social theorist Michel Foucault (1926–1984) contends in "On the Genealogy of Ethics" that we should strive to create ourselves as works of art. Similarly, Henri-Louis Bergson (1859–1941), one of the most influential French philosophers of the late nineteenth and early twentieth centuries, claims in *Creative Evolution* that "for a conscious being to exist is to change, to change is to mature, to mature is to go on creating oneself endlessly." Yet man is also the entity capable of *not* creating himself, of being an existential couch potato. A conscious being can make a conscious decision not to change, or to change in regressive or destructive ways. Even for those who continually create, not all acts of creation are inherently good, as Bergson implies. Man is also the being who can create in ways that undo, that unravel.

How do we break out of the grip of those proclivities that impel us to negate others? Put in a much more positive light, how do we best go about cultivating our most humanizing creative impulses?

The timeless lesson imparted by the Buddha and Socrates, by Epicurus and Dewey and Spinoza, is that we are bundles of habits, and we can rid ourselves of those that do damage, no matter how stubborn and resistant they are. The odds are more likely that we'll succeed once we understand that destructive habits practiced toward others are also self-destructive. In her moving meditation *Upheavals of Thought: The Intelligence of Emotions*, Martha Nussbaum notes that nearly all ethical traditions across the ages and cultures equate good character with sound habits of action and emotion. What this means is that if you want to act in virtuous ways as an individual or a society, you have to understand how emotions, individually and collectively, drive your actions. "All emotions have ethical content," she maintains, "since all concern our evaluation of things and people as extremely important for our well-being." Nussbaum's compelling claim is that emotions aren't alien forces that upset our rational thoughts and plans, but are—or should be—part and parcel of them, once we learn how rationally to explore, evaluate, and judge them. Once we can do that, we can change harmful emotional habits and replace them with healthful ones. That requires not only a great deal of will, but of imagination, so we can see ourselves acting in new ways, and then map out ways to achieve this. First and foremost, we have to decide which emotions we should consciously cultivate, and which we should discard. To Nussbaum, if we make it a habit to value and practice emotions such as love, compassion, and grief—not just toward those in our immediate circle, but to those we don't know and will never know—we can't help but create more humane societies, since our individual and group actions will as a matter of course reflect our deep concern for and interest in others.

Second Birth

Hannah Arendt makes the intriguing assertion that our entrance into this world as newborns is not what matters most when it comes to matters of personhood. While our beginning as an individual, she asserts in a stirring note of hope near the end of her *The Origins of Totalitarianism*, "is guaranteed by each new birth," this is but the first step; there must be an ongoing birthing process, a "second birth," which she claims can only be had if we develop a political stance in the world, and have the freedom to act on this stance. This is the moment of true birth, Arendt contends, because it's the moment when the possibility for true self-creation and liberation arrives. We can take our place as a unique self in a world among other unique selves. As she puts it in *The Human Condition*, "with word and deed we insert ourselves into the human world, and this insertion is like a second birth." When we are denied the ability to insert ourselves, when we are kept from taking our place at the political table (or family table, for that matter) as one among equals, we are existentially stillborn; we can't become full-fledged persons. Those on the receiving end of deliberate acts of rejection and exclusion will never be treated as equals unless and until those denying them their place at the table come to realize that they are also keeping themselves from being full-fledged persons. Their acts of inhumanity not only prevent the unfolding of others, but of themselves.

Chapter 6

Sweet Child of Mine

Baby On Board

It is a postcard-perfect spring Sunday. Ceci and I are at a French bistro on the periphery of Philadelphia's Rittenhouse Square. We sit beside large open windows, and hold hands across the table as we engage in a favorite pastime, people-watching. There are a lot of people to watch today, what with nearly every inhabitant in the city milling about outdoors after a long and bitter winter.

We're celebrating our fifteenth wedding anniversary. Ceci is thirty-three weeks pregnant, her ballooning belly a beauty to behold. The newest addition to our family, Cybele Margarita—named, respectively after the Greek goddess of nature, fertility, and healing, and my mother—will soon make her debut.

Several months after she'd had a miscarriage, Ceci made an appointment to have an IUD inserted, after she and I decided that it was best to remain a family of three. Except, one member of the family hadn't been consulted. Cali wasn't happy about our decision. She might not yet be versed in how a kid is made, but she knows it's up to us to make one, and she made it clear that she wanted us to keep trying. Ceci and I explained to her how we came to our decision. Cali, arms crossed, lower lip jutting out, was the picture of disapproval. Ceci's appointment was scheduled to coincide with her period. It never arrived. We bought a pregnancy kit. "Oh, yes," she reported. She held out the stick, and there was the bold pink line, a sure sign of the "pregnancy hormone" in abundance.

I did all my jumping up and down on the inside—unlike the first time around, in November 2005, when Ceci bounded out of a restroom at an Arizona interstate truck stop, waving the pregnancy stick back and forth in the air like a mini-baton. Cali was on her way. This time around, when Cali realized that the pink line on the stick meant Mommy was pregnant, she made a cry of pure exultation. Then she became not sad, but serious. "Will we lose the baby again?" she asked. Cali had experienced too many losses in the past year—both of her adored grandfathers died within a stretch of six months, and then Ceci's miscarriage. I wasn't sure Ceci did the right thing when she assured Cali that the groups of cells, already exponentially growing and differentiating within her uterus, would result in a baby brother or sister. In hindsight, she was justified.

Irene passes us by on the street. She is pushing two white poodles in a fancy baby stroller. Such a sight is not unusual in Philadelphia, where people outdo one another mollycoddling their pets. About a year ago, I'd started a Socrates Café in central Philly. At our inaugural gathering, none other than Irene—a charter member of the first Socrates Café I started in Montclair, New Jersey, in 1996—bounded in, fashionably late, just as our dialogue was gaining steam. I stopped what I was saying in mid-sentence, jumped off the swivel stool on which I was perched and made my way through the group encircling me to give Irene the kind of hug reserved for long-lost friends. Before I could ask her what in the world she was doing in Philadelphia, she told me what in the world she was doing there: She'd moved in with her two sisters, Esther, eighty-six, and Ethel, eighty-nine, who'd been living together for the last fifteen years, in their childhood row house home in Center City, ever since their spouses passed away. For years, her sisters had urged Irene—at age eighty-three, the youngest of the trio—to move in with them, and at last she'd decided to do so.

Irene was the only sibling who'd ever left Philly. She had enjoyed a memorable career as a singer in New York, at cabarets and also the occasional off-Broadway musical. She had been married seven times. She never had a child. Irene was fond of saying that the stage was her child.

Ceci and I call out to her. Irene puts the brakes on her stroller, and leaves two whimpering poodles to make her way indoors. Ever the attention-getter, she enters the restaurant with a flourish, her loud clothing, generously applied bright makeup, and red bouffant hairdo enhancing her larger-than-life aura. She refuses our invitation to sit down after we tell her it's our anniversary. Irene stands over us and says, "And to think your romance was sparked the one week I didn't come to Socrates Café." At the Socrates Café in question, Ceci was the only attendee. That night, we explored, "What is love?," proposed by Ceci, who'd just recently arrived in the US to study for her master's degree in education. We married less than two years later. We ended up living on and off for more than a decade in Chiapas, Mexico, where Ceci resumed her activism for indigenous rights, and where I held a number of life-altering dialogues.

Irene touches Ceci's abdomen. She feels a pat-pat-pat against the palm of her hand—a foot, a knee, perhaps an elbow, compliments of Cybele. Her face lights up. "Oh my."

Soon afterward she says, "Newborns are a sign of hope, of new beginnings." Looking at me, she then says, "At one of the first Socrates Cafés you held in Montclair, we inquired into the question, 'What are the best beginnings?' The person who asked it was pregnant. She was curious and nervous as one chapter in her life was ending and another was starting. I remember one answer, from a woman who'd managed to raise five children by herself. She said that babies are the best sort of beginnings because they represent new possibilities for humanity itself.

"I'm glad you decided to have another," she says next. "The world needs more Phillipses." She leans down, smothers each of us in an embrace, and takes her leave.

I stay silent afterward. Ceci says after a while, "What? What is it?"

I don't want to put a damper on our special day. On the one hand, I find myself wondering if the world really needs any more Phillipses. On a radical swing to the other, I am struck by the bittersweet thought that this will be the last child the love of my life and I will conceive. "I wish there still was time to have a little Christopher Amado," I tell Ceci. If we had a boy, that's the name we'd long ago picked out. Amado, which means 'loved,' is the name of Ceci's grandfather. "*You* are my Christopher Amado," she says. Her eyes and smile envelop me; they are all about warmth, love, comfort.

Ceci was born six weeks premature in a public hospital in Mexico City. Her condition was so precarious that a priest was called to perform last rites. It's impossible to imagine my life without her. No matter how trying the times, with Ceci as my partner, life has a magical intent. I think of the day we exchanged vows at San Francisco's city hall all those years back. Our pockets were too threadbare to afford a photographer; the only images we have are etched in memory: that day in late spring 1998, Ceci has on the entrancing hand-sewn white dress, made by an indigenous woman, that she wore the first day we met. She stands across from me, rocking back and forth on her heels and toes, her wide, expressive brown eyes moist and exhilarated. Our arms are extended as we clasp one another's hands and recite the vows we each prepared, our voices a welter of love and joy and anticipation. We do so in the presence of a judge who hails, of all places, from Montclair, New Jersey. The day we married was a liberating experience. When we had our first child, it further set me free, expanding my sense of possibilities for all I might still do and be. No doubt the day Cybele arrives will be another liberation day.

I wonder what Cybele will look like, will be like. Her soon-to-be big sister has wondered out loud with me about this too, even as Cali focuses her energies on being a personal welcome wagon. She has taken a class on being a sibling to an infant, can change a diaper like a pro, and has taken infant CPR. In our cozy apartment, her crib and co-sleeper at the ready, Cali has taped to it a "Welcome Cybele" sign with a picture of her baby sister, as she imagines her, lying in a crib, surrounding by her adoring family members. Even before she has officially entered the world, Cybele is filling out our family.

I can't wait to meet Cybele in the flesh, can't wait to begin the journey with her, to learn and grow from and with her. She is a new beginning for me, for our family, and a new beginning, as every child should be, for the world.

New Beginning

John Dewey's heartfelt belief, expressed in his book *Construction and Criticism*, is that every human being heralds a world of new possibilities.

> I have always been struck by the interest taken in small children, in their doings and sayings. Discount as much as we will the doting fondness of relatives, yet there is something left over. This something is, I believe, the recognition of originality; a response to the fact that these children . . . bring something fresh into the world, a new way of looking at it, a new way of feeling it. And the interest in this freshness . . . indicates that adults are looking precisely for something distinctive of individuality. They are sick of repetition and duplication, of opinions that are stereotyped and emotions that are pale stencils of something that someone else has once experienced.

There is little disputing that wanted children are doted on. But Dewey's claim that our youngest are more distinctive and original individuals than adults is cause to take pause. Does individuality tend to become less discriminate as we grow older? If so, why? Does it have to be this way?

Perhaps our response to children who invite us into their world as full participants offers clues about how we might put ourselves back on the road to achieving genuine newness of self. When we immerse ourselves in the world of a child, a world made up of unbounded imagination and wonder, we feel the world, see it, are part of it, in a fresh way. As with Dewey, to Rachel Carson, a child's world is necessarily "fresh and beautiful, full of wonder and excitement." Her lament is that "it is our misfortune that for most of us that clear-eyed vision, that true instinct for what is beautiful and awe-inspiring is dimmed and even lost before we reach adulthood." It is the misfortune of too many children that this true instinct of theirs is dimmed from the outset. Born into an uncaring world, they are robbed of the chance to experience the wonder and awe that is woven into their being. The ancient Greek ethos of *arete* is based on the belief that none of us can fully flower unless we create conditions that make it possible for others to do so as well. In fact, this "creating of conditions" is a big part of what it's all about; it's arete in practice. If the spirit of arete was revived and made widespread, each day would represent a world of new beginnings for all of us.

What Child Is This?

In *Thus Spoke Zarathustra*, Friedrich Nietzsche describes three types of human spirit. He likens the first to that of the camel. Obedient and ascetic, the "camel spirit" doesn't question tradition and authority but instead goes along to get along. Resigned and resentful, a person with the camel spirit carps about his lot in life but makes no real effort to change it. The second type, according to Nietzsche, is the "lion spirit." Someone with this spirit goes his own way by saying "no" to any strictures not to his liking. That's the extent of his resistance to existing mores; the lion spirit doesn't create anything new. Most of us, Nietzsche claims, have one of these two spirits.

There is a third and higher type, which Nietzsche considers the summit of human being: "the child spirit" breathes new life into life, creates new possibilities for his own existence, for human existence, for the universe itself. He has a distinctive attitude, stance, regard that transcends conventional modes of being in the world. Nietzsche describes one with the child spirit as a "dancing wheel," a "play," "joyfulness." His accolades know few bounds: "The child is a new beginning, a sport, a self-propelling wheel, a first motion, a sacred Yes." One who fits the bill for a child spirit can even create new values. "To create new values—even the lion is incapable of that," Nietzsche asserts. A child spirit dispenses with careworn value-laden concepts like "sin" or "shame" that keep a person or society down, and replace them with more life-affirming ones. One with the child spirit has weathered slings and arrows, yet has emerged not just unbowed, but further liberated: "Pure is his eye, and no loathing lurks about his mouth. . . . He has become a child, an awakened one."

Malala Yousafzai is a child spirit on an exalted scale. The Pakistani school pupil at age fourteen was shot in the head and neck by the Taliban for her activism advocating education rights for children and women's rights. She survived the assassination attempt, and after intensive rehabilitation she went on to become one of the world's most beloved, impassioned, and effective advocates for children's universal right to education. In her first public speech after the attack, she said:

> The terrorists thought they would change my aims and stop my ambitions, but nothing changed in my life except this: weakness, fear, and hopelessness died. Strength, power, and courage was born. . . . I am not against anyone, neither am I here to speak in terms of personal revenge against the Taliban or any other terrorist group. I'm here to speak up for the right of education for every child. I want education for the sons and daughters of the Taliban and all terrorists and extremists.

A child spirit of whatever age and walk of life is a model of a certain kind of transformation. Each has tasted hopelessness, anger, bitterness, and despair, but refuses to be identified by them. If likened to a blossoming flower, the clusters they grow are an ideal blend of the best attributes of a child and adult, youth and baby. The crosses they've had to bear did not stunt their growth, but made their spirit lighter and brighter, gave them a greater sense of possibility, for themselves and for humanity. They are, as Nietzsche puts it, "still child enough, an eternal child!"

Nietzsche was no Buddhist, needless to say, but he would find appealing the faith's comparison of people who flourish in the face of formidable obstacles to a lotus. The tiny and fragile flower starts out its existence at the bottom of a dark and murky pond. It struggles against oppressive elements to make its way toward the sunlight above. If it manages to get to the surface, the lotus blossoms in breathtaking fashion. Similarly, many who set themselves free in ways that also emancipate others have undertaken a difficult upward journey from a dark place way down low. Nelson Mandela recounted "many dark moments when my faith in humanity was sorely tested." To Mandela, one can only overcome such moments by "keeping one's head pointed toward the sun, one's feet moving forward." Mandela would agree with William James's assertion in *The Varieties of Religious Experience* that if you can manage this, you will experience "a second birth, a deeper kind of conscious being than [you] could enjoy before." The day he was released from prison, many who had waited for hours outside of the prison gates to witness history wore T-shirts adorned with a youthful image of their hero. But the look on the seventy-one-year-old Mandela's face that day, a mixture of radiance, exuberance, and anticipation, made him seem even younger in person than on those emblazoned images.

Rarest of all is for a civilization itself to "child." Yet one can point to two times in Western history when most members of an entire society managed the feat—in Florence during the Renaissance, when there was unrivalled artistic, scientific, and humanistic flourishing—as epitomized by Leonardo da Vinci (1452–1519)—and in ancient Athens. Nietzsche offers a panegyric to the Greeks' "childlike nature."

> They live unconscious of the genius they produce. Enemies of constraint and stupidity. . . . Their way of intuitively understanding misery, combined with a sunny temperament, genial and cheerful. Profundity in understanding and glorifying everyday things (fire, agriculture). . . . Unhistorical. . . . The individual raised to his highest powers through the polis.

They were exuberantly childish, with a wide-eyed gaiety that wasn't inoculated to misery, but that saw it as a fact of life that could, when tapped into in the right way, lead to further discovery, appreciation, joy. They'd fully "childed," with new figurative blossoms arising from fresh inner ones—the new replenishing the old, and vice versa. They were one another's parents and progeny, originals one and all, and the result was unprecedented thriving on manifold scales. The Athenian polis experienced a wholesale collapse from within when oligarchs convinced the rest to let them till the soil of the polis for them. This ended up stunting everyone's growth.

After Athens became a shell of its former self, flourishing wasn't done away with altogether. By the time Socrates was an adult, he was part of the remnant, the antithesis of a contemporary Athenian adult and his "weight-bearing spirit." Nietzsche described him as "a genius of the heart . . . who smoothes rough souls and lets them taste a new yearning."

He was the definitive "childult." Those who were in his company became infused with his spirit, with the yearning to be more than they were at any given moment. Socrates had the gift of divining "the hidden and forgotten treasure, the drop of goodness . . . from whose touch everyone goes away richer, not having found grace nor amazed, not as blessed and oppressed by the good of another, but richer in himself, opened . . . less sure perhaps . . . but full of hopes that as yet have no name."

Like a child who loves to hear the same story again and again, scholar Laszlo Versenyi (1928–1988) writes in *Socratic Humanism*, the questions Socrates entertained with others were "merely different ways of asking the same fundamental question"—namely, "What is man?"—and that Socrates was asking "not only the same question, but the same about the same . . . circling around the same center, approaching the same thing from seemingly different directions." While I believe that Socrates was also asking, "What is man capable of becoming?" I agree with Versenyi that Socrates never tired of plumbing the same question—not because (no more than a child would) he delighted in its repetition for the sake of it, but because with each inquiry he and his fellow inquirers gleaned novel points to ponder, fresh insights, about the world at large, and about themselves.

What should you expect—of yourself, of your life—when you're childing? To live life with more purposeful abandon. To be a co-creator of the universe. To craft a story about yourself that is more intentional than aimless, more colorful than monotonous, more open-ended than predictable. To give life everything you have, but to temper earnestness with playfulness, even whimsicality, knowing full well, as Puck puts it, "what fools these mortals be."

Does achieving the soaring state of a child spirit seem too daunting? Most likely, with some honest reflection, you'll discover that you've already childed more than you give yourself credit for. To do so to an even greater degree, become the "trapeze artist within" and let go of the bar. You need nothing but the midair of imagination to keep you grounded. The important resolution you must make is to be resolved, come what may, to keep moving forward and upward, despite moments of despair, dread, and setback. When I decided in 1996 to change my life radically and, among other things, start Socrates Café on a wing and a prayer, I almost ended the adventure before it began. In a moment of paralyzing indecision, I pulled out of my wallet a slip of paper with a quote from an 1835 translation of Goethe's *Faust*. The lines from the manager in the play's "prelude at the theatre" read in part:

> indecision brings its own delays,
> And days are lost lamenting over lost days.
> Are you in earnest? Seize this very minute;
> What you can do, or dream you can do, begin it;
> Boldness has genius, power and magic in it.

I dispensed with further hesitation and delay. Ever since, I've become more adept at realizing life while I live it. Yet Emily Webb, a central character in Thornton Wilder's *Our Town*, after having the epiphany that most of us never really examine how we go about living out our days—wonders whether this is possible: "Do any human beings ever realize life while they live it?—every, every minute?" The Nobel Prize–winning Russian poet and novelist Boris Pasternak (1890–1960) has this response in his novelette *The Adolescence of Zenya Luvers*: he observes that "there are few who know and feel what shapes them, forms them, and links them with one another. Life lets but a few people in on what it is doing to them." Perhaps that's because few beyond their childhood years care to be continually in the know about what life is doing to them. Or perhaps you can only know what life is doing to you by doing something to life, by shaping it as it shapes you, and doing so in a way that links you more to others, and to life itself, even as you feel less sure, more open. For such a person, as Nietzsche puts it in *Beyond Good and Evil*, "his world becomes more profound; ever new stars, ever new riddles and images become visible for him." He is in a regular state of arrival and takeoff. He comes full circle again and again, even as he returns to a starting point that is never the same, because he is never the same. The point of every meaningful personal journey is to return yourself, understand yourself more deeply, and in a way that leads you to take wing still again. A person who practices this philosophy lives in accordance with this passage from T. S. Eliot's *Four Quartets*,

> What we call the beginning is often the end
> And to make an end is to make a beginning.
> The end is where we start from. . . .
>
> We shall not cease from exploration
> And the end of all our exploring
> Will be to arrive where we started
> And know the place for the first time.

Psalms 103:15–16 tells us that "the days of a human life are like grass: they are as short-lived as the flowers in a field. The wind passes over it, and it is gone, and its place knows it no more." But the place does still know it. What we say, do and make has a ripple effect long after we are gone. What we must do is our utmost to make sure our days are spent keeping the human field abloom in ways that nurture everyone and everything else. In doing so, as underground writer Charles Bukowski (1920–1994) put it, "the people look like flowers at last."

And Baby Makes Four

It is a little after 4:00 a.m. when Cybele gives a plaintive cry. After rocking her for a half, she'd at last fallen asleep. We are semi-reclined on the family room sofa. Cybele is splayed across my chest, arms spread out on each side. Just shy of a month old, she still isn't attuned to the difference between day and night. I'm giving Mommy a respite. But when she's hungry, she's hungry, and that brings her awake after an hour and a half has passed.

Our sapphire-eyed infant, with a spray of reddish-brown hair and the cutest dimples (if I do say so myself), was born on July 2.[29] Ceci and I

---

29 Our nation's "real" Independence Day, as those who've read my *Constitution Café* know.

arrived at the birthing suite at Pennsylvania Hospital, the nation's oldest, with little time to spare. Her water broke during the taxi ride. Not only did the driver refuse the extra money I offered to have the seat cleaned, he refused his fare. "I'm part of your birth story," he said. "That's priceless." Once in the birthing suite, Ceci put her know-how in natural childbirth and mindfulness training to work. She was inside herself yet fully present, traversing the divide between the two like a virtuoso performer completely in her zone. Ninety minutes later, she pushed Cybele into the world. A midwife and I were there to catch her. We placed Cybele on Mommy's chest, where she began feeding at once.

Feeding is what baby wants now. I take her to Ceci. More than half asleep, she smiles, turns to her side, and cradles Cybele, who latches to her nipple, feeds for a while, then falls asleep while still sucking away. On the other side of Cybele is Cali. Though sound asleep, her hand stretches out and rests on the crown of her baby sister's head. The first time Cali met Cybele in the flesh, she said, "This is the most special moment of my entire life." I take a lingering look at my littlest muses. Being a parent is not for the faint of heart. Neither is being a child, for that matter. While I hopefully have a long way to go in this thing called life, I find myself wondering how they'll remember me. Will they remember me mostly for those acts I most regret, or for those of which I'm most proud? Will they be glad, in balance, that Ceci and I brought them into the world?

Such thoughts do not induce sleep. I go to my office to work on this book. At first I don't notice when Cali comes in. "Why aren't you sleeping?" I ask. She shrugs. She has something on her mind, but she's not yet ready to share. After a while, she says, "Daddy, do you think that lady and her baby who'd been in the hospital room with Mommy and Cybele are okay?"

A woman who'd given birth two days earlier was our neighbor for the briefest while in the room where Ceci and Cybele spent their first night (and where Cali and I stayed till the wee hours, thanks to a friendly nurse who bent the rules). When we entered, she was speaking with a social worker. She was pleading to her to let her stay for one more night. She said she wasn't ready to go home, that she was still in discomfort. From the back and forth, I gleaned that she had a teenage son at home whom she was raising alone. The social worker said it was impossible for her to stay any longer, that they'd already given her an extra night. When she left, the woman got on the phone and spoke to her son. She told him to put the one air conditioner they had in their apartment in her bedroom, so she and the baby would have a respite from the unbearable humidity when they arrived home that night. He must have refused. She cursed him roundly, hung up the phone, then burst into tears.

She took her time packing, still crying, but softly now. On her way out, she apologized for her language. I didn't know what to say. Cali knew what to do. She offered her some cookies and also gave her two chrysanthemums from the floral arrangement beside the bed where Ceci and Cybele already were fast asleep, both gifts from my mom. The look on the woman's face was one of incredulity. Then she accepted the gifts, and hugged Cali tightly. Cali is not normally one for extended hugs, but she let the woman hold onto her for a good while. Cali somehow understands that at any time, it might be her turn, or our turn as a family, to be in great need of caring concern.

Just two weeks before she gave birth, Ceci and Cali went on a morning shopping trip to the Salvation Army store in downtown Philadelphia. The following day, at precisely the hour they'd been inside, the building collapsed, killing six and injuring fourteen. Among those killed were college students, a newlywed, and an employee who'd just started working there that day. It was dumb luck that my family hadn't been in the store. I can never feel the pain of those who lost loved ones, but for a flickering, the enormity of their loss is palpable. What if the unthinkable had happened? Would I want to go on living, much less continue trying to make something meaningful of whatever time I have left? Would "childing" all of a sudden seem absurd, even inane?

Several years earlier, dear friends of mine, lost both their children—their biological child, Harrison, and Mara, adopted as an infant—in a car accident. Soon set to graduate from college, they were on their way home for a weekend visit during their exam study period. The person who rear-ended their car was texting while driving over ninety miles an hour on the interstate. He didn't see their car in front of him, stopped at a traffic accident, in time to brake. He somehow emerged from the accident with minor injuries, but he robbed Harrison and Mara—and their parents, Emmanuel and Tracy—of their future. While they remain outraged over the senselessness of what happened and continue to grieve deeply, they have established a foundation in the name of their children. Donations are channeled to the causes that Harrison and Mara held most dear. They've also joined a group made up of parents whose children's lives were tragically truncated. They are there for one another in a way that no one else can be.

A few days after Cybele was born, Emmanuel called. He knew this was around Ceci's due date, and he wanted to know how we were. His genuine joy over our good tidings filled my heart with a gratitude that mingled with a great ache for him and his wife. He told me that he and Tracey were going to China to volunteer for several months at the orphanage where they'd adopted Mara. They wanted to spend time at the place where she was lovingly cared for during the first three months of her life, and to be of some service, as a small gesture of thanks for the joy Mara had given them. If I ever face similar unthinkable circumstances, would I be capable of such grace?

Friedrich Nietzsche lauded our attempts to give meaning and value to suffering. While Walter Kaufmann, the most important Nietzschean scholar, went to lengths to distance his own philosophy from that of Nietzsche, he is philosophizing in a "Nietzschean" vein when he asserts in *The Faith of a Heretic* that we should "try to fashion something from suffering, to relish our triumphs, and to endure defeats without resentment." Kaufmann even believes there is an artistry to such fashioning: "The great artist is the man who most obviously succeeds in turning his pains to advantage, in letting suffering deepen his understanding and sensibility, in growing through his pains." Kaufmann's words hit home with full effect after I began this book, when I was on the receiving end of several deliberate acts of almost unimaginable meanness. Over time, these acts deepened my understanding and sensibility of how some might be so damaged that they not only try to cause afflictions in others, but even gain pleasure from it. The greatest test is to empathize with those who themselves are incapable of it. Most of all, these acts deepened my appreciation for having in my family constant sources of love and empathy that others are deprived of. If you can pass such a test, a new kind of artistry for living is born from it.

I tell Cali now that I've also wondered whether the woman and her baby are okay. I wish I'd asked her for her name and address. I wish I'd offered to be of help. I take Cali back to the bedroom. I sit on the bed's edge and stroke her hair until she falls asleep. Soon Cali makes a long and deep sigh in her sleep, a sound of contentment that she's been making since an infant. At that moment, I think of all those who live in circumstances that make it impossible to make such a sound.

Cali, for her part, is determined to do what she can to make ours a world in which all hearts beat as one. Her philosophy of caring is kindred to that of Confucius (551–479 BC), the Chinese philosopher who taught that seemingly small actions—like giving cookies and flowers and a hug to a woman in crisis—have a ripple effect that changes the course of someone's world, which changes the course of the world as a whole. It's my experience that Cali is a pretty typical child in living by this insight of Rousseau's in *Emile*: "Human beings are by nature neither kings nor nobles nor courtiers nor rich. All are born naked and poor, all are subject to the misfortunes of life, to difficulties, ills, needs, pains of all sorts." While some are far more subject to the misfortunes of life than others, we are all a step away from humility. None of us knows when tragedy might come our way. Somehow Cali, as Rousseau puts it, "understand[s] well that the fate of these unhappy people can be [yours.]" But she also understands that she has it within her heart to make their fate happier. If this everyday child spirit of hers and most other kids rubs off on the rest of us, what a world ours will be.

Acknowledgments

This book, and the serendipitous circumstances that led to its birthing, wouldn't have been all it might without the encouragement and support of these dear people, kindred spirits who have made it possible for me to move forward in the direction of my dreams: cherished friend Paul Martin; best buddy Dennis Dienst, who has been there for me through thick and thin; Stewart Harris; Justin Holley; Jim Burke; Linda Pierce; the poet Wolfgang Somary; Barry and Bettylou Kibrick; novelist and philosopher Ron Cooper; Michael Burri; Ralph Lewin, executive director of the Mechanics' Institute; Shirley Strum Kenny; Sophia Chryssanthacopoulou; Paul O'Brien; the late Margot Adler, who performed an unforgettably moving chant at the baby shower of my oldest daughter; my mentors, the late Matthew Lipman, Ann Sharp and Philip Guin; Sam Fairchild; Rachel Hollon; Liz Tullis; Don Carlson; Genevieve O'Shea; Maria Colavito; Margo Martin; Phil Jenkins; Peter Schoonmaker; Giancarlo Ibarguen; Lelia Green; Danielle Olson (see her masterful work on our Declaration Project—DeclarationProject.org— which has given a voice to young people who are typically unheeded); Jake Baer; Charlynn Duecy; John Thornell; the late Henry Outlaw; Eric Liu; Michael Ostrolenk; Alane Mason; Bill Reynolds; Paul Stahl; Felicia Eth; Kirk Boyd; Uncle Sheldon Kelly; Maryann Watson; V. Chapman-Smith; Lori Crockett; Hajera Karim; Jorge Lopez Campos (who will become a proud papa just before this book comes out); Peter Sparber; dear friend Bobbie DeLeon; Kathy Cadwell; Patty Reyes; gifted teacher Fran Brethel, who has been using my children's book *The Philosophers' Club* with her elementary school charges for over a decade; Omar Akhil, Suhail Arastu, and T. J. Mayes; all those who have served on the board of our nonprofit DemocracyCafe.org, which in essence seeks to make it possible for us all to "child" optimally; and all the thousands of inquisitive souls with whom

I've had the privilege of engaging in philosophical give-and-takes. Special thanks to my agent, Andrew Stuart, for his unswerving faith in this book, and my fabulous editor, Julia Abramoff, for her enthusiasm for this project and her expert guidance in making the book far better. My family—my life partner, Cecilia Chapa Phillips, and daughters, Cali and Cybele, who will always be my bundles of joy—gave me the boundless love, patience, and understanding needed to complete my book in the face of sometimes daunting circumstances. My mom, Margaret Ann Phillips, and my dad, Alexander Phillips, who passed away in 2011, several months after I began this project, are indelible influences and inspirations in my life. I also have a measure of gratitude for those who, to paraphrase Nietzsche, did me some good, despite all attempts to the contrary.